CHILD VITIMS OF CRIME
PROBLEMS AND PERSPECTIVES

CHILD VITIMS OF CRIME
PROBLEMS AND PERSPECTIVES

Editors

M.C. Gupta
K. Chockalingam
Jaytilak Guha Roy

GYAN

ISBN : 978-81-212-0741-6

Published, 2018

Published by

Gyan Publishing House
5, Ansari Road
Daryaganj, New Delhi-110002
Phone: 011-47034999, 9811692060
www.gyanbooks.com
E-mail: books@gyanbooks.com

Printed at: G. Print Process, Delhi.

Contents

Foreword

Children are the future citizens of a country. The progress and prosperity of a country are, therefore, dependent on the well-being of her children. Unfortunately a large chunk of India's children remain the victims of physical and sexual abuse, abduction, trafficking and various other types of crimes despite legal and administrative measures for their protection. Hence, child victimisation calls for greater societal concern. As we prepare ourselves to meet the challenges of the 21st century, protection of children from victimisation of crimes is bound to figure prominently on our national agenda for good governance. As a first step towards fulfilment of this urgent requirement the Indian Institute of Public Administration (IIPA) had organised the Third Biennial Conference of the Indian Society of Victimology on November 26-27, 1999. The theme of the Conference was 'Child Victims of Crime: Problems and Perspectives'.

This edited volume consists of a number of papers presented by eminent academicians and administrators and also young scholars at the Conference. It seeks to contribute to a better understanding of the multi-pronged challenges, need and strategies of protection of child victims of crime. Various issues on this subject such as nature and patterns of child victimisation, neglect of child victims of crime, child's rights to protection from sexual exploitation and abuse, strategies and innovations for protecting child from victimisation have been analysed and studied from national as well as global perspectives by a wide cross-section of public opinion and experience.

The subject of the present volume is absorbing; its relevance is profound; and the cause is therefore of national significance. I would like to take this opportunity to convey my warm appreciation to Shri M.C. Gupta, Prof. K. Chockalingam and Dr. Jaytilak Guha Roy for their commitment and contribution to this project.

I am sure this publication will be a very useful addition to the literature on Victimology.

New Delhi
January 1, 2001

S.B. CHAVAN
Chairman, IIPA

Editors' Note

The III Biennial Conference of the Indian Society of Victimology (ISV), held at the Indian Institute of Public Administration (IIPA), New Delhi, during November 26-27, 1999 was a remarkable success which encouraged the Indian Society of Victimology (ISV) and the Indian Institute of Public Administration (IIPA), the organisers of the Conference, to compile the contributions and make it available to academicians administrators and other the world over.

The Conference had two sub-themes, *Victimisation of Child—Various Forms and Patterns* and *Protection of Child from Victimisation: Strategies and Innovations.* Each of the issues dealt with invites readers to share their ideas and experiences relevant to the book's topic. We thank our many colleagues at the ISV and the IIPA for their constant encouragement and positive support.

The United Nations General Assembly celebrated the 30th Anniversary of the Declaration of the Rights of the Child. On the same day, the international community extended the protection afforded under human rights to one of the most vulnerable groups of the society, namely children, by adopting the 'Convention on the Rights of the Child'. It is the first international legal instrument to spell out guarantees to the entire field of children's rights. Even after a decade of the adoption of this instrument by the United Nations and almost universal ratification of the same by 191 States, violence against children is on the rise. According to UNICEF data, over eleven million children under the age of five die each year from hunger, disease, war, or inhumane treatment suffered at the hands of adults. This number does not include children who are the victims of abuse, neglect or exploitation.

Child abuse and neglect in India have been gaining the attention of the policy makers and researchers in the recent years. Child abuse, when not fatal, can hinder a child's growth and development. Documented data on child abuse shows emotional and physical damage suffered by abused and neglected children. These children can experience developmental delays, memory lapses, anxiety and an inability to control violent outbursts. This supports the fact that these children are more likely to become juvenile delinquents and turn sub-social. Most recent data and reports on child victims have revealed that the number of victims (below the age of 16 years) have been showing a steady growth in the last decade. At the ISV, we are committed to doing everything we can to reduce this growth and change the trend. There are several NGOs, highlighted in this volume, having prevention programs aimed at preventing abuse or neglect before it occurs and providing assistance to victims of crime. Throughout this book, you'll read more about child abuse, the various patterns of child abuse and the prevention of child abuse and neglect. I invite you to explore the resources and information available in this book and do your part in saving child victims.

Status of the Victim in the Criminal Justice System

The Hon'ble Union Minister of State for Home Affairs, I.D. Swamy, in his inaugural address under the title, *Victims and the Criminal Justice System*, had most rightly said, "You have to be a victim to know what it feels like". He gave due importance to the United Nations initiatives to help crime victims and specifically mentioned the Declaration of the Basic Principles of Justice for Victims of Crime and Abuse of Power. Even after fifty-three years of independence, he said, India is yet to listen and respond to victims of crime. He appreciated the efforts of the ISV and mentioned that due importance will be given to the Bill on The Victims (Criminal Justice) Right to Assistance -1996, drafted by the ISV.

In the Presidential address delivered by K. Chockalingam on *An Agenda for Victims of Crime during the 21st Century,* he has highlighted the national and international developments on Victimology in the recent years. At the international level, the Declaration on the Basic Principles of Justice for Victims of Crime and Abuse of Power, 1985, is a 'Magna Carta' for victims, according to him. Most recently, the two documents viz., 'Handbook on Justice for Victims' and 'Guide for Policy Makers', brought out by the United Nations in 1998 and disseminated to all nations need to be taken seriously by the practitioners in the criminal justice system and the policy makers, if victim's position has to improve, particularly in the developing nations. At the local level, he has focussed the efforts of the Indian Society of Victimology particularly by creating awareness among different sections of the society, about the rights of victims and the responsibilities of the criminal justice professionals towards the victims. He has concluded his paper by setting certain priorities of action towards justice for victims, with a special emphasis on assistance to victims.

The approach paper by P.S. Bawa, on *Neglect of Victims of Crime and What can be Done*, clearly visualizes the inclination of the criminal justice system towards the criminal in India since independence, just as all other criminal justice systems in the world did. He lays down the various safeguards that are provided by the law for criminals, pointing out the neglect of the victim. The victim, besides being neglected by the criminal justice system when the crime occurs, is re-victimised by the same system and the society at large, even during the aftermath of the crime. A powerful justification for the rights of the victim, in the criminal justice system, has been laid down with principles of law and basic human rights.

A Panorama of Child Victims in India

The works of other social scientists including a few young researchers included in this volume reflects the status of child victims in India. The victimisations range from female infanticide to domestic abuse and child labour to other forms of man made crimes. The opening paper on *Child Victims of Crime: Issues and Prospects* by S.P. Srivastava, gives an insight to the reader on what victimisation of a child means, in the legal and general sense, and the typology of the victimisation of children. The text helps one to understand the nature of hidden criminal victimisation of children in India. The legal status of the child victim has also been described, eliciting one's concern and the need for change in legislations.

Victimisation of children is a universal phenomenon but victimisation, especially between the developed and the developing countries, is varied in nature and extent. The various forms and patterns of child abuse have been examined and analyzed, with special reference to the Indian context, by Jaytilak Guha Roy in his paper on *Victimisation of Child: Various Forms and Patterns.* Crimes like female foeticide and infanticide on the one side and child labour and child slavery on the other are typical examples of victimisation of children in countries like India. More common among the Asian countries are crimes such as child trafficking and prostitution, besides drug trafficking and substance abuse. There are empirical studies presented in this volume on almost every such form of child victimisation.

Another paper, which stresses on the rights of the children and the deprivation of these rights, is the text by Tushar Kanti Saha on *The Issue of Childhood Deprivation and Survival Worldwide.* The experienced author of this paper supports his views with elements from the UN Convention on the Rights of the Child, India's National Children Policy (1979), the Indian Constitution and various other special Acts. Children are deprived of things, not necessarily monetary, right from birth. They are deprived of their mere survival before being born, and the "lucky" ones who survive are deprived of their health, schooling and all or any of the basic necessities.

Victimisation of the Child before and after Birth

As mentioned earlier, victimisations of a certain kind are exclusive to countries like India. Poverty and unemployment force parents to commit foeticide and infanticide of the girl child. Yatish

Mishra in *Crime Against Unborn Child*, has explained the severity of these crimes by statements of moral and legal support. He has quoted relevant sections of the law and the Medical Termination of Pregnancy Act (M. T.P. Act), bringing about their inadequacies while comparing them.

T. Chakraborty, in his paper on *Curse to Victim—Foeticide and Girl Child Problems and Prospects*, has explained in detail the causes for such crimes in India and also the problems the girl child faces—child marriage, abuse and neglect. Psychological studies in India on child victims have also been quoted by the author, in support of the trauma that children undergo even after several years of their abuse. He has mentioned a few relevant prevention methods adopted and services offered, by the Governmental and Non-Governmental Organizations, to child victims of crime. An effort has been made in this paper to offer some suggestions to parents in order for them to understand and to help their children.

Latha Krishnamurthy, in her paper on *Female Child—Victim of Gender Bias and Crime*, has dealt with gender bias and the specific victimisation of the female child. The history of such bias, in Indian families, has been noted with relevance to their social structure. Sensational cases have been quoted in this descriptive paper bringing out the trauma of the girl child in this society at large. She has traced the history of child prostitution till the present day, depicting to the reader the part played by social values in modern society.

Women—Victims of Violence from Womb to Tomb by K.Shanthi expands on the victimisations that are faced by the girl child when she grows to become an adult. She talks of the various forms of violence the female undergoes in her life cycle. These range from foeticide, infanticide, child labour, child prostitution and trafficking to domestic violence after marriage and even communal violence. The paper includes statistical data on the subject to support the author's views.

Sexual Victimisation of the Girl Child

Rape is a crime, which leads to serious repercussions on the social and psychological life of the victim. When it occurs in the life of a child, her life is doomed. S. Sanyal in her paper, *Traumas of a Child Victim of Rape*, diagnoses the myths of child rape. The author clears the several presumptions that are held in general without any scientific basis. The long-term psychological effects of rape on a child have been spelt out clearly with citations from various psychologists. While understanding the trauma of a child victim, it is necessary to simultaneously study the profile of the offender. The author has dealt with the typical characteristics of a rape offender in her paper. The legal implications of rape and the rehabilitation of the victim and the offender have also been touched upon. She has rightfully stressed the need for treating the offender, especially when it involves a child, thus highlighting a possible method to prevent the habitual occurrence of such crimes. Besides this, the author has suggested several measures that could be adopted to prevent child rape. More significant among them being the need to create an awareness and develop healthier attitudes about sex among the children.

Statistical and a spatio-temporal analysis of this issue has been vividly dealt with—by Tahir Hussain and Mary Tahir. Their paper, *A Spatio-temporal Analysis of Child Rape in India*, statistically analyses the trend in crimes against children in India in the period 1993-1997. The authors have also given a state-wise picture, which shows that the incidence of rape in the metro-cities is highest in the capital city, Delhi followed by Mumbai. They have explained the geographic occurrences of such crimes, answering questions such as who commits such crimes and why such crimes are committed.

The rising trend in sexual crimes against children has over the years raised questions on the inadequacy of the laws. Raghunath Patnaik has given a judicial scrutiny of the laws relating to the prevention of child abuse in India, quoting several Supreme Court judgements in his paper, *Judicial Scrutiny for Protecting the Child as a Victim from Sexual Abuse.* This judicial scrutiny has pinpointed the very refusal to act on the testimony of the victim of a sexual offence, in the absence of corroboration, as an insult to the injury sustained by the victim. In a cited Supreme Court case, the Court recognised the right of the victim for compensation and even to the extent of payment of interim compensation in certain cases. In the suggestions that have been furnished in the paper, the main argument is that the society should come forward to restore the human dignity of the victim and the payment of interim compensation is a poor solace to the victim.

Child Labour in India

Victimising children by employing children for domestic and hazardous industrial jobs is to date the pressing concern of the Government and several NGOs. It is common knowledge that data on child labour are extremely scarce. The reason for this is the absence of an appropriate survey methodology for probing into the work of children, which for the most part, is a "hidden" phenomenon. Studies have shown that the less developed a country is, the greater the proportion of the child population who work. It is also clear that the more elementary the type of economic activity or the kind of occupation that does not need specific skills, the larger the relative size of the working children in that particular industry or occupation. These factors influence the level of distribution of the total number of working children by branch of economic activity or by occupation in any specific country. Being tender physically, children are susceptible to various work—related injuries and illnesses more than adults doing the same kind of work. Besides this, they are not yet matured mentally, they are less aware, even completely unaware, of the potential risks involved in their specific occupations or at the workplace itself. As a result, a large number of working children are affected by various hazards. Many of them suffer actual injuries or illnesses that even stop them working permanently. Malay Dewanji's paper on *Child Labour*

Problem in India is a comprehensive one on the issue of child labour. Child labour in different industries has been clearly explained with statistical data. The paper also mentions the various causative factors that lead to child labour in a developing country like India. Several amended Children Acts and other relevant special laws have been analyzed with important Supreme Court and several High Court judgements. The readers will be benefited by the list of welfare measures that has been listed out from the National Policy on Child Labour (1987).

This next paper on *Child Labour in Beedi Industries: A Case Study,* by S. Ramdoss and A.Mathan Raj explains the extent of child labour and bonded child labour in Southern India. The sample included 30 children from the beedi industry. A major finding of the study was that nearly 95% of the sample had parents working in the same industry. More interesting is that majority of the children were between 5-8 years. The study has emphasised free and compulsory education for children, besides a few other recommendations.

Victimisation of Children by Child Abuse and Neglect

Children land on the streets either due to poverty or abuse or neglect by parents or others. It is a disturbing fact that these children are exposed to further forms of victimisation that eventually turn them into delinquents and criminals. R. Thilagaraj and Prasanna Poornachandra in *Deviant Behaviour as a Consequence of Child Abuse and Neglect among Street Children in Chennai* have empirically researched this area. The study explains to the reader, various forms of victimisations in the life of a street child and the consequence of which sometimes makes the child a delinquent and a prospective criminal. Diagrammatic representations of the phenomenon facilitate the understanding of the problem even to a layperson.

Another study, with relevance to abuse and neglect, is the paper on *A Study on Child Beggars in the City of Chennai* by S. Latha, S.

Ramdoss and A. Mathan Raj. This study with thirty beggar children from Chennai city as sample provides the reader with the different categories of beggars and the causes for their condition. Child abuse and neglect, poverty and unemployment are some of the causes that are identified by the researchers, as the reasons for a few taking to beggary.

Presenting Child Victimisation

Despite several laws and the establishment of NGOs solely functioning for children in difficult circumstances, the problem of child abuse and several other kinds of victimisations are still on the increase. Bharati Sharma, in her paper on *Preventing Child Victimisation—Some Strategies*, analyses the causes of child victimisations and suggests strategies to combat them. The societal changes, structure of the modem family and inter-generation relationships have brought out the responsibility of the family and targeted it as the main factor for the victimisation of children. She highlights the various stages of a child's life and the effects of victimisation in each of these stages.

Jyotsna Chatterji's paper on *Child Protection*, gives the reader an insight into the rights of the child in the light of the UN Convention on the Rights of the Child and the National Policy for Children, 1974. She has taken the pains of giving the various definitions of a child under different Indian special laws and the IPC. All existing laws that relate to the child have been mentioned in this paper. This is followed by a list of ways that could be adopted to protect children from victimisation.

Another paper in this area is that of Pradeep Kumar Bhardwaj on *Protecting Child from Victimisation: Strategies and Innovations.* The paper gives an overview of the plight of crime victims and highlights the fact that the victims of crime in India, unlike in other western countries, remain neglected at every stage of the criminal justice process. The responsibility for crime prevention cannot remain with one agency, what is necessary is a consolidated effort by all—the police, social service organizations, health organizations, the probation service, the community and the role of parents.

Sneh Lata Tandon, in her paper, *Protecting Institutionalized Child from Victimization: Strategies and Innovations*, has emphasised the responsibility of the Juvenile Justice Act in protecting the institutionised children from secondary victimisation by the Juvenile Justice System, as the realities in such institutions are totally different and ineffective to achieve the goals of the Act. She has quoted several cases and emphasised that institutional care should be the last resort for such children. She has made several recommendations in order to improve the working environment of the children's institutions besides strengthening the Non-institutional programmes, diversion programmes and preventive programmes.

Children as Victims of Parental Behaviour

An understanding of the victimisation of children, affected by their parents' behavioural problems due to alcohol abuse, is the focus of the paper on *A Study on the Victimization of Children of Alcoholic Parents*, by Gia Coombes and Prasanna Poornachandra. The study was conducted in the city of Chennai with a sample of 28 children, above 11 years and below 16 years of age. The results reflect the effect of parental alcoholism on the parent-child relationship, children's education, child's behaviour and psychological well being of the child.

Children as Victims of War

The empirical study on *Child Refugees—Socio-Psychological Aspects of their Victimisation*, by K. Chockalingam, Prasanna Poornachandra and R. Hema, brings to the public view the trauma undergone by child refugees in the Sri Lankan refugee camps of Tamil Nadu. The sample includes 31 children from various age groups and both sexes. The tragic causes of ethnic conflict in Sri Lanka have been the cause of the uprooting of its population with internal and external ramifications. The study makes understanding of the trauma undergone by these children, before and after leaving their motherland, easier through flow charts given at the end of the paper. Besides many others, the main focus of interest would be on the recent trend of adolescent marriages in the camps. The recommendations suggested are practical and are arrived at from the findings of the study.

As concluding part of the book, *Recommendations of the Third Biennial Conference of the Indian Society of Victimology held at the Indian Institute of Public Administration, New Delhi, on 26-27 November 1999*, have been included which would facilitate all those interested in providing a better deal to child victims, to follow up the recommendations with a view to implementing them. On the part of the Indian Society of Victimology, these recommendations have been forwarded to all the State Governments and the concerned Ministries of the Central Government for implementation.

New Dolhi
January 1, 2001

M.C. GUPTA
K. CHOCKALINGAM
JAYTILAK GUHA ROY

List of Contributors

Shri I.D. Swamy
Hon'ble Minister of State for Home Affairs
Government of India

Shri M.C. Gupta, IAS (Retd.)
Director,
Indian Institute of Public Administration
New Delhi

Dr. K. Chockalingam
Professor & Head
Department of Criminology
University of Madras

Shri P.S. Bawa, IPS (Retd.)
Formerly, Director General of Police, Sikkim
Presently, Consultant to the Lt. Governor, Delhi

Dr. S.P. Srivastava
Professor
Department of Social Work
Lucknow University

Dr. Jaytilak Guha Roy
Reader in Criminal Justice Administration
Indian Institute of Public Administration
New Delhi

Dr. Tushar Kanti Saha
Reader in Administrative & Constitutional Law
Indian Institute of Public Administration
New Delhi

Dr. Yatish Mishra
Research Scholar based in Delhi

Shri T. Chakraborty
Assistant Director
Bureau of Police Research & Development (BPR&D)
Ministry of Home Affairs
Government of India

Dr. (Ms.) Latha Krishnamurthy
Lecturer & Head
Department of Humanities
Priyadarshini College of Engineering & Agriculture
Nagpur

Dr. K. Shanti
Department of Criminology
University of Madras

Dr. (Ms.) S. Sanyal
Reader (Sociology)
National Institute of Criminology & Forensic Science
New Delhi

Tahir Hussain
Research Associate
Department of Geography
Jamia Millia University
New Delhi

Dr. (Ms.) Mary Tahir
Lecturer
Department of Geography
Jamia Millia University
New Delhi

Dr. Raghunath Patnaik
Reader
P-G Department of Law
Utkal University
Bhubaneswar

Shri Malay Dewanji
Secretary
Liberal Association for Movement of People (LAMP)
Calcutta

Shri S. Ramdoss
UGC Research Fellow
Department of Criminology
University of Madras

Shri A. Mathew Raj
Research Fellow
Department of Criminology
University of Madras

Dr. R. Thilagaraj
Professor
Department of Criminology
University of Madras

Shri Prasanna Poornachandra
Doctoral Scholar
Department of Criminology
University of Madras

Sh. Ms. S. Latha
UGC Research Fellow
Department of Criminology
University of Madras

Dr. (Ms.) Bharati Sharma
Professor of Management
(Organisational Behaviour & Behavioural Science)
Indian Institute of Public Administration
New Delhi

Ms. Jyotsma Chatterji
Director
Joint Women's Programme
New Delhi

Shri Pradeep Kumar Bhardwaj, IPS
Deputy Commissioner of Police &
Joint Secretary, Pratidhi
New Delhi

Dr. (Ms) Sneh Lata Tandon, Readers
Department of Social Work University of Delhi

Ms. Gia Coombles
Master's Student
Department of Criminology
University of Madras

1 Victims and the Criminal Justice System

I.D. Swamy

As we look forward to the beginning of a new millennium with new challenges and new opportunities, let us look back at the neglected issues of protecting crime victims. Our Government wishes to recognize the importance of the rights of victims of crime. "Justice", henceforth, "marches to a different beat".

I have always wondered what victims of crime have to go through in the Criminal Justice System and about their feelings and experiences as a victim—imagine these issues when the victims are children—the most vulnerable section of any society. Perhaps, you have to be a victim to know what it feels like.

Although we are not dealing with 'natural victimization' my heart goes out to the hundreds of people, especially children, who have been victimized by the cyclone-hit districts of Orissa. A deathly lull has crept over the entire state where over one and a half crore people have been rendered homeless and at least ten-thousand people are either killed/injured or missing. We are yet to recover from the most horrendous train tragedy in North India, sometime ago, that claimed hundreds of lives of innocent victims including women and children due to the negligence of a couple of human minds. The lesson that these tragedies teach us is that we need to have better appreciation in disaster management. How can we be more careful in the future and prevent such victimizations? What can we do to assist the living victims?

Though general victimology is a scientific study of all kinds of victims, the scope of victimology here is limited to crime victims. When a person is harmed by a criminal act, the agencies that make up our criminal justice system have a moral and legal obligation to respond. It is their responsibility not only to seek swift justice for the victims but also ease their suffering in a time of great need. Victimologists are concerned with the interaction between victims and offenders, victims and the criminal justice system, victims and the society and victims and the environment. This field has been increasingly recognized as an international field of research and action, transcending many cultural and legal systems in the last few years.

It is fifty-three years since our nation has got its independence and we are yet to listen and respond to victims of crime and their advocates. The victims of crime are virtually invisible in the laws and policies that govern our criminal justice system. Tremendous strides are being taken by various legal and social bodies and also the Indian Society of Victimology, to enact victims' rights laws in our country. Hopefully, the Bill on The Victims (Criminal Justice) Right to Assistance - 1996, drafted by the Indian Society of Victimology, will be given due importance and consideration by the present government to frame a national legislation to assist victims of crime in tune with the United Nations Declaration of basic principles of justice for victims of crime and abuse of power.

During the past two decades, the United Nations has undertaken a number of initiatives to address myriad needs of crime victims at the international level. The Declaration of the Basic Principle of Justice for Victims of Crime and Abuse of Power was adopted by consensus in the United Nations General Assembly in

1985, reflecting the collective will of the international community to address the interests and concerns of victims of crime. Considered as a 'Magna Carta' for crime victims around the world, the Declaration is based on the philosophy that victims should be treated with compassion and respect for their dignity. And that they are entitled to access the mechanisms of justice and to receive prompt redress for the harm they have suffered. India is proud to be a signatory to this Declaration.

Each year, millions of children are directly experiencing or witnessing increased violence and abuse in their homes, neighbourhoods and schools. Children from broken homes, abandoned and destitutes are easy targets of unscrupulous elements. Their tender age, innocence, lack of experience and absence of any guidance add to their vulnerability. The general penal code of this country and the various protective and preventive 'Special and Local Laws' specifically mention the offences wherein children are known to be victims. The statistical analysis in the 'Crime in India', 1997, discloses that there has been a gradual increase in the incidence of child rape in the figures of five years from 1993-97, followed by kidnapping and abduction, exposure and abandonment and the procuration of minor girls. Other crimes against children are infanticide, foeticide, buying and selling of girls for prostitution, abetment of suicide and child marriage. These are the only statistics that seem to be available on child victims. What we lack is a national repository of all child victimizations that is published every year. In spite of the lack of exact data, the available statistics suggest that child victimization is a crisis of national importance.

Though accurate figures are unavailable, each year there are thousands of children who enter the multi-million dollar illegal sex market. Children are coerced, kidnapped, sold and deceived or otherwise trafficked into enforced sexual encounters. The damage, commercial sexual exploitation causes to the children is unquestionable. Children are robbed of their natural sexual development and their sense of dignity and self-esteem as well. Their physical and mental health are put at tremendous risk, their rights are violated and their only support may come from those who exploit them. Where have we gone wrong in our sense of priorities and responsibility, when children of a prosperous society like ours, are selling their bodies to supplement their livelihood and find a ready market in the flesh trade?

Over the past decade new manifestations of child victimization have emerged. Advances in technology have brought serious threats and potential harm to children. Video cameras are increasingly used to produce child pornography. Computers equipped with scanners and access to the internet are used to disseminate child pornography worldwide and to solicit children for sexual encounters.

Research also reveals new information about intergenerational cycle of violence. A link between early victimization and the later involvement in violent crime has been identified. Witnessing violence at home and in the community also have adverse effects on the child's mental health and development, including an increased likelihood in some children to become directly involved in violence, whether as victims or perpetrators, as they mature.

Such tragedies are not just a day's happening. They happened yesterday; they are happening today; and they will happen again tomorrow—unless the nation decides to give priority to what can now be done to protect the victimization of these vast sections of its children.

In dealing with the victimization of children, the role of law enforcement agencies is most crucial as any effort taken even in the best interest of the children should not cause secondary victimization. This calls for a sensitization of the personnel of the criminal justice system, particularly, the police as they are the first agency to come in contact with the child victims. Sensitization programmes should cover the prosecutors, lawyers and even the judges at all stages of the criminal proceedings. In fact, I would go one step further and advise that sensitization programmes should extend to the legislators and policymakers.

In the given situation, time is ripe to address the unique needs of child victims and outline the legal rights that can protect children from physical and sexual abuse, child abduction, trafficking and other types of crimes against children.

Victimization is a serious threat for Indian children and youth. Many State laws now exist to protect children from physical abuse. Reforms on issues based on children have taken place at every step of the criminal justice process. But today, like all other victims, not even a fraction of the nation's child victims receive much needed services such as emergency financial assistance, crisis and mental health counselling, shelter, information and advocacy within the criminal justice system. There are many victims and their families who do not actively participate in the criminal or juvenile justice processes. They are denied meaningful participation in the judicial system and services to get justice done to them. Policies, therefore, have to be formulated to protect the rights of the child victims and improve their treatment. The Indian Society of Victimology has already ignited the kind of legislative response necessary. It is therefore, a challenge to the nation to renew and refocus the treatment of child victims of crime. There should be a comprehensive plan regarding how the nation should respond to child victims. Today, we have, besides academicians and scholars, a broad cross-section of the criminal and juvenile justice and allied professionals and workers in the victim service field. Let your voices be the guiding force for the hundreds and thousands of crime victims who go unheard every year. Let us develop a strategy for providing justice and comprehensive services to child victims of the 21st century. I urge every Indian who interacts with victims, from police officers to prosecutors, from judges to correction officers, from politicians to bureaucrats and business leaders to join this force and implement programmes and reforms that make sense for their own communities. Over these years the doors of justice have gradually opened to some victims of crime. It is my great hope that our nation will move closer to the day when the doors of justice open for all victims of crime.

The Indian Society of Victimology is dynamic in evolving innovative approaches to help child victims, find justice and assistance for child victims and their rights through this conference. It is this dynamism that ensures response to the evolving understanding of the needs of the child victims. This is not the final word, it is a sound compass that will help hold the course true in the years to come. Let us have faith that legislation will improve in favour of child victims of crime in near future.

2
An Agenda for Victims of Crime During the 21st Century

K. Chockalingam

Introduction

When a crime took place, concern of the criminal justice system all over the world till the middle of the 20th century was to prosecute the accused and punish the guilty. Victims of crime and the problems faced by them during the investigation, trial and after the trial have been completely neglected since the State took over the responsibility of the criminal justice system. The orientation of the criminal justice agencies all along has been to focus on the phenomenon of crime, its perpetrator and to prove the guilt of the perpetrator and to get him a conviction. Only in the early 1940s, realization about the role of victims in crime and the need to undertake scientific research about crime victims began after the introductory expositions made by the pioneers in Victimology such as Hans von Hentig and Benjamin Mendelsohn. Since then, several milestones have been made in the development of the science of Victimology and on the advocacy for the recognition of victims of crime in the criminal proceedings.

The first among the major landmarks in the field of Victimology was the collectivity of victim advocates comprising of various sections of the society such as researchers and academicians interested in Victimology and practitioners in the fields of criminal justice system in Jerusalem in 1973 for the first time in the First International Symposium on Victimology and their decision to meet once every three years to share and discuss the developments in the field[1].

The plight of victims of crime and of illegal abuse of power has been arousing increasing concern in recent years. Proliferating instances of victimization, both of individuals and of vulnerable groups, have provoked feelings of empathy, of shared vulnerability and the need for effective preventive and remedial action. Though the response still lags far behind the need, there seems to be a growing recognition that the common bond of humanity and self-interest as well as the climate of insecurity and fear in which so many people live, require strengthened ties of social solidarity and joint action to reduce the suffering and damage which criminal and other illicit acts inflict.

The second landmark is the founding of the World Society of Victimology in 1979 during the third International Symposium on Victimology in Germany to promote empirical research on victimology, and to focus attention of the nations and criminal justice systems of the world on the need to render justice to victims. Since the founding of the World Society of Victimology, Triennial International Symposia on Victimology have been sponsored by the society and organized the participation of researchers and practitioners in the criminal justice system, with the unanimous view to uphold the human rights to victims of crime and abuse of power. Criminologists and Victimologists of the world have consistently felt that when the rights of offenders, suspects and accused have been protected through several international instruments such as the United Nations Standard Minimum Rules for the Treatment of Prisoners and provisions in the national constitutions, there was nothing at the international or at national level in most of the countries to protect the rights of the victims of crime and abuse of power. Realizing the precarious conditions of victims of crime, the World Society of Victimology prepared a draft Victim Bill in consultation with experts from different countries of the world and after long deliberations at the Fifth International Symposium on Victimology at Zagreb in 1985 pressed for its adoption by the Seventh United Nations Congress on the Prevention of Crime and Treatment of Offenders held in Milan in September, 1985. For the first time in the history of the U.N. Congress on Crime Prevention, victims of crime and abuse of power became an item of the agenda for deliberations by all the countries leading to an intense debate resulting in a consensus among all the countries to have a declaration on victims with certain modifications. Finally, the Declaration on the Basic Principles of Justice for victims of crime and abuse of power was unanimously adopted by the General Assembly of the United Nations on 29th November, 1985. The adoption of the Declaration on victims by the United Nations is the third significant landmark and this instrument is a "Magna Carta" for the victims[2].

The Declaration on victims envisages four important aspects of rights of victims of crime and abuse of power, *viz.*, Access to justice and fair treatment, Restitution, Compensation and Assistance. A review of the position of victims of crime in the national criminal laws and the progress in the implementation of the U.N. Declaration on Victims by the United Nations revealed that even after a decade of adoption of the Declaration by the General Assembly, not much attention was paid by majority of the nations to implement provisions of its, more particularly among developing countries.

Handbook on Justice for Victims and Guide for Policy Makers

Concerned about the inaction and slow progress in the implementation of the U.N. Declaration on Victims, the U.N.

Commission on Crime Prevention and Criminal Justice in May, 1996 adopted a resolution to develop two international documents, *viz.*, (i) A Handbook on Justice for Victims[3] and (ii) Guide for Policy Makers[4] with the help of experts from different countries. Several groups of experts met four times during the last four years and the Fourth Expert Group meeting convened at Washington D.C. in April, 1998, in which the present author was also a member, finalized the two documents. The Handbook on Justice for Victims is an elaborate document meant for the different practitioners including the frontline professionals in the criminal justice system, *viz.*, police, prosecutors, judiciary and correctional departments and other victim assistance professionals providing methods and techniques by which victims could be handled and assisted. On the other hand, the brief document, *viz.*, the Guide for Policy Makers lists out the objectives of the U.N. Declaration on the Basic Principles of justice for victims of crime and abuse of power and the State's responsibility to implement the declaration by enacting new laws or incorporating new provisions in the existing laws to assist victims of crime and abuse of power.

Developments in the Field of Victimology and Victim Assistance in India

Realizing the plight of victims of crime and abuse of power in India is all the more high, due to the vast differences in the socio-economic conditions and discrimination perpetrated in the name of caste, creed, sex and religion, illiteracy and many other factors by people among themselves and also by the agencies of the government in its various administrative functions, a national organization in the name of Indian Society of Victimology was established in Chennai in 1992. Its main objectives were to promote victimological research, victim assistance and dissemination of knowledge about the rights of victims of crime and abuse of power and to bring together people who are interested in victim empowerment.

During the last eight years, the Indian Society of Victimology has endeavoured to disseminate the victimological principles among the members of the general society and the agencies of the criminal justice system through its seminars, symposia and conferences. Two significant events in the annals of the Indian Society of Victimology deserve special mention here. Due to the consistent efforts of the Indian Society of Victimology, the Government of Tamil Nadu has established a "Victims Assistance Fund"[5] since 1995 through which three specific categories of victims of violent crimes, *viz.*, murder, rape and grievous hurt are eligible to get a compensation of Rs. 10,000, Rs. 5,000 and Rs. 5,000 respectively, recognizing the need of the victim, though this is only a token amount. The Government of Tamil Nadu has allocated one crore rupees in the year 1995 (the same is renewed year after year) and effected some amendments in it in 1997[6]. In May, 1999, the Government of Tamil Nadu has extended the compensation to three more categories of victims, *viz.*, women victims of kidnapping and abduction (Rs. 5,000) victims of attempted murder in dowry harassment (Rs. 5,000 if the victim dies), children of victims who commit suicide (Rs. 10,000) and women who are permanently disabled in a dowry harassment (Rs. 5,000)[7].

Not being content with this State scheme and also recognizing the need for a national level law for victim compensation, the Indian Society of Victimology prepared a Victims (Criminal Injuries) Right to Assistance Bill, 1996 drafted by an expert committee consisting of some retired judges of the Supreme Court, High Court, Criminal Lawyers, Professors of Criminal Law and Criminology under the chairmanship of Justice V.R. Krishna Iyer, which was sponsored by the National Human Rights Commission. This Bill was considered as an immediate measure to be taken at the national level to provide monetary compensation and other assistance to victims of crime and the same was forwarded to the then Prime Minister, Home and Law ministers of the Government of India for adoption as a national law for victim assistance. Justice V.R. Krishna Iyer also addressed letters to the then Prime Minister, the Home and Law ministers to consider the Bill for adoption as a national law. The United Nations Commission on Crime Prevention and Criminal Justice also supported the initiative of the Indian Society of Victimology and wrote to the Government of India, in April 1998, for bringing out a national level legislation in tune with the U.N. Declaration on the Basic Principles of Justice for Victims of Crime and Abuse of Power, to assist crime victims in India but so far it has not been done.

Biennial Conference of the Indian Society of Victimology

The National Conferences of the Indian Society of Victimology have always served as fora to project the cause of crime victims in India. The First Biennial Conference held in Chennai in 1994 took up the subject of women as victims of crime as one of its main themes for deliberations, whereas the Second Biennial Conference held at the National Law School of India University, Bangalore had deliberated on the only theme of 'A Comprehensive Victim Bill for India' and adopted the victim bill prepared by the expert Committee constituted by the ISV[8,9].

The main theme of the third Biennial Conference was "Child Victims of Crime: Issues and Prospects" with the following two sub-themes:

1. Victimization of Child : Various Forms and Patterns.
2. Protection of Child from Victimization: Strategies and Inncvations.

The preamble of the United Nations 'Convention on the Rights of the Child'[10] states the significance of childhood and the need to protect it in the following words: The Universal Declaration of Human Rights, 1948, has proclaimed that the childhood is entitled to special care and assistance. The family, as the fundamental group of society and the natural environment for the growth and well-being of all its members, particularly children, should be afforded the necessary protection and assistance so that it can fully assume its responsibilities within the community. For the full and harmonious development of his or her personality, the child should grow up in a family environment in an atmosphere of happiness, love and understanding. The child should be fully prepared to live an individual life in society, and brought up in the spirit of the ideals proclaimed in the Charter of the United Nations, and in particular in the spirit of peace, dignity, tolerance, freedom, equality and solidarity.

The need to extend particular care to the child has been stated in the Geneva Declaration of the Rights of the Child of 1924 and in the Declaration of the Rights of the Child adopted by the General Assembly on 20th November, 1959, and recognized in the Universal Declaration of Human Rights, in the International Covenant on Civil and Political Rights and in the Statutes and relevant instruments of specialized agencies and the international organizations concerned with the welfare of the child. The Declaration of the Rights of the Child states that the child, by reason of his physical and mental immaturity needs special safeguards and care, including appropriate legal protection, before as well as after birth. The Declaration on Social and Legal Principles relating to the protection and welfare of children, with special reference to foster placement and adoption, the U.N. Standard Minimum Rules for the Administration of Juvenile Justice (The Beijing Rules) and the Declaration of the Protection of Women and Children in emergency and armed conflicts, recognize that, in all countries there are children living in exceptionally difficult conditions and that such children need special consideration; take due account of the importance of the traditions and cultural values of people for the protection and harmonious development of the child; recognize the importance of the international cooperation for improving the living conditions of children in every country, particularly in developing countries.

Extent and Forms of Child Victimizations—International and National

The background paper for the workshop on the prevention of violent crime presented by the United Nations in its 9th U.N. Congress on Prevention of Crime and Treatment of Offenders held in Cairo in April, 1995 states that "in the U.S.A. homicide is one of the five major causes of death in young children". The same study quotes some alarming figures. In Brazil, four children are murdered each day, representing an increase of forty per cent over the year 1993; in the Philippines, Sri Lanka and Thailand, there are estimated to be more than five lakhs cases of child prostitution. In the U.S. in 1992, 7,000 children were killed using firearms. At least ninety per cent of domestic violence in Canada is targetted at women and children. In Asia, it is reckoned that one hundred million women are estimated to have 'disappeared'. According to the experts, this figure may be partly attributable to the selected destruction of foetuses, infanticide, and the abandonment of female children.

A recent study on the prevalence and consequences of child victimization sponsored by the National Institute of Justice in U.S. in 1997 and conducted by the National Crime Victims Research and Treatment Centre at the Medical University of South Carolina among 4,023 adolescents and their parents indicate that a significant number of the youth of today have been victims of sexual and physical abuse and have personally witnessed incidents of violence against others.

Extrapolating the findings of this study to the national adolescent population as a whole suggests that of the 22.3 million adolescents in the age of twelve to seventeen years in the U.S. today, approximately 1.8 million have been victims of a serious sexual assault, 3.9 million have been victims of a serious physical assault, and almost 9 million have witnessed serious violence. Nearly 2 million have suffered from Post Traumatic Disorder Syndrome (PTDS), and about 3.4 million have been drug or alcohol abusers as well. Analysis of the survey information indicates a strong correlation between drug abuse and delinquency. Further findings indicate that more females than male adolescents had been sexually assaulted with 13 per cent of females in contrast to 3.4 per cent of males. Also young males had significantly higher rates of physical assault than females, with 21.3 per cent versus 13 per cent. The data also revealed that the youth from lower income groups experienced higher rates of sexual and physical assault than those from middle and higher income groups[11]. The trend of these findings may be similar in many other countries too, including India.

In India, the child victimizations or child abuse have been found to take several forms—physical, sexual and emotional. The perpetrators of violence on children range from the friendly neighbour to the tough schoolteacher to the child's own parents. Some perverted streak in men and women impel them to hurt and injure children both physically and mentally.

The abused children are hesitant to talk about their experiences because they are unable to comprehend or articulate what has happened to them and also because the people who abuse them have threatened them with dire consequences if they reveal it. While physical abuse takes the form of beating, inflicting burns, strangulation, battering and bites and is most prevalent among child workers and children in alcoholic families, emotional abuse is very common and happens in many homes everyday.

Affluent families are not an exception for the prevalence of child abuse. Parental favouritism, constant negative comparisons and castigation for being "under-achievers" can nag a child into depression. Often, it is the sheer neglect on the part of parents to identify the symptoms of abuse in their children that leads to extreme situations. While children may not be able to explain what has happened to them in detail, they give off certain signals that must be watched out for. Physical indicators such as unexplained bruises, welts, bite marks, fractures, torn or bloody undergarments, difficulty in walking and sitting, venereal diseases and fatigue must be investigated. The more subtle behavioural disorders such as delinquency, violence, withdrawal symptoms, chronic depression, shying off physical touch, suicide attempts and hysteria over a prolonged period are also indicators that the child may be undergoing victimization or abuse.

Priorities of Action towards Justice for Victims

Creation of Awareness

Criminal Justice systems have a moral and legal responsibility to make all efforts to prevent crime victimization and also to provide relief and satisfaction to the victims. In India, creating awareness at all levels is the basic and immediate need to recognize that the sufferings of victims are unfortunate and the society condemns such sufferings and to motivate the society and people at large about the importance of preventing victimization and taking care of victims. Even in developed countries where victim support and service systems have been sufficiently established, awareness campaign is an ongoing process. For example, in the United States, Congress designates one week each year usually in late April, as "National Crime Victims Rights Week" for the last two decades and it is declared by the President of the United States each year to highlight the needs of crime victims and the types of rights and services that could respond to those needs. Declarations are signed by many leading politicians such as State Governors and Mayors. During the week, national awards are presented to outstanding victim service providers from across the country. The week also provides opportunity for local communities to pay tribute to crime victims. The U.S. Department of Justice sponsors the development of a Public Awareness Resource Guide for victim assistance programmes to use in planning "National Crime Victims Rights Week" activities. Hundreds of ideas to increase public awareness of victims issues have been presented in the guide. They include runs, rallies, memorial walls and sapling plantings; conducting forums, publishing editorials and broadcasting public service announcements; displaying posters and distributing brochures and other information in court buildings, school libraries and local retail establishments. Europe celebrates each year a "European Victims Day" with new initiatives being announced. In 1997, the European Forum for Victim Services issued a "Statement of Victims' rights in the process of criminal justice" which focused on the rights for the victim to:

1. Respect and recognition at all stages of the criminal proceedings.
2. Receive information and explanation about the progress of the case.
3. Provide information to officials responsible for decisions relating to the offender.
4. Have legal advice available, regardless of their means.
5. Protection both for their privacy and for their physical safety.
6. Compensation both from the offender and from the State.

In the Netherlands, Victim Satisfaction Surveys (like customer satisfaction surveys) are regularly conducted by the office of the public prosecution.

A peer review system in the Police Department has also been established in the Netherlands in which, after the victim has been questioned by a police detective, a second detective inquires of the victim regarding how he or she had been treated by the first detective. The responses are used to improve their training further. In Japan, a number of questionnaires regarding the treatment of citizens by the police are carried out both by the National Police Agency and some prefectural police forces. These are used as a means of improving the police treatment of victims and civilians.

The United States has created a separate section as Office for Victims of Crime (OVC) in the Federal Department of Justice and many other countries have also created a section for victims in their Home or Interior Ministries. On the similar lines in the Home Ministry of the Government of India and the Home Departments of all the State Governments and Union Territories, a separate section to deal with issues of victims of crime should be opened. This could be the first step to recognise the problems of victims of crime and to chalk out programmes to alleviate their problems, to collect information and disseminate information about victim issues.

Victim Assistance is the Need of the Hour

What is most important in the case of victims of crime, particularly, child victims is the immediate assistance to be rendered to them to relieve them from victimization. Experiments have been initiated in Maharashtra, Tamil Nadu and a few other states to provide rescue to the children in difficult circumstances. For example, as early as in 1994, the Indian Council for Child Welfare, Chennai, set up a Crisis Intervention Centre to "intervene, prevent, rescue and rehabilitate children from all kinds of abuse". The Directorate of Social Defence, Government of Tamil Nadu has started a twenty-four hour phone outreach programme called "CHILDLINE" for helping children in distress in Chennai from April 30, 1999 onwards with a toll free telephone number of 1098. Any child in distress or an adult who sees a child in distress can call the number and provide details to the volunteers attending the call. Any child who is abandoned, runs away, requires help, lives alone on the streets, needs a place to stay, is abused or needs help to go back to the family can call the number for help.

While the Directorate of Social Defence is the nodal agency for the "Childline" services, two NGOs, *viz.*, Indian Council for Child Welfare and Don Bosco Anbu Illam function as the collaborating agencies receiving the calls and providing immediate assistance to the child. The response mechanism had been activated in such a way as to render assistance to children, depending on the needs of each case, within fifteen minutes of receiving the call. A log book records all calls received, details regarding the nature of intervention, action taken and subsequent follow-up activities, in an effort to build up a data base of problem children in Chennai. Childline is funded by the Ministry of Social Justice and Empowerment.

When we are at the threshold of the third millennium, it is the duty of the State and Society to care for its crime victims and treat them with human dignity. Such duty is more paramount when it comes to child victims of crime who are defenceless in majority of the cases. I hope that the Indian Society of Victimology and other organisations, NGOs through deliberations will pave way for the statutory recognition of rights of victims of crime in general and child victims in particular.

References

1. Chockalingam, K. "A Review of Victimological Developments In India", *Japanese Journal of Victimology,* Vol. 3, No. 20, 1995, pp. 78-95.
2. United Nations Declarations on the Basic Principles of Justice for Victims of Crime and Abuse of Power, U.N. General Assembly Resolutions, 40/34, 1985.
3. United Nations Handbook on Justice for Victims—on the Use and Application of the United Nations Declaration on the Basic Principles of Justice for Victims of Crime and Abuse of Power, 161 Pages, 1998 A.
4. United Nations Guide for Policymakers—on the Implementation of the United Nations Declarations on the Basic Principles of Justice for Victims of Crime and Abuse of Power, 31.
5. Government of Tamil Nadu "Creation of Victims Assistance Fund" Home (Police-XII) Department, G.O.M.S. No. 1258, dated 21.8.1995.
6. Government of Tamil Nadu (1997) "Victims Assistance Fund Reviewed" Home (Police-XII) Department, G.O.M.S. 89, dated 24.1.1997.

7. Government of Tamil Nadu (1999) "Victims Assistance Fund—Provision of Relief to Certain Women Victims of Additional Crimes Against Women", Home (Police-XII) Department, G.O.M. S. No. 629, dated 10.5.1999.

8. Indian Society of Victimology, "The Victims (Criminal Injuries) Right to Assistance Bill" Draft Bill prepared and presented at the II Biennial Conference of the Indian Society of Victimology, at the National Law School of India University, Bangalore, October 5-7, 1996.

9. Chockalingam, K. "March Towards Implementation of Victim Bill in India" in 'Society and Politics—Issues and Perspectives' (Ed) T.P. Sankaran Kutty Nair, Indian Institute of Police Studies, Thiruvananthapuram, 1998; pp. 550-68.

10. United Nations (1989) "Convention on the Rights of the Child" in Compendium of United Nations Standards and Norms in Crime Prevention and Criminal Justice, United Nations, New York, 1992, pp. 271-78.

11. Kilpatrick, "The Prevalence and Consequences of Child Victimisation", NIJ Research Preview, April, 1997, p. 8.

3

Neglect of Victims of Crime and What can be Done

P.S. Bawa

A victim of crime is a pathetic sight. Not only does he suffer losses, loses dignity, or undergoes privation of having a traumatic experience of being a victim of crime when he feels diminished in all respects, he also sees no hope, in near future, of his being fulfilled, satisfied, or compensated. He is heavy with guilt because of the missed opportunity in preventing the crime or protecting himself against it by not following a lonely street or carrying money without adequate precaution or care. He thus suffers guilt, stress, trauma, fear, emotional upset, and psychological distress.

Crime imposes heavy cost upon society in terms of the personal loss (indicated above), the insurance costs, medical expenses, man-days lost, impairment, death, systems costs, etc. It is a drain upon economic resources as the product is usurped by the ineligible and, unauthorized persons who ought to have contributed to the economy. It is also a strain upon the economy to the extent of costs required to meet the challenge of crime in terms of the infrastructure of the criminal justice system comprising the police, the prosecution, the judiciary, the correctional services, and the prisons. The institutions of the system are expensive and cost the exchequer, ultimately the tax-payer.

So there are two categories of victims of crime. One category pertains to those suffering the direct impact of crime. The other includes the society that bears the cost of the institutions designed to deal with crime in its various phases and processes, even those dealing with crimes that have not happened or been committed; *i.e.*, the preventive action.

Both these categories are pushed to the background in the rush of events when the search for the criminal becomes a predominant management objective for police. Though this is meant to find out the truth of the incident, yet this process is impersonnel, unidirectional and related to the victim only to the extent he helps in identification of the culprit or the circumstances under which the crime was committed. Sometimes, this relapse into memory of the unpleasant event creates unpleasantness every time the victim reconstructs the scene for the benefit of the investigating officer.

It is only after the police has succeeded in apprehending the criminal that the response of the court and the efforts of the prosecutors come into play. Since both these institutions have not seen the victim in his raw, original, shattered state, they are remote, methodical, impersonal, and aloof in responses which, at times, appear to be wooden, devoid of any milk of human kindness, or any streak of sympathy.

Whatever be the extent of responses of the system, the moot point is that it is loaded in favour of the criminal. In the process, victimology is a victim of the proverbs which give direction to the functioning of the system. Quotes from the jurisprudence are like proverbs which are not only unhelpful to the victim but also contradictory thus neutralizing the functioning of the system. Proverbs were conceived by the 'wise' to guard against the arbitrariness of the autocrats, and yet-to-be-just regimes. These are short crisp sentences which etch deeply in the psyche of the law enforcement officers, the judiciary, and all others concerned with the system. These are polestars, touchstones, astrolabes, guidelines, and tests of the system.

There is a large category of the safeguards for criminals in the form of proverbs.

- he is innocent till proved guilty
- he is entitled to benefit of doubt
- bail is his right (bail and not jail)
- the case has to be proved beyond reasonable doubt
- let 99 criminals get away but not one innocent person indicted
- he is entitled to all rights under the Constitution
- since he is a citizen, he is entitled to all the basic needs in the prison, including the legal aid.

All these principles are couched in the beautiful, jargonized language, very convincing, well reasoned out. Taken one by one, there is a lot of force in these tenets. All by themselves, they stand erect. But they are too solid to meet each other, bend for a compromise and make for a coherent system. They clash. They are uncompromising because their interests come into conflict. If a criminal is innocent till proved guilty, then why is he incarcerated as an 'undertrial' awaiting the finalisation of the case. If 'bail and not jail' is the principle, how is it that so many (perhaps 85 per cent) prisoners are languishing in prisons. And how does one trace out a criminal released on personal bond? Why should 99 criminals be left out? Why should, the criminal who has rights, not perform his fundamental duty of eschewing violence or following the law? And then after a prolonged incarceration, he gets benefit of doubt and all traces of criminality are washed from his face.

Victim of crime is a fact; criminal is a conjecture. Not much effort is required to know the plight of the victim. But law has to protect the innocent who can be a victim of a conjecture. Since the criminal is unknown, the law enforcement agency has to be circumspect and ensure against miscarriage of justice upon the innocent. Yet who can deny that there are criminals. After all, crime is a matter of fact; so is a victim. But the criminal either eludes or deludes under the support of the jurisprudential shibboleths. No surprise that many get scot free after a protracted trial which is more gruesome for the victim than a criminal for the former loses and the latter gains. The processes of the system are a zero sum game. It is here that the distinction between truth and proof is necessary. The truth shall come out and it does. But the proof is elusive because witness may not be available, may become hostile, may not cooperate, may forget the incident thus introducing contradictions and creating a scope for incredibility. So in spite of the fact of crime, the perpetrator escapes from the net.

The large scale latitude shown to the lot of the criminal is responsible for a low rate of conviction and search for a parallel system of justice. It is equally a powerful tenet that justice delayed is justice denied. But the distribution of justice does get delayed. Hence the denial, leading to frustration, and then personal initiatives to seek justice as per one's will. This is a symptom of desperation. This has been the cause of Bhagalpur incident and continues to intrigue the police under pressure to 'show results' and resort to short cuts and other unauthorized practices. It will not be far fetched to suggest that brutalization of force is attributed to delay and then denial of justice. The rise of the parallel system too can be attributed to the vacuum caused by the system's inadequacies and limping progress.

At the initial stage when crime is committed or has come to light, the state is all for the victim of crime. The police swoops over the site of crime, speaks to the victim, gets his report and then evidence, is all anxious to 'work out' the case, as the detection of crime is called. And then other institutions are responsible to complete the process. But with the lapse of time, the concern for the victim decreases. The element of time works as a scourge.

Time heels the wounds of the victim and the sensitivities of the enforcement agency.

More the time, less the concern; less the time, more the concern. The result is that the victim is not heeded to when he wants to find out the progress of the case. He has no response from the inaccessible court whom he cannot, for fear of contempt, even ask

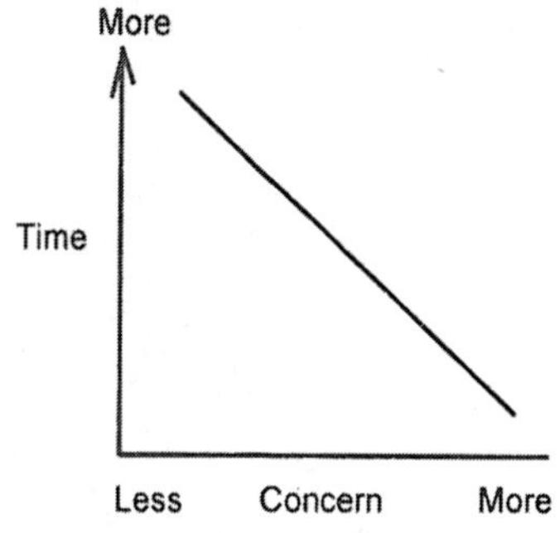

the reason for delay or make a suggestion for an expeditious disposal.

The other reason for diminishing interest is the piling up of cases with all agencies. The latest in time pushes the earlier ones backwards. The new gets the priority. The fresh is in lime light. Hence resources have to be expanded upon the most recent. The 'more' engulf the one which may be the concern of the individual but not that of the organization.

Third factor that lessens the interest is the element of familiarity. Once the case is familiar to the officials, it loses its sting. The victim then subsequently becomes a burden to be avoided. It mostly happens when the case is not worked out and the victim is compelled to knock at the door of police, even if for the purpose of satisfaction. With time, the victim also gets acclimatized to deprivation, loss, humiliation. Mental adjustment is made, justification provided, and coping strategies devised.

Under the incomplete system, the problem is how to create a

sense of justice. There are two aspects which must be considered. The CJS is expected to produce justice which means speedy, sure and sufficient disposal of case and penalties where necessary. We must get over the overbearing influence of the proverbs[1] which have succeeded in creating a mindset, and found a theory of justice that satisfies the victim, the criminal, and the social order. This is an intricate task. However incomplete and inadequate, an attempt

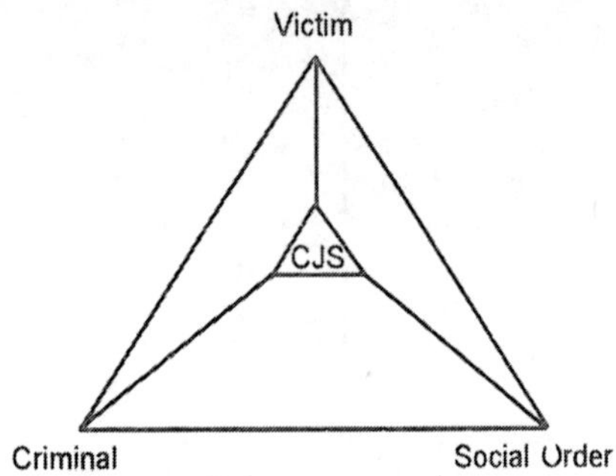

must be made.

Let us examine the system as dealing with three parties when crime is committed.

In appears that the system has accountability to all three participants. Whereas its role towards the criminal is well defined in the shape of crisp short sentences, its role to the victim and social order is excluded in the scheme of things. The safeguards granted to the criminal are given, cannot be altered because each one is well reasoned and stands on its firm feet. There is thus a need to search roles that appease or satisfy the victim and take care of the public interest and social order. The present system is loaded in favour of the criminal. There is a need to balance and bring about an equalization. How to do this? We may try a few principles.

1. **Rule of the prima facie:** This principle is based on the preponderance of evidence. It is this which puts the criminal in the dock to face a trial. If it is risky to see an innocent

being punished, it is equally unjust to let a criminal go by in spite of the preponderance of evidence. And what is the sanctity of the benefit of doubt? Why only in favour of the criminal? Why not to assist the victim? Truth is a fact whereas proof is a construction. If construction fails, the ground must not give way. It is well known that statements u/s 161 Cr PC are not signed, that witnesses turn hostile, often become forgetful, develop a soft corner for the criminal, enter into compromises, are cajoled, threatened and endangered. In the light of all these possibilities, how is it that the 'principle of innocence' should be so overbearing as to stifle the fact. So the probabilities cannot be set aside and circumstances doubted every time the evidence whittles down under the various pressures to the disadvantage and disappointment of the victim who is left in the lurch by all around him. The prosecution might fail, but the victim loses. The victim is betrayed by the process. The majority works against him as his testimony is said not to be supported by evidence. In spite of the fact, he becomes unreliable. Such is the power of the rule of corroboration. The so-called corroborators are not victims; so they can shift their allegiance, leaving the victim high and dry, not to be counted upon. He appears an unreliable wretch.

2. **Right to be heard:** Every victim of crime has a right to be heard. Often this right is denied to him by means of subterfuges practised by police who are reluctant to register cases not realizing that the process of investigation cannot start unless cognizance of crime is taken. This is, in fact, a fundamental right, subsumed under the rubric of 'equality before law and equal protection of laws'.

There shall be no denial of registration with regard to any cognizable crime. Law must take its course, whatever be the compulsions (statistical, resource, work-load) of the police.

Similarly, he has a right to be heard by the court which is more indulgent in giving adjournments, generally on the request of defence counsel. Every postponement of the trial is a pain to the victim who gets feeling of being ignored by the system.

3. **Right to know/information:** The victim has every right to know the progress of his case both from police and the court. Though the channel of communication in the court is one-sided, *i.e.*, from the court to the client, with no questions or doubts permitted, yet this does not satisfy the victim who must seek court's indulgence and patronage in being heard and his problem resolved. The plight of the victim and the witnesses in the corridors of courts is well known. The atmosphere is impersonal, remote from compassion, sympathy, balmy touch. It is formal, standardized, commercial and matter-of-fact, at times verging on the insensitive. It is here that the victim is grilled, harassed, put to inconvenience, not cared for by anyone, and running from pillar to post.

   The anxiety of the victim must, therefore, be appeased by the police or court informing him of the progress or reason for delay. He must not be in doubt about the efficacy of the system and must understand its genuine compulsions or else he shall have his own interpretations of the unjustness which he is a prey to. This requires a sensitive approach.

4. **Right to decent treatment:** The system is required to decide the problem expeditiously. It involves three things. One, it must not permit delay being caused; two, it must deliver the result; and three, it must be humane to the victim till the process is complete. This analysis highlights the need to give decent treatment to the victim who undergoes privations till the decision of the case. If the processes cannot be expedited, the least that the system can do is to extend a proper treatment to the victim and not humiliate him by asking him to come again and again or refusing to inform him of the progress or considering him as a burden, an imposition, or denying him

the basic facilities of waiting, toilet, clarity of orders, giving him copies, if he so desires, etc.

5. **Minimization of pain, inconvenience, humiliation:** One of the methods of coping with plight of victim is to minimize the inconvenience caused by procedures and processes. This can be done by the sensitization of the agents to the travails of the victims. It involves two things. First, not doing what is not permitted. If a woman or a child under the age of 15 years is not to be called to the police station, this should not be done (Sec. 160 Cr PC). If statement of the complainant is to be taken, it must be done at the earliest so that he gets the feeling that it has been done. Often, the statements u/s 161 Cr PC are written later on, based on the FIR. Statements, should not only be taken at the earliest, but also appear to be recorded by giving this feeling to the victim. If the victim has an appointment to meet the investigation officer, this must be honoured or the victim should be informed of the change, if it is unavoidable.

This aspect also includes the compensation to victims and all efforts which are necessary to secure it. For instance, a victim of road accident or the survivors must be assisted in getting the solatium, insurance on self, insurance as per third party commitment, and other support which the Accident Claims Tribunal can provide. All this requires copies of police reports, documents, certificates and other supporting material which police and others concerned must provide without hassels. In this aspect is also relevant the issue of Final Report so that the victim can get relief. Even getting the postmortem expedited in unnatural death cases is a great succour to the survivors.

The principle involved is getting the victim what is due to him. If there are various proverbs which come to the assistance of a criminal, there ought to be a few which help the victim. One of these can be 'do not do unto others what you do not like to be done to you.' This is a negative moral ethic propounded by Sandra Pralong[2], a totally practical rule and in consonance with Popper's principle of 'minimizing avoidable suffering', propounded in his book *The Open Society and its Enemies*.

6. **Training in sensitivities:** The agencies must be made to realize that the principles are important, practical, desirable, and enforceable. The officials at all levels must be sensitized to the problems of the victim. Policing, which had so far concerned itself with the crimes and criminals, must extend its concerns to the victim. So at every incident, there are two things which it has to do. Firstly, make efforts to catch the criminal. Secondly, to give all possible support to the victim of crime.

This sensitization will come to a sensitive person only and not every one. So while dealing with organization, one must institutionalize inputs and drill in the attitudes to be converted into behaviour.

7. **Monitoring and follow up:** The conversion of attitude to behaviour is possible only when the senior officers ensure that along with efforts to trace the perpetrators of crime, efforts are made to alleviate the condition of the victim. The latter endeavour does not require many resources. It only requires a proper handling. All that ought to be done for the victim must be done because it is in ones control, whereas catching a criminal is a big adventure, a riddle, a charade.

Notes and References

1. The concept of 'proverbs' was used by Herbert A Simon in Administrative Behaviour; The Free Press; New York, 1976.
2. Sandra Pralong; Is there an ethics of the Open Society in Popper's Open Society after 50 years; ed. Ian Jarvie and Sandra Pralong; Routlege; 1999.

4

Child Victims of Crime: Issues and Prospects

S.P. Srivastava

I

The contemporary victimological vision is expanding its horizons to visualise the trials and tribulations of a wide variety of those victims of crime about whom the justice-oriented policy perspectives with regard to their plight and problems are far from being clear. The indifference of traditional victimological vision to unravel the ground realities of children's abuse and exploitation is one such area where empirical insight is both partial and perfunctory. To make up for this deficiency of our current knowledge on the subject, victimologists are trying hard to build a substantial data-base largely on the non-criminological forms of child abuse and exploitation—globally, nationally, regionally and locally.

Having resolved to look at the problems and predicaments of child victims of crime, the victimologists everywhere are trying to understand and analyse the situations under which criminal victimization of children occurs. In fact, the subject of juvenile victimization has not yet been extensively discussed and debated in India.

II

The victimization of children is by no means a new phenomenon, in fact, history is replete with examples of various forms of child abuse and exploitation. What is new is the recognition of the problem. The growing societal concern about the problem, the forms it has taken—and the cruel realities that these forms often reflect—are due to a number of developments, prominent among them being: (i) the recognition of the rights of child and the ratification of these rights by large number of nations and, (ii) the world declaration on the survival, protection and development of children. In conformity with these developments, governments across the globe are now feeling sufficiently concerned with the preservation, protection and promotion of children's rights and to the prevention, control and eradication of all forms and practices derogatory to children's rights and injurious to their safety, health and well-being. In consonance with the concerns voiced both globally and nationally, everywhere the governments have now come up with policy statements, legal instruments, programme formalization and the implementation of the State's agenda for the care, protection, treatment, training and development of the children. The commitment that has arisen out of the concern for some of the atrocious and unthinkable forms of juvenile victimization offers hope for a better deal to children who are helpless victims of adult abuse and exploitation, and in some extreme cases, of barbaric brutalization.

The issue here is not the presence or absence of the beautifully worded policy statements and rhetoric on the rights of the child. The issue indeed is how far the policy and programme related rhetoric have travelled to the realm of a progressive and positive empirical reality for children in general and victimised children in particular. When we look at the children's condition in the developing countries, we come across a depressing reality—a situation that makes us hang our heads in shame. Millions of children in many of the developing countries of Asia, Africa and Latin America are silent sufferers of mass poverty, wide-spread malnutrition, hunger, hopelessness, illiteracy, ignorance, dearth, desertion, destitution, disability, disease and death. We know of the harsh reality and the misfortunes of millions of children woefully trapped into conditions of life from where there is no escape, except for a degrading, disgraceful and dehumanised existence.

Children's situation in India is no better and we cannot afford to be complacent about it. Anyone who is familiar or concerned about the disadvantaged children, or children in especially difficult circumstances, knows that there is a problem galore. The brazen and bizarre incidents of children's abuse and exploitation occur with frightening regularity compelling us to think of our hypocrisy about the nation's commitment to those constitutional commandments which obligate the state to do so many good things for children. The deeply disturbing realities of child abuse and exploitation give a lie to a defining sentence in the National Policy for Children: "Children are supremely important assets and their nurture and solicitude is the nation's primary responsibility".

The magnitude of the problem of child abuse and exploitation is so gigantic, the causes so complex and confounding, the resources so limited, the indifference and unconcern so wide-spread and the states' unwillingness to act in a determined manner so obvious, that there is an all-round disappointment and despondency. Majority of us are becoming cynical because most of our past and present policy statements do not invite credibility any more. The huge expenditures on several programmes and activities of child development have not brought us any closer to solutions. It is no wonder then that we have a huge problem of child abuse and exploitation on hand.

This work intends to delimit the outreach of the discussion to the problem of "Criminal victimization of children", namely, the analysis, examination and articulation of the problems, policies, programmes and the current perspectives on combating the menace of criminal victimization of juvenile, in other words, the unravelling of issues and perspectives on child victims of crime.

The victimologists (included criminologists) may not be in position to competently analyse or examine some of obvious, yet very important non-criminological manifestations of the problem of child abuse and exploitation. The reference is to the problem of child labour, or to the problems of street children, handicapped children, destitute children, neglected children and other varieties of children vulnerable to non-criminal victimization. Let us, therefore, avoid any detailed discussion on non-criminal aspects of juvenile victimization, and better concentrate on criminal victimization of children, which, in itself, is a big subject for deliberations. Let us also avoid getting bogged down to problems and issues concerning children's well-being and move on to the specific varieties of criminal victimization of children.

III

The fact that children in all societies and at all times have been loved and loathed, healed and hurt, protected and punished, endeared and endangered, shows that benevolence for and violence against children runs parallel throughout history. Crimes against children continue to be committed everywhere, perhaps in the same manner as before. The criminal victimization of children in its subtle and bizarre form continues to be the burden of societal benevolence towards children. The victimization of children through various forms of violence—physical and emotional, social and economic—has been the persistent and pervasive problem of the past and continues to be the problem of the present. It is a different matter though that most of the societies (including Indian Society) have long ignored violence against children as a tolerable aberration of certain families troubled by the traumas of domestic disorganisation.

Domestic violence against children has, therefore, not been recognised as a problem of any serious concern. It continues to be perceived as a private family matter not fit to be discussed with any outsider. Talking about it is incongruent without idealised notions of paternal care of children. Subjecting children to harsh disciplinary measures is still the parents' privilege and supposedly the surest way of teaching a child the early lessons of discipline and obedience. The issue of cruelty does not figure prominently in the large portion of parental violence directed against their own children. But herein arise certain questions; whether domestic violence is a private issue, or a matter of public concern? Should parental violence against their own children be regarded as 'disciplining' or be treated as a form of child victimization? Or, where and under what circumstances parental violence ceases to be beneficial or benevolent and assumes that character of victimization? These questions, in Indian context, defy easy explanations and continue to be problematic. It is for reasons of cultural conditioning that one tends to ignore child-centered domestic violence and refuses to treat it as a problem.

Another issue for consideration is: whether child-centered domestic violence has reached such serious proportions that treating it as a social problem has become necessary? There are no straight answers to this question, at least for now. Many of us will not feel comfortable to follow the western (basically American) line of thinking where children have been privileged to approach police against parental mistreatment, cruel or unusual treatment or punishment.

Against this backdrop, we often come across an empirical reality which makes sordid revelations about the cruelties (read crimes) being inflicted on children in certain families. The bizarre incidents of family-centered juvenile victimization make us confused about how to help such victims of domestic violence. These incidents also make us overwhelmed by the seeming impossibility of intervening into the situation and rendering some help or succour to the child. Our feelings towards the plight of such children are often passionate and intense, involving emotional concern, quite often outrage, but that is where our concern ends and helplessness takes over.

Since an overwhelming number of such incidents go unreported and never enter the official police records, we are in no position to gauge the actual extent or the magnitude of the problem. We do not know the names or the numbers of such children or the whereabouts of their victimizers (parents and employers). The cases that come to the knowledge of official agencies—hospitals, nursing homes, police stations, etc., just reveal the tip of the iceberg. Given the kind of social milieu we live in, the extent of domestic victimization of children is impossible to be deciphered. As yet, we do not have reliable data to tell us as to where such families are and where are such agents of juvenile victimization? Whatever rudimentary awareness we have about such children and their victimizers, we do not know how to deal with them. This is in reality dilemma of the situation.

The problem of latent criminal victimization of children is perhaps as much disconcerting as is the problem of child victims of crimes reported in the Crime in India figures. It is therefore, imperative that we should also understand the nature of hidden criminal victimization of children, since that alone would help us devise some practical measures for prevention and control. Devising preventive, combative or corrective strategies without fuller understanding of the dark figures of domestic crimes against children would only turn out to be a futile academic exercise.

IV

The offences committed against children, or the crimes in which children are the victims, are called 'crimes against children'. The Indian Penal Code and various protective and preventive "Special and Local Laws" specifically mention the offences wherein children are known to be the victims. The cases in which the children are victimized and abused are categorized under two broad heads: (i) crimes committed against children which are punishable under Indian Penal Code; and (ii) crimes committed against children which are punishable under special and local laws.

The crimes which are punishable under the Indian Penal Code include: (a) foeticide (crime against unborn child) Sections 315 and 316 IPC; (b) infanticide (crime against newly born child) Section 315 IPC; (c) exposure and abandonment (crime against children by parents or others to expose or leave them with the intention of abandonment) Section 317 IPC; (d) Kidnapping and abduction for exporting, Section 360 IPC; kidnapping for ransom, Section 363 read with Section 384 IPC; for camel racing, Section 363 IPC; for begging, Section 363-A IPC; to compel for marriage, Section 366 IPC; and for slavery Section 367 IPC; (e) procurement of minor girls (for inducement to force or seduce to illicit intercourse), Section 366-A IPC; (f) selling of girls for prostitution, Section 372 IPC; (g) buying of girls for prostitution, Section 373 IPC; (h) rape and unnatural offences.

Crimes against children which are punishable under special and local laws fall under the ambit of: (a) Immoral Traffic Prevention Act 1956; (b) Child Marriage Restraint Act 1979; (c) Child Labour (Prohibition and Regulation) Act 1986; and (d) Juvenile Justice Act 1986.

Whilst the available official statistics on crimes against children (as annually reported in Crime in India) do not indicate the actual extent of the criminal victimization of children owing to a large number of cases remaining unreported or unregistered, these statistics, however, provide us a peep into the nature of crimes which come to the knowledge of the police.

A report of (1997) Crime in India tells us that amongst the 10 types of crime against children, child rape tops the list followed in descending order by kidnapping and abduction; procuration of minor girls; selling of girls for prostitution; buying of girls for prostitution; abetment of suicide; exposure and abandonment, infanticide; foeticide and marriage of minor children.

Child rape (up to 16 years) has shown noticeable size in its reported incidence from 1993 to 1997, and percentage variation has been 8.1 per cent over 1993 figure. Almost similar increase was noticed in other crime heads. A further probe into the rising incidence of child rape revealed that: (i) of all the victims in rape cases during 1997, children alone accounted for 28.8 per cent; (ii) the cases of rape of children below the age of 10 years were on a rise every year in the country sence 1993; (iii) for the first time in the last 5 years, the year 1997 witnessed a sharp rise of 26.6 per cent, a rise of 4.0 per cent in victims in the age group of 10-16 years; (iv) the child rape victims below 10 years reported steep increase in 1997 over 1996.

Having shown a continuous rise in the reported cases of crime against children, the Crime in India report called for a "humane approach" to issues relating to child victims of crime. This is a very relevant observation coming from a Home Ministry outfit, namely, the National Crime Records Bureau. Before we come to question of approaches and strategies, let us understand the multi-faceted character of criminal victimization of children.

V

For purposes of clarity, patterns of juvenile victimization must be preceded by some kind of an operational definition of 'victimization'. Keeping in mind the fact that non-criminal victimization (victimization arising out of exploitation and abuse which is illegally forbidden, though considered bad, evilsome and problematic) is not the central issue, we can have this tentative definition: "Criminal Victimization" is the process and outcome of conditions/circumstances emerging out of crimes/criminal acts committed against the child that cause him/her the physical, mental, sexual, social and economic hardship, hurt, humiliation, inconvenience, discomfort or annoyance. Subject to acceptance of this definition, I may like to add that criminal victimization of children includes cruelty, injury, pain, suffering, shame, humiliation, rejection and other kinds of social denigration. On the basis of these physical, psychological and social ramifications of crimes committed against children, we may construct a tentative topology of their victimization. This topology may comprise of the following five broad forms of victimization.

1. **Physical Victimization** includes putting (forcing) children to hard physical labour under hazardous conditions, causing ill-health, physical injury, permanent or temporary disability or, in worst cases, death. Victimization of working and street children neatly fits into this category. The most brutal and inhuman form of physical victimization is the crime of maiming (kidnapped) children for purposes of begging.

2. **Sexual Victimization** includes exposing or exploiting children for immoral and sexual purposes; forcible child rape; child prostitution; paedophilia, incest involving children; and child pornography. The most reprehensible form of sexual victimization is the problem of child prostitution.

3. **Psychological Victimization** includes different types of emotional deprivation, rejection or treating the child in manner that he or she may feel unwanted.

4. **Social Victimization** includes parental/familial neglect, abandonment or turning the child out of home.

5. **Economic Victimization** includes cornering the earning of the child; denying the child the payment of adequate or prescribed minimum wages; keeping him as bonded labour and taking the economic advantage of the work done by the child.

The forces conspiring to cause the aforesaid forms of

victimization depend upon the number of factors which govern the existential conditions/circumstances may also be dependent upon: (i) child's family milieu-disorganisational domestic conditions; poverty and penury of parents, and the parents' attitude and of behaviour of neglect, ill-treatment, etc. and (ii) external conditions making the child vulnerable to be victimized by persons other than parents/family members. Therefore, the forms that juvenile victimization takes depend on the child's social and economic background; situations of destitution and disability and conditions conducive to the criminal victimization of the child.

The etiology of each of these forms of juvenile victimization needs separate discussion. However, some discussion must take place on the kidnapping of children for criminal purposes and disgraceful sexual exploitation and abuse. Child prostitution is one such form which has already assumed menacing proportions. This problem needs to be discussed with a sense of urgency. A thought may also be spared for assessing the devastating psychological/ social impact of victimization on the personality of the children. The Western researches on the subject show that most of the victimized children develop such sense of hostility against their victimizers or society in general, which in future years, may well be channelled into violence. These researches also aver that there is a high probability that victimized children may turn out to be tomorrow's victimizers, or perpetrators of crime and violence. We certainly need some empirical data to prove or disapprove these western assertions.

VI

Having explained the problems of the child victims of crime, and having understood the forms and patterns of juvenile victimization, we finally need to address ourselves to the mechanisms and measures which could prevent victimization of children, and help us devise effective strategies and approaches to combat with the problem. Coming straight to the question of strategy, we should keep in mind that complexity of the problem does not permit any further room for complacency and does not allow us to look for simple quick-fix solutions. Good intentions and bold policy statements have outlined their utility, for, we had enough of rhetoric on child welfare, child development and the rights of child. There is a need to develop a long-term view and evolve possible potential solutions as opposed to short-run crisis management, Band-Aid approach--all too common in popular thinking and official responses. We need to devise, develop and operationalise variety of approaches—social, psychological, and legal to prevent juvenile victimization and to protect children from the traumas of their abhorrent abuse and exploitation. Without being more elaborate in describing the three major approaches, let us outline their salient features.

The Social Approach includes launching of public campaigns designed to call nations' attention to the problematique of children's criminal victimization. Organised social movement, involving mass action is the prerequisite for mobilizing the support of the powerful members of society who can exert profound influence and activise the state to take effective action, in respect of preventing child abuse and exploitation and promoting children's care, protection, treatment, education, training and rehabilitation. Providing assistance of an advocate (legal counsel) to the victim is one of the most important requirements, and, as such, services of a lawyer should be considered mandatory, right from the beginning. The Supreme Court of India, in the case of Delhi Domestic Working Women's Forum vs. Union of India and Others (Crl.WP No. 362/93), has laid down the broad parameters in assisting the victims of rape. Some of these parameters are relevant in case of child sexual abuse as well. The Court had laid down that: (a) Legal representation should be provided to the complainants of sexual abuse; (b) competent, sensitive and child friendly advocates be appointed by the Court to represent the indigent/needy complainants; (c) legal assistance to be provided at the police station itself; (d) the police has to inform the victim about her right for legal representation, even before any questions are asked; (d) the cases of sexual victimization be tried in an atmosphere where anonymity of the victim could be maintained as far as necessary; and (f) a list of child friendly and willing lawyers should remain available at the police station.

Law-Enforcement Approach requires the demonstration of greater sensitivity in the handling of the complaints of the child victims of sexual abuse. For example, child victims of sexual crimes should be examined in seclusion and in a child-friendly domestic environment, which is congenial for the child to be examined. Basic decency and courtesy should be maintained while examining the child victims of crime, especially the victims of sexual abuse. The case should be taken to ensure that the secondary victimization be avoided and human rights of the child victim are not violated.

To ensure a sensitive and humane handling of child victims of crime, low-level police functionaries have to be specially trained in child-friendly methods of policing. The proposed special 'child-friendly' training of police functionaries at the cutting edge level should also include imparting knowledge about the procedural and substantive laws relating to various offences against children, not only in the Indian Penal Code but also under various special and local laws. This is being repeatedly emphasized in view of the fact that on many occasions majority of the lower level (Thana level) police functionaries have been found to be blissfully unaware of the large number of laws relating to children. It is also desirable to get prepared a compendium of procedural substantive and local and special laws and make it available at all police stations.

These approaches no doubt hold the promise of providing a better deal to child victims of crime. But given the all-round inertial and indifference, bordering on hopelessness and helplessness, it is unrealistic, however, to believe that the existing preventive, protective, curative and rehabilitative policies and programmes run both by the governmental agencies and large number of non-governmental organisations in the field of child welfare, would produce results better than before.

The police and child serving agencies, valuable as they are, can only treat the symptom and not the roots of the problem. What is needed, therefore, is a more fundamental approach of correcting the societal conditions that make millions of our children vulnerable to abuse and exploitation. This would certainly necessitate catching the culprits and subjecting them to their just deserts.

VII

Let us be little more hopeful and confident that notwithstanding the pessimism over the grim child situation in the country, and the seeming impossibility of combating the problem of juvenile victimization, we must maintain hope that there always exist potentials for easing out the problems of criminal victimization of children. Although we might desire more pleasant picture of child situation in the country, we cannot avoid encountering many difficult problems. We should not think that being realistic about these problems is any reason for inertia. Quite the contrary, confronting these problems demands creative as well as critical thinking about the possible solutions. The experience of the developed countries (where incidents of juvenile victimization are far too less) indicate that children can be spared the exploitation and abuse if the country is determined to do so, regardless of constraints and difficulties. This is possible only when clear priorities are set, concerted efforts are made, existing programmes are restructured, and other available, but often underutilized resources, are mobilized to energetically tackle the task at hand. Only with persistent efforts at finding pragmatic solutions, we can hope of creating a more just and humane society. Finally and most importantly, an optimistic vision is important, because there is always light at the end of a dark tunnel.

5

Victimisation of Child: Various Forms and Patterns

Jaytilak Guha Roy

Prologue

Any study on victims of crime poses two major problems. Firstly, official criminal justice records hardly provide any data on the victims since they logically relate to the offenders as principal clients. Secondly, the non-official surveys on crime victims which have so far been carried out mostly in developed countries are prone to some forms of "response error". In such a scenario one can easily assume how difficult it is to highlight the problems of crime victims including victimisation of child in a developing country like India. There is no denying the fact that children in the developing countries are much more vulnerable to crime as compared to their counterparts in the developed countries primarily because of their sufferings from poverty and illiteracy on one hand, and inadequate state and societal responses to victimisation of child on the other. Keeping in view these major constraints, a modest endeavour has been made in this article to examine and analyse various forms and patterns of the victimisation of child with particular reference to the Indian context.

Who is a Child?

There is no uniform legal definition of 'child'. Different laws define it differently. Under the 1860 Indian Penal Code, child usually refers to a person under 12 years of age. The Juvenile Justice Act, 1986 defines 'juvenile' as a boy below the age of 16 years and a girl below the age of 18 years. Under Child Marriage Restraint Act, 1992 a male child means a person who has not attained 21 years of age while a female child is a person who is below 18 years of age. The Factories Act, 1958 and Child Labour (Prohibition and Regulation) Act, 1986 define child as a person who has not completed 14 years of age. Such varying legal definitions notwithstanding the commonly perceived norms prescribed a person below the age of 16 years as a child, between 16 and 18 years as a minor and above 18 years as a major. According to UN Convention on the Rights of the Child (CRC), every human being under 18 years is a child unless majority is attained earlier under national law.

Female Foeticide

Undoubtedly, the worst form of child victimisation is female foeticide as it results in the killing of a female child before she is born. It is most unfortunate that even after entering the new millennium preference for the male child remaining such a predominant socio-economic factor that in a large section of our society, including the middle and upper class, the female child, to quote an official of Indian Medical Association (IMA), "is still considered an avoidable social burden". The increasing misuse of technical advancement in medical science such as sex determination tests with ultra-sound scan is evident from the fact that the ratio of women to men has gone down from 972:1000 in 1901 to 927:1000 in the 1991 census which is 63 less than the world average. In Punjab and Haryana the unethical practice of sex determination tests and abortion of female foetuses appears to be so widespread that a 1997 survey showed the sex ratio having dipped to 750. A recent newspaper report outlines the following facts/data which are indeed a matter of great concern:

- IMA activists estimate that 5 million female foeticide operations are conducted every year.
- India has about 20,000 ultra-sound clinics, mostly unregistered and staffed by doctors unqualified to conduct these tests.
- In Punjab, Haryana and Uttar Pradesh mobile vans have taken such sex detection tests to the villages.

Female Infanticide

Female infanticide is another worse form of child victimisation which has been practised in our patriarchal, male chauvinistic society for the past several centuries. In fact, female infanticide was one of the agenda of the social reforms movements in India during the eighteenth and the nineteenth centuries led by Raja Rammohun Roy (1772-1833), Ishwar Chandra Vidyasagar (1820-91) and other great social reformers. It may be partly due to the impact of these movements that the female-male ratio was much higher in 1901 as compared to 1991. Another reason for such higher ratio in 1901 may be due to non-availability of sex determination tests in those days. The lower sex ratio in the 1991 census indicates that in all probability the cruel practice of female infanticide still exists in our society alongside female foeticide.

According to an estimate of the United Nations Children's Fund (UNICEF), biologically 105 boys are born for every hundred girls. However, with higher death rates among the boys in the first year of life, these figures should be more or less equal. Since this is not the case in India, it implies that many of the girl children who are born normal may subsequently go missing as victims of female infanticide. Majority of those who survive in this process later become the victims of gender bias prevalent in their domestic and social life. They are generally subjected to indifferent and inferior treatment as compared to their male counterparts.

Child Abuse and Neglect

Child abuse and neglect are universal phenomena. They have a two fold effect in the sense that these are not only offences against society's most vulnerable sections but may also sow the seeds of crime perpetrated later in life by the victims themselves. In fact, the violence committed by youths quite often is traced back to the abuse and neglect they suffered in their early years.[1] Survey results in some countries have established the link between child maltreatment and later criminal behaviour by its victims. Such linkage results in growing acceptance of the concept of a "cycle of violence" that starts with child abuse and neglect. One recent national study in USA revealed that being the victim of abuse and neglect as a child increases the chances of later juvenile delinquency and adult criminality by forty per cent. Even among children who are neglected but not abused, one in eight would later be arrested for a violent offence.[2]

Child abuse and maltreatment are not confined to family life alone. They occur more frequently far from the victim's own house or in its vicinities. Schools, formal and informal custodial institutions, working places (in case of child labour) and streets (in case of homeless children) are common places of victimisation.

The worst form of child abuse is rape, sodomy or sexual assault. One recent research study in USA showed that more female than male adolescents had been sexually assaulted (13 per cent of females in contrast to 3.4 per cent of males). It also revealed that youths from lower income groups experienced higher rates of sexual assaults than those from middle and higher income groups.[3] Similar data relating to India are not readily available since "victimisation surveys have still not gained complete recognition by researchers of victimology in India".[4] Nevertheless, "scarcity or absence of statistics on the toll of abuse in developing countries", according to an observer, "does not mean that child abuse does not occur there".[5]

Our real life experiences may also lead us to contend that victimisation scenario is more or less same in India as elsewhere. For instance, the crime trend in urban areas in recent years reveals that children living in slums or on the streets are more vulnerable to rape or sexual assaults and other forms of child abuse as compared to children from middle and higher income groups. It is also found that in many cases, the sexual assaults on children are committed by those who are close or known to the victim's family.

Other forms of child abuse of neglect could be identified as:

- Physical assaults including "being attacked" or "threatened".
- Verbal assaults
- Child battering
- Mental injuries or emotional abuse
- Parental neglect
- Neglect by caretaker
- Witnessing violence in real life
- Kidnapping children and mutilating them for begging purposes
- Exploitation of children in the form of child labour and child slavery etc.

Another worst form of child abuse is genital mutilation which is widely prevalent in African countries. According to a recent report of Amnesty International on CRC, "two, million young girls are subjected each year in Africa to genital mutilation and without anaesthetic: it is painful, terrifying and traumatic".

It needs to be emphasised that although all forms of child abuse and neglect do not come under the purview of law and justice, they must have deleterious effects of various kinds on the victims. A lot of research needs to be undertaken by scholars in Victimology to analyse why child abuse is rampant in developed as well as developing countries.

Child Labour and Child Slavery

The term child labour has been aptly defined by Homer Folks as "any work by children that interferes with their full physical development, their opportunities for a desirable minimum education or their needs for recreation".[6]

The term, therefore, applies to "children engaged in all types of activities whether these be industrial or non-industrial but which are detrimental to their physical, mental, moral and social well-being and development".[7]

In developing countries a large number of children from poor families are victims of the exploitation of child labour. According to International Labour Organisation's Bureau of Statistics, there are now 120 million children between 5-14 years of age who are fully at work, while there are about 250 million children for whom work is a secondary activity. Of these, sixty-one per cent are found in Asia, thirty-two per cent in Africa and seven per cent in Latin America. India has the highest number of child labour. As per 1991 census the number of working children is estimated to be 17.36 million in the country. In real terms, the figures must be much more than the estimated figures. For, the National Sample Survey Organisation estimated the numbers at 17.58 million way back in 1985.

The worst form of child labour is child slavery in the form of bonded labour which still exists in some parts of rural India. It is the end product of an extreme form of economic indebtedness which compels the parents to engage their children in household and agricultural work under inhuman conditions of a debt bondage. Although the incidents of child slavery have declined considerably in recent years due to governmental and non-governmental efforts, this socio-economic evil has not been eliminated altogether. This is why, on November 11, 1997 the Supreme Court had brought under the purview of National Human Rights Commission (NHRC) the task of supervising the implementation of all laws relating to abolition of bonded labour. In response, the NHRC constituted a group to study various aspects of bonded labour and submit periodic reports to the Supreme Court.

In the socio-economic context of a developing country as ours child labour is often considered as a necessary social evil resulting from economic necessity of a poor family. Although the conditions under which the children work vary widely across activities and between different sectors, the fact remains that child labour not only leads to denial of education and recreation for the working children but also they are often exposed to various types of occupational health hazards that reduce their average life span. Children engaged in mines, quarries, glass, bangle, fireworks, carpet, metal and match factories and other such hazardous occupations under unhygienic working and living conditions are the worst sufferers of child labour.

Sexual Harassment of Working Children

The working children, both male and female, are also subjected to exploitation in the form of sexual harassment by the employees and their associates. There are various forms and patterns of sexual harassment. As per the Industrial Employment (Standing Orders) Rules, 1946 as amended recently, any behaviour or any other unwelcome physical, verbal or non-verbal conduct of sexual nature shall be construed as sexual harassment.

Child Trafficking and Prostitution

The United Nations General Assembly, in 1994, defined trafficking as "the illicit and clandestine movement of persons across national and international borders, largely from developing countries, with the end goal of foreseeing women and girl children into economically oppressive and exploitative situations for the profit of recruiters, traffickers and crime syndicates". The UN Convention on the Rights of the Child, defines child prostitution as "sexual exploitation of a child below the age of 18 for remuneration in cash or kind".

Child trafficking and prostitution are the commercial sexual abuse of children resulting in denial of human rights of the victims. According to Amnesty International's report on CRC, "On just two established routes, from Nepal to India and from Bangladesh to Pakistan an estimated 9,000 girls a year are trafficked." Girls in other developing countries are also not free from this menace.

Child prostitution is the worst form of child abuse and exploitation. Its nature and type vary from one country to another, one society to another and from one age to other age. They may even vary in a society due to different religious and cultural practices of different social groups.

A recent study conducted by a Delhi-based NGO, Joint Women's Programme, reveals that most of the children engaged in prostitution are not paid for the first 5-10 years. Mental and emotional trauma apart, they are tortured, burnt and beaten. Many of them are to live with unwanted pregnancies, riddled with diseases or die of maternal mortality. The stigma of illegitimacy stubbornly persists, often propagated by the parents who live off them.[8]

There is wide variation in regard to numerical data on child prostitute. One study estimated a total of 100 million sexually abused children in the world, but did not distinguish between the categories of child prostitutes and sexually abused children.[9] According to an estimate by End Child Prostitution in Asian Tourism (ECPAT) in 1993, there were 1.5 million prostitutes in India with 20 per cent of them under 16 years of age.[10]

Children as Victims of Drug Trafficking and Substance Abuse

India is placed between world's largest drug growing areas—the Golden Crescent on the border regions of Pakistan and Afghanistan and the Golden Triangle on the borders of Myanmar, Thailand and Laos. India has become a conduit country for drugs moving from the Crescent and the Triangle to the western world, especially during the past one decade. Drug trafficking is now closely linked to terrorism and supply of deadly weapons and arms for terrorist activities.

Children in India and countries on the Crescent and the Triangle are increasingly engaged in drug trafficking, especially as carriers. Children in large number, particularly from the lower strata of the society, have also become the victims of the menace of drug abuse in India and other developing countries. The menace, according to an empirical study conducted in Delhi a few years back,[11] afflicts the children and the young persons, especially in the age group of 15 to 25 years, under the peer group pressure, the sense of curiosity and spirit of experimentation. "The contribution of the modern technological age," observes this study very forthrightly, "is that the more potent derivation of narcotic drugs and other synthetic drugs and psychotropic substances are a trap from which even the casual experimenter can seldom escape without professional help."[12] The menace of drug abuse was initially confined to urban areas. But of late, it has spread its tentacles over semi-urban and rural areas too.

Children of developed countries are no less prone to substance abuse, i.e., a combination of drug and alcohol abuse. A recent study reveals that about 3.4 million adolescents aged 12-17 in USA have been drug or alcohol abusers.[13]

Children as Victims of Wars and Civil Conflicts

Another worst form of child victimisation has its roots in today's armed conflicts in which children themselves have been compelled to become instruments of war. They are lured or kidnapped to serve as soldiers as is evident from armed conflicts in Angola, Chechnya, Eritrea, Ethiopia, East Timor, Guina Bissau, Kosovo and Kashmir, to name a few. In Colombia, observes the recent Amnesty International Report on CRC, "child soldiers are sometimes called 'little bees', because their size and agility enable them to move quickly and 'sting' their enemy."

Children are even exposed to vicious hate campaign as in Rwanda, Burandi and Bosnia. For, almost all the major wars today are civil conflicts, and as observed by a commentator very poignantly, "they are fought among people who know each other well. Compatriots and neighbours are engaged in combat with each other."[14] Children's exposure to hate campaigns in these wars have left them with severe psychological trauma. As this commentator observes further, "in the innocent mind, categorisation of separation on religious, ethnic and racial lines are introduced. Even when fighting stops, children live with the psychological trauma of war. They need sustained assistance for rehabilitation, though today their needs are largely ignored."[15] Children are also being used as instruments of war by militant organisations like the LTTE in Sri Lanka and the Talibans in Afghanistan.

Impact of war on children is multiple and severe. It leads to deprivation of children of their basic security, food, education and access to health. During war, the girl children are especially vulnerable to sexual abuse, rape and forced prostitution. War also compels the children to live a miserable life as refugees. The majority of todays 11.5 million refugees are women and children.[16] Armed conflicts in countries like Angola and Sierra Leone have even produced a large number of limbless children, the victims of land mines. As Olara A Otunnu, Special Representative of the UN Secretary-General for Children and Armed Conflicts observes:

Children are truly blameless victims of conflict... Yet, today we are witnessing unspeakable abominations directed against children in situations of conflict... Over the last decade, two million children were killed... over one million made orphans, over six million have been seriously injured or permanently disabled and over 10 million have been left with grave psychological trauma."[17]

Migrant Children

With rapid urbanisation in developing countries as India, there has been large-scale migration of rural families to urban towns and cities. The children of migrated families have not only become the victims of instability and insecurity but also exposed to various forms of abuses and exploitation. They are subjected to "abusive employment practices and, worse still, are forced to work under conditions which are dangerous to their health and physical and mental development."[18] They are to live either under inhuman conditions in slums or near their workplaces outside the orbit of the family. As a result, they become vulnerable to the vices of urban life—sexual and other abuses and also social and economic exploitation. Many of them are also lured by criminal gangs and ultimately become adolescent offenders.

Child Torture

Child torture is another worse form of child victimisation. Unfortunately, child torture though being one of the most insidious evils against humanity, has not been defined in the law, not even in the UN Convention Against Torture. In developed as well as developing countries, children are often subjected to insidious and informal types of torture as in children homes. The working children in developing countries are often the victims of this kind of torture by their employees. The Indian police has earned notoriety in inflicting torture or other cruel inhuman degrading treatment not only against accused children in its custody but also innocent children to extract information about their parents who are suspected to have committed offences.

Epilogue

It is most unfortunate that victimisation of child in various forms and patterns continues to occur in developed as well as developing countries even ten years after the United Nations drew up its Convention on the Rights of the Child which has been adopted by all but two countries (Somalia and the US) in the world. Consequently, there exists a wide chasm between universal acceptance and universal observance of this humanitarian international instrument concerning protection and promotion of human rights of the child. No wonder that the rights of tens of millions of children all over the world are being flouted on an enormous scale. Contemporary human civilisation and world community are yet to traverse a long, long way in their tryst with a new world order which will ensure human rights of the child victims.

References

1. Earle, Ralph B., *Helping to Prevent Child Abuse and Future Criminal Consequences,* National Institute of Justice (NIJ): Program Focus, Washington DC, US Department of Justice, October 1995, p. 2.
2. Widom, Cathy Spatz, *The Cycle of Violence,* NIJ Research in Brief, Washington, DC: U.S. Deptt. of Justice, 1992, 3; Widom, *Victims of Childhood Sexual Abuse—Later Criminal Consequences,* NIJ Research in Brief, Washington, DC: U.S. Department of Justice, 1995, 4. See also, Earle, *Ibid.,* p. 3.
3. Kilpatrick, Dean and Saunders, Benjamin, *The Prevalence and Consequences of Child Victimization,* NIJ Research Preview, April 1997.
4. Singh, D.R., "The International Crime (Victim) Survey in Bombay", in Zvekic, Ugljesa and Frate, A.A.D. (eds.), *Criminal Victimisation in the Developing World,* Rome, UNICRI, Publication No. 55, 1995, p. 96.
5. Suman, Somen K., "Child Abuse in India" *Social Welfare,* Nov.-Dec. 1985, p. 22.
6. Quoted, Stein, Emanuel and Davis, Jerome (eds.), *Labour Problem in India,* New York, Farrar and Rinchart Inc., 1940, pp. 12-13.
7. Kulshreshtha, Jinesh C., *Indian Child Labour,* Delhi, Uppal, 1994, p. 4.
8. For further details, see Ramaswamy, Anindita, "The Ultimate Abuse" *The Hindustan Times,* November 12, 1999.
9. Gathia, Joseph, *Child Prostitution in India,* Delhi, Concept, 1999, p. 15.
10. *Ibid.*
11. Prashant, Saroj, *Drug Abuse and Society,* Delhi, Ashish, 1993.
12. *Ibid.*, p. 159.

13. *Supra*, n. 5.
14. Panicker Lalita, Traumatised Children of Deadlier Wars, *The Times of India*, Delhi, September 17, 1999.
15. *Ibid.*
16. *Ibid.*
17. Quoted, *Ibid.*
18. ILO, *Report of the Director General*, International Labour Office, Geneva, 1983, p. 10.

6

The Issue of Childhood Deprivation and Survival Worldwide

Tushar Kanti Saha

In the vast sea of humanity, children are the most vulnerable section living on the edge of mercy of others, nearly as animals. "Children are all around us. They represent about a quarter of the world's population. They are not equipped to defend themselves. They depend on what is given to them. They are victims of circumstances. They bring us joy, they bring us tears, they are our reason to hope. They are your children, they are my children, they are children of the world", said Eddie Adams.

The philosophy behind the UN Convention on the Rights of the Child is that children, too, are equals but they are not alike. This calls for extension of special support to childhood in the best interests of the child. Article 3.1 thus enjoins all responsibility in the following words:

"In all actions concerning children, whether undertaken by public or private social welfare institutions, courts of law, administrative authorities or legislative bodies, the best interest of the child shall be a primary consideration."

India's (now) outdated National Children Policy (1979) declared that "The Nation's Children are a supremely important asset. Their nurture and solicitude are our responsibility. Children's programme should find a prominent part in our national plans for the development human resources, so that our children grow up to become robust citizens, physically fit, mentally alert and morally healthy, endowed with the skills and motivations needed by the society. Equal opportunity for development to all children during the period of growth should be our aim, for, this would serve our larger purpose of reducing inequality and ensuring social justice."

Now, how we have treated our "supremely important asset" in all these years? Even at the micro level children's interests and rights are no longer identical with those of their parents. In Indian context, the twin blades of poverty and greed play a rather antipathetic role in many such relationships. Yet the general defence of paternalism by the Master of the Rolls in Re S (1993) is understandable where he claimed, "... a child is, after all, a child."

"The reason why the law is particularly solicitious in protecting the interests of children is because they are liable to be vulnerable and impressionable, lacking the maturity to weigh the longer term against the shorter, lacking the insight to know how they will react and the imagination to know how others will react in certain situations, lacking the experience to measure the probable against the possible".

Indian Constitution provides for the foundational framework of the care and protection of the Child in Articles like 24, 39 (e) and (f). In backing up these constitutional provisions, general legal framework has not been evolved although piecemeal legislations like Factories Act and Child Labour Prohibition and Regulation Act take a little care of the field. According to Art. 24 'No child below the age of fourteen years shall be employed to work in any factory or mine or engaged in any other hazardous employment'. This solemn declaration, is hardly respected and regularly violated.

Nearly 11 million children are forcibly employed in hazardous sectors like fireworks and bangle making industry. In Sivakasi alone which has some 200 units producing 90 per cent of the country's fireworks employ 1,25,000 children in the age group of 10-14 years by perpetuation of the system of contracting and sub-contracting. In the process, children are exploited "and sacrificed as flies in the fine plays of the adult from the blast to the bursting. Nearly one and a half lakh children inhale substantial quantity of gunpowder in their workplace, making them unsuitable for jobs in later day life as they suffer from respiratory diseases, says CRY report (Asian Age dt. 5.11.99). Then finally, who are the majority of victims of fireworks at funsport? Dewali—a festival of light meant darkness for life to many child victims who were treated among 220 burn patients admitted within a span of 3 hours in Ram Manohar Lohia Hospital, Delhi recently. This number has remained almost the same for last six years. Delhi High Court in its Order dated 5.10.99 instructed the Government Hospitals to make special arrangements with additional manpower, dressing material, linen and medicines for treatment of burn patients being a repeat of the Order on yearly succession (vide Order dt. 9.10.98). According to a study made by a Bio-medical Engineer of IIT, Delhi, 77 per cent of the burns caused by fireworks otherwise considered safe by the people are due to e.g. *Anars*—flower pots, *chakris*—rotating wheels—again mostly used by the children.

Article 39 (e) speaks in terms of health and strength of the workers and seeks to raise a protective shield against abuse and exploitation of the tender age of children. This age is a formative stage best protected by parental care and schooling and insulation from the uncaring labour market of domestic servitude and wayside cantons of canteen. Obviously, Art. 39 (f) sounds hollow and rhetoric although its lofty spirit is undisputably a piece of the moon everybody aims at. The demand "that children are given opportunities and facilities to develop in a healthy manner and in conditions of freedom and dignity and that childhood and youth are protected against exploitation and against moral and material abandonment" has to be looked into with a free mind and fresh outlook. Childhood belongs to the child. Let us return it back to him. 'Mankind owes to the child the best it has to give" (UNDRC).

Deprivation of Childhood Health

Deprivation, in this context, includes a wide range of material and non-material entitlements or benefits and more than just monetary wealth. Natural disasters and calamities apart, parental and societal deprivation of the children are rampant throughout the world. Orphanage total or partial either in a loss of father or mother, early separation from them in-house or outward, absence of company for long hours or even neglect at home are not quite uncommon. Since the development of an individual is affected not only by his geographical and physical environment but also by psychological and social factors, our concern should be to see how best to avoid or minimise the extent of deprivation of early childhood of the children. Parents' care is the best insurance against a variety of deprivations due to bio-medical reasons. The degree and quality of attention, affection, association and appropriation are impartible by outside agencies and cannot therefore, be imparted. What is needed most is to understand and accept that the mother is central figure and force to reckon within any scheme of orderly planning of parenthood. A child is born from the mother's womb. What goes on before the birth of the child determines the health of the child to be. Drinking, smoking, drugs with their side-effects tell tons on the congenital defects and disability of the children. If that be the case, thalasemia is preventable by blood tests before marriage whereas medical check-up is yet to form part of the legal framework for instituting marriage. Nutrition is a major determinant of child's health in his life-long episode beginning from the foetal growth in mother's womb. American Journal of Clinical Nutrition reporting results of research by a team of scientists of the University of Amsterdam on women reveals that mothers conceived during the period of famine of 1944-45 after Nazi occupation gave birth to children among whom the female group developed obesity in their fifties relatively higher than the general group—an inheritance from the mothers of malnutrition. Obesity, surely then is not merely a by-product of living style of the rich due to environmental and societal contribution. Nutrition Foundation of India in its study 'Prevalence of Obesity in Urban Delhi' identified obesity as fast emerging health hazards of the rich but the poor mothers of the slums will have their own contribution to the problem in generational legacy through the process of inheritance. (HT dt.13.11.99). The problem of Acute Limphoblastic Leukaemia (ALL) of children is a disturbing feature of the child health scenario globally. Results of research published in 'the Lancet' claims that Cancer Research Institute, London has found first direct evidence that child leukaemia is not inherited but is caused by a gene defect (mutated or altered) which takes place during the development of blood cells in foetus which again is affected by environmental conditions such as pollution. So, if the children are to be saved from this fatal disease, remedial measures must address to the source of attack. Children are also to be protected against inheritance of HIV virus which is playing havoc with a large number of innocent children. According to UNAIDS' estimate about 1000 infants are infected with HIV virus each day although prenatal HIV is preventable currently by ZDV drug treatment.

School at Early Age and Early School Hour

Children are booked for admission to school at a very early age sometime below or around the age of 2 years while large number of grown-up children are not sent to school. This Indian experience of thoughtless handling makes the children victims for life. Paediatricians now warn that it is injurious for the children's long-term interest to force the learning process too early, that too, with overload of books physically and the pressure of homework mentally. The fear of getting up early in unearthly hour leads to constant anxiety. Exposing the child to bitter dawn cold results in upper respiratory tract infections. Irregular food habits cause listlessness, low stamina and poor concentration. The daily trauma can seriously harm the health of the child in the form of blood sugar, anaemia, stress and bowel disorder. The general pattern of ill-treatment met by children at the hands of their parents is indicated by the following rituals:

- Dragging the child out of bed while it is pitch dark .
- Literally force-feeding him or her, often without success.
- Waiting at the bus stop in the cold and darkness, or dangerously driving through fog.
- Making the child wear shorts even in winters as some schools insist children below a certain age cannot wear long pants.
- Have the child return with bronchitis because he or she has attended morning assembly or been made to stand in the 'late line' out in the cold and fog .

It is surprising to gauge the extent of tolerance stretching to the extreme, probably unique to India. In England schools are gifting alarm clocks to young children to remove their anxiety as a measure of incentive to come to school punctually. Yet, more than 100,000 children run away from home in Britain each year, according to the Children's Society Survey. These run-aways did not fit the stereotype image of being from poor, inner city homes. The problem was spread almost evenly across society, children having been forced to leave in many case. Emotional conflicts, neglect, apathy and indifference are the root cause for isolation of the children in the lonely island in the uncaring crowd of the family. Here again, blaming the parents is not enough. It has been observed that the kind of support networks available to mothers working or not, are crucially important for social and cognitive development of the child. All it means, conditions at home must be right for the children. Children want to live with nature and be natural, to be aware of the seasons, to smell trees, grass and flowers, and to hear and see birds. Freedom with check can only assure their well-being. "In the little world in which children have their existence, whosoever brings them up, there is nothing so finely perceived and so finely felt as injustice" finely cut by Charles Dickens.

The Issue of Survival

The principle most directly related to children's economic and social rights is formulated in the right-to-life Article. The Article in the UN Convention goes further than just granting children the right not to be killed. It definitely includes the right to survival and development with dignity. Art. 6.2 says:

"State shall ensure to the maximum extent possible the survival and development of the child".

The extensive meaning conferred to the-word 'survival' points to the need of preventive action such as immunisation. While immunisation is good and necessary, the overburden of vaccination has been ignored totally and their side-effects side-lined from the point of view of long-term safety.

Girl Child

According to 'Save the Children' Report* published recently even in Australia 3733 children with a sizeable percentage belonging to the age-group below 10 years are selling the body merely to survive. Of the total number of rapes in US about 30 per cent of the victims are below 16 years—747 (5.4 per cent) are reported to be below 10 years and 3320 (24.1 per cent) belong to 10-16 years age group.** Whereas throughout the world, girl child, rarely finds the right kind of assurance with regard to a safe dwelling abode, sanitary and wholesome provisions of privacy. The mother-child life cycle starting with the girl child is a disturbing lot of an affair. The goals of the UN Convention have been earmarked as survival, development, protection and participation. It gets first shock at prenatal stage of the USG Table. Only the lucky ones are allowed to see the light of the day. There is none to speak on behalf of the unborn child—the child *en ventre sa mere*. The neglect starts with the growing girl child, the mother to be in the form of deprivation of the correct level of nutrition at post-natal stage. As a result, out of 200 million children under five from the developing countries, 36 per cent have been found to be underweight (1989-90 ACC/SCN 1992). In India, the launching of the ICDS(1975) programme made no difference to the situation qualitatively. The programme expanded from its original objectives, failed to take care of the girl children on the street. A modest step in the right direction has been the effort of IPER schools. In Calcutta, the Child in Need Institute runs home shelter of the street girl children—a limited scale of laudable venture.

Specific needs of the Street Child

- Privacy and Toilet
- Residing place
- Night Shelter
- Clothing
- Protection against sexual harassment
- Educational Facilities and Access to Sporting Activities

We talk a lot about right to privacy. The question of survival of the street children especially of the girl children is the prime consideration. Of course, the NGOs like Sulabh International can extend the convenience of toilet and bathing facility to the girl children on the street to bring a shade of sanity and improvement to the situation further. More shelters need be constructed and it can serve multiple objectives in view of the devastating cyclonic disasters recently experienced in Orissa which brought miseries to 15 lakh children.

Poor children's clothing should be part of the kit given free of cost and their timely supply is equally important as delay in procurement of warm clothing this year is going to affect large number of poor students of the capital city itself.

Mobile school scheme for street children can be initiated. The main handicap is posed by the economic-value of the time investment in education by this unfortunate lot of street children working as rag-pickers. Alternative jobs or allowances as incentive to registration for schooling is now less attractive as the opportunity cost for them is too high. Thus, an NGO's plan to introduce this measure remained still-born, after all the need of the moment is immediate and children are unwilling to accept Rs. 1,000 as monthly dole against their current earning level of around Rs. 3,000 in Calcutta. In this regard, Delhi High Court judgment upholding the banning order on recycling of plastic material is a correct one as it kills two birds with one stone.

Sexual harassment to street children should be made a separate category. They are the most unprotected species as far as rape victims are concerned. In the US nearly 30 per cent rape victims are children below 16 years.* If they are on the street, the probability of harassment is even greater everywhere.

Conclusion

A heartening note to be taken into account is that of the 183 ILO conventions 19 relate to child labour of which seven has been satisfied by India as against only three by Germany and only one by the USA. But there is a difference at the ground level situation. In the US- several legislations are in the pipe-line notably, Child Labour Deterrence Act which seeks to prohibit use of products made by child labour. The Child Labour Free Consumer Information Act (s.554) imposing labelling standard (Rugmark as a monitoring body and symbol) is going to be enforced and effective as the certification procedure stipulated is quite rigorous. These legislative measures are of relevance and significantly important to our Indian exporters. A strategy to free the market from child labour and their rehabilitation in a concerted fashion with a collaborative and cooperative approach from the industry and the government will have to be devised in larger national interest.

One positive step taken by the Government at the behest of the Human Rights Commission in the form of amendment of the Civil Service Rule prohibiting employment of children below certain age as domestic hands is a charitable gesture setting the mode in top gear for a welcome change, can bring salutary effects in course of time. We should now think about forming an independent Children Rights Commission to take care of the entire gamut of children's issues cropping up in the new millennium.

References

Nagar, Divya, *Deprived Children* (1992), Printwell, Jaipur.

MacPherson, Stweart, *Five Hundred Million Children* (1987), Wheatsheaf Books, Sussex.

Devasia Leelamma, *Girl Child in India* (1991), Ashish Publishing House, New Delhi.

de Souza, Alfred, *Children in India* (1979), Mandhar, New Delhi.

Franklin, Bob, *The Handbook of Children Rights* (1995), Routledge, London.

S. Nayana Tara, *Integrated Child Development Services* (1988), Ashish Publishing House, New Delhi.

Kewalramani, G.S., *Child Abuse* (1992), Rawat Publications, New Delhi.

Chopra, Kamala, *Reinforcement Among Infants* (1983), National Psychological Corporation, Agra.

Ginzberg, Eli, *The Nation's Children* (1960), Columbia University Press, New York.

Muthayya, B.C., *Child Welfare* (1972), National Institute of Community Development, Hyderabad.

Yudkin, Simon and Holme, Anthea, *Working Mothers and their Children* (1963), Michael Joseph Ltd., London.

Archard, D., *Children; Rights and Childhood* (1993) Routledge, London.

Aries, P., *Centuries of Childhood* (1993), Jonathan Cape, London.

Deakin, N., *A Voice For All Children* (1982), Bedferd Square Press, London.

Dworkin, R. *Taking Rights Seriously* (1977), Duckworth, London.

Asian Age, Dated 11.11.99.

Shelter: Vol. 2, No.1, Jan, 1999.

Shelter: Vol. No.1 Jan., 1999.

7

Crime Against Unborn Child

Yatish Mishra

We have a fundamental right to life. But surprisingly we don't have a fundamental right to be born. In the womb, we don't enjoy even the status of a human being and that is why the killing in the womb is not considered homicide. What to talk about culpable homicide! By implication, we don't have even rights in the womb.

One can ask a question, is it true? The answer to this question is provided by the Indian Penal Code itself. There are, of course, certain provisions to check foeticide, but the Section 299 clearly says that it shall not amount to homicide to kill inside womb. What is the net result? We are going on killing unborn children, legally and illegally, in the womb. Since the illegality of foeticide does not attract severe punishment as compared to homicide, we are going on even identifying the sex of the child in the womb and then at times we kill it if the doctor says it is female child. There are large number of such cases creating a serious threat to the sex ratio and leading towards creation of an unsafe society, especially for women, and ultimately it turns against all human beings.

A question which demands an urgent answer is—Does an unborn child enjoy any rights, whatsoever? The question should be addressed immediately not only for the reason mentioned above, but for other reasons concerning the basic rights. After introduction of artificial insemination and appearance of surrogate mothers, some children lose their basic rights, of even knowing their parents. It is important, more so because the child loses other rights regarding property, for which the child is otherwise entitled to, in case of natural parents.

The term 'crime' largely signifies offences which are serious in nature. But this meaning will not do, because, it excludes the acts of omissions and commissions which are not so serious in nature as to constitute a crime. Therefore, for current discussion the word 'crime' should be replaced by the word 'offence' under Section 40 of Indian Penal Code which are made punishable by law and are in force. Therefore the word 'crime' here, has been handled in a way so as to encompass the word offence, so that the meaning of the word 'crime' should include the whole gamut of our discussion. It would naturally include all the abuses and inhuman treatment which may not constitute a crime but victimise a child.

Now, the term 'child victims' come. A child can be a 'victim of crime' in two different ways. First, when the offence is directed against the child and second, when the offence is not directed against the child, but affects the child. For example, if a girl child is raped, the incident comes in the first category and if the girl witnessed her mother being raped in front of her and consequently traumatised, the incident comes in the second category. Now, the word 'child' comes in our consideration.

Here, we are totally confused. More so because its very definition varies from one act to the other, from one scholar to the other, and from one branch of knowledge to the other. It is a matter of great concern that in most of the laws the word 'child', has a meaning which covers the age only after birth.

It is common knowledge and which is also endorsed by linguists, semantics and lexicographers that a 'child' is a person who is below the age of 14. However, this knowledge does not lead us to the appropriate place except while we understand it or express it in common parlance. For each and every specific purpose, and it will not be an exaggeration to say that for almost all the practical purposes we come across a different meaning of a 'child'. The different laws give the meaning of a 'child' ranging from the upper limit of 12 years (Section 376 IPC) to 21 years (for marriage of a male child), but child in the womb, is not considered a child.

However, in the Indian Penal Code the Section 312 gives us the expression 'woman with child' which means a pregnant woman. We derive from there that the existence of a child starts from the womb of the mother. With the existence of the child he or she may face the danger of victimisation which has also been perceived in the Indian Penal Code. But unfortunately they are improperly protected against the various crimes other than miscarriage and their killing. There are only five sections (312-316) under the Indian Penal Code, which deals with miscarriage and death of an unborn child.

Even injury which may severely hurt the child in the womb but not cause killing or miscarriage is not considered a crime against the child under Indian Penal Code. No police officer or prosecuting authorities are filing such type of cases in our country. At the most they consider it as an offence against the woman with the child. Thus it is proposed that the separate identity of the child even in the womb must be considered and appropriate laws should be framed to fully protect them against all types of victimisation—criminal or otherwise. Mainly because we know of many cases of civil and criminal nature which hurt the interests of the unborn child.

Now another question arises here that endangering the life of a child in the womb below the age of the fourth or the fifth months of pregnancy when the woman be 'quick with child' i.e., the peculiar sensation which for the first time the woman feels, is prevalent in our society, under the garb of Medical Termination of Pregnancy

Act (MTP Act) which provides for the termination of pregnancy by a registered medical practitioner where its continuance would involve a risk to the life of a pregnant woman or grave injury to her physical or mental health or where there is a substantial risk that if the child were born, it would suffer from such physical or mental abnormalities as to be seriously handicapped. Where the pregnancy is alleged to have been caused by rape or as a result of failure of a contraceptive used by a married woman or her husband, it would be presumed to constitute a grave injury to the mental health of the pregnant woman.

The MPT Act heavily protects the woman but not the 'child'. If the pregnancy is unwanted and is the failure of contraceptive, the woman suffers a grave injury to her mental health but if the pregnancy is terminated the child loses his or her life. The mental health of a woman can be restored later on but can the child who lost its life be restored by any means?

While asking this question we are well aware of the problem of population we are facing. Yes, any civilised person would like to limit the population of the world but not by means of cruelty. Should killing be the means of population control? Enthusiasts of the population control policy are continuously making efforts to control the population by adopting such a cruel mean against the helpless unborn child. They also insist on amending the Indian Penal Code in the light of MTP Act. But, it has not been amended till date. However, the practice is going on and we are unable to protect even the innocent child in the womb, which has not been conceived by any other way but in the wedlock of husband and wife. The ground for termination is that their contraceptive failed. It is another matter that they may not have used contraceptive at all. In this connection we can see Section 91 of the Indian Penal Code which refers to causing miscarriage as an offence, unless caused in good faith for the purpose of saving the life of a woman, independently of any harm which it may cause or be intended to the human.

Therefore, it is not an offence by reason of such harm; and the consent of the woman or of her guardian to the causing of such miscarriage does not justify the Act. Now under Section 3 of the MTP Act pregnancy can be terminated. What a cruel practice it is?

Let us take an example:

X has been 'presumed' to be causing a grave injury to the 'mental health' of Y. Y wants to kill or terminate X on this ground. Can any justice system grant a permission to terminate X? And if the permission is granted, can we call it a justice?

To put the record straight we would like to mention here that X has done nothing wrong to Y. The answer to the question would obviously be in negative. Mainly because X has a fundamental right to life. Therefore we cannot do anything which leads to victimisation of X.

But, if Y is a woman and X is in her womb below the age of four weeks and if X is legally conceived, MTP Act may grant permission to terminate X on the ground that contraceptive measures failed or X is conceived without their intention or X is unwanted. X has obviously done nothing wrong and if there is anything wrong, it is on the part of X's parents. However, on the submission of the woman or parents that X is causing mental suffering to them, the competent authority may presume under the MTP that X is causing mental suffering to them. In this way the child is even prevented from the right to born. Its certainly against the natural justice of the child because human beings enjoy a right to born. However, in the Indian Penal Code proper amendments to this effect is awaited. Many jurists are of the opinion that it is the failure of justice for the child. Does the killing of the child in the womb not constitute the violation of human rights?

The unborn child is not protected fully from any type of victimization other than miscarriage. We can take example of an unborn child who is injured in the womb but is not miscarried. At best the authorities may file cases against the guilty for hurting the woman but the victim child is generally ignored because people do not think that the child in the womb has also a separate identity. In this way, if a pregnant woman is killed the FIR against the culprit is invariably filed for killing of the woman but not for the killing of the child in the womb. It is generally treated as a single murder.

As far as other laws are concerned mainly regarding compensation and insurance, the loss of woman is generally compensated but the child in the womb is simply ignored. Does our Constitution not provide assurance of a right to life even in the womb?

Now, we can take another example of victimisation of an unborn child when the crime is not especially committed against the child but against the woman who bears the child. The woman suffers and consequently the child suffers. But what we are doing for the child?

Let us see Section 299 of the Indian Penal Code which is for culpable homicide. The explanation no. 3 of the Section says that the causing of death of a child in the mother's womb is not homicide. This homicide is culpable only when any part of the child has been brought forth though the child may not have breathed or been completely born. A funny thing is that the killing of the child in the womb is not even homicide. That is why, we are compelled to file cases of this nature in Section 312 of the IPC for causing a woman to miscarry and the culprit rewards only a minor punishment of a term not beyond three years or a fine or both. And if act is done with intent to prevent child from being born alive or cause it to die after birth, the guilty can be booked under Section 315 IPC but the punishment is comparatively less than killing of human being. Even when the act amounts to culpable homicide of a child unborn the Section 316 provides lesser punishment. Only when the woman is "quick with child" the offence rewards imprisonment, which may not extend to seven years and of course shall also be liable to fine.

Clearly while law makes provision for the woman, the child in the womb is ignored. Under the comment on the Section 299 some definitions are given. 'Causes death' is one of them. Here 'death' means the death of a human being as defined under Section 46 of the IPC. But this word does not include the death of an unborn child as we have seen in explanation no. 3 above.

There are other things like immoral, illegal and unethical practices prevalent in our society hampering the development of born and unborn child which have not been covered under the Cr. P.C., esp need to be catered through social, educational, religious and other platforms.

8

Curse to Victim—Foeticide and Girl Child Problems and Prospects

T. Chakraborty

Introduction

The issue of child victims especially the girl child needs a humane approach as it has become a curse to the country—crime graph of which is increasing in galloping way. Of different facets of crime against girl child, problem of female foeticide has been cropping up seriously in our country. Despite the law against sex determination enacted in 1994 (The Prenatal Diagnostic Technique—Regulation, Prevention, and Misuse Act), female foeticide is still a serious menace. This article deals with pros and cons of the problem of foeticide and girl child and tries to suggest some measures to control the problem.

Problem

India is one of the few countries where the sex ratio is adverse to females because of high female mortality rate. While 12 million girls are born in India every year, almost 50,000 female foetuses are aborted in a year after sex determination. If this is the situation when the prenatal diagnostic technique act is expected to go a long way in tackling this menace, the gravity of the problem cannot be measured and for this millennium it may pose as one of the important crimes of the country. Despite the fact that such crimes are viewed as social evil and bad, the reported incidents of such crimes continue to rise in magnitude. This calls for greater involvement by the society with greater awareness and attitudes towards such crimes to fight and contain this menace.

No less telling is the fact that despite banning sex determination tests, the Governments of Madhya Pradesh, Maharashtra, Rajasthan, Delhi and Haryana have not been able to check this evil. The National Crime Records Bureau (NCRB) being the only source of getting authentic statistical data on such crime, this article mainly referred to the NCRB data in focussing the grievousness of the situation. We do not know how far the information is correct as only reported crimes are taken into account. NCRB, in its latest edition of 'Crime in India'—1997 figured that the incidence of foeticide crime in India in 1994 was 45; in 1995 it was 38; in 1996, although the figure rose up to 39, increase in 1997 was remarkable, i.e., 57. The percentage of variation from 1997 over 1996 was recorded as 46.2 per cent, which shows an exorbitantly increasing trend. So far as the state-wise contribution of this crime to the national figure is concerned, Madhya Pradesh was leading with 36.8 per cent; Maharashtra contributed 33.3 per cent and Bihar with 7.0 per cent. Haryana, Rajasthan and Delhi shared 5.3 per cent during 1997.

Even though the decade started with the celebration of International Year of Girl child, female child continues to get a raw deal, even the birth of a girl in the Indian society is also not welcomed properly. This is mainly because of the structural set up of the Indian society and the social attitudes towards the birth of girl-child. Although things are constantly changing, the old thinking of higher the education of the boy, greater is his matrimonial value in the matrimonial market and the parents accordingly want to exchange the boy for a girl with sufficient amount of immovable property, jewellery, hard cash and other items still persist in the country.

Disagreeing with the system leads to serious crimes like dowry death, wife beating etc. Thus, the attitude towards girls in India has not changed over the decades which stands in the way of economic, social and cultural developments of our national life.

In several parts of rural India, a mid-wife's fee is lower when the newborn baby is a girl rather than a boy. This practice is symptomatic of a widespread preference for male child among Indian parents. While an imaginative scheme, announced on the golden jubilee of Independence, entitles parents of a new-born girl to a grant of Rs. 500, it has delivered little, if anything, in terms of positive influence on parental behaviour. Although the scheme endorses anti-female stereotypes but it does give parents an incentive to keep their daughters alive at least temporarily. In any case, grants for female births are a clumsy way of addressing to the problem of plight of the girl-child.

In the front of social status also, female children are more victimised comparatively to male children. In the imparting of social benefits like health care, education, nutrition etc., greater care is bestowed on boys rather than on girls. One of the important primitive ideologies among the poor parents which still exists, is that girls suffer from poor education. In most of the poor families, parents find little meaning in sending girls to schools. One of the important reasons of depriving the girls of enrolment in the schools are their dual role in the family—first as domestic helper and second as baby sitter and to help their parents in a wide range of family vocations and in unorganised sectors like agriculture, animal husbandry, weaving, sericulture, beedi-making and so on. The main reason lies in poverty and environmental factors. Due to this, in most cases girls become the victims of several crimes like forced prostitution, trafficking, child marriage, etc. Their future depends on the whim of their parents. Child marriage not only deprives girls of health and nutrition but also education too.

The Child Marriage Restrain (Amendment) Act of 1978 prevents marriage of a girl below eighteen years and a boy below twenty-one years. The NCRB report focussed that the child marriage occurred highest in Gujarat (37.2 per cent), and simultaneously in Bihar (29.5 per cent), Rajasthan (12.8 per cent), Himachal Pradesh (7.7 per cent) and Kerala (5.1 per cent). The latest report (Crime in India-1997) also reveals that of the seventy-eight cases reported under this Act in 1997, twenty-nine cases were reported from Gujarat followed by Bihar twenty-three and Rajasthan ten. Even though the offence is non-cognizable, the police can take the offenders into custody. It is reported that the police disposed off seventy-two cases in 1997 out of one hundred seven cases including pending cases from investigation of previous year. In sixty cases, chargesheets were laid by the police. Of the two hundred seventy-four cases for trial, sixty-five cases were decided by the courts, in which thirty-seven cases ended in convictions.

A recent research by SAKSHI, a Delhi-based Non-Government Organization (NGO) reveals that eighty per cent of women from all classes experienced some form of sexual abuse in their childhood. More than fifty per cent of these women experienced abuse within their own families or from acquaintances. Over twenty per cent of them have undergone serious and continuing form of sexual abuse by close relatives. So, the female victims are mostly affected in the society. World Health Organisation (WHO) states that one in every ten children is sexually abused. A few case-studies of victimisation of girl child are cited here for exemplifying its gravity.

(A) A case, reported in the *Tribune* (January 7, 1993) tells of Amandeep Singh, a student of class VII, who was made to crawl four times along the fifty metre corridor of the boarding house and then canned on his thighs and knees. The reason is that she had forgotten to take her T-shirt from the store room for a rehearsal.

(B) The *Tribune* cited another incident occurred in the month of November, 1997. Sonu, an eight-year-old girl-child who was living at home with her parents, was often beaten, sometimes for a mistake and many times even when she made no mistake.

(C) Lovely was seven year old. Her uncle, who used to visit often, used to put his hand under her dress to touch her whenever they were alone and sometimes asked her to touch him too. He said that he loved her very much. That was their secret... He would be very angry if she told anyone.

Like Amandeep, Sonu and Lovely, there are so many female children in our country who are victimised of neglect, physical, emotional and sexual abuse. SAMVADA, a Bangalore-based NGO, surveyed on the different emotional reactions of victims of different types of assault or depression, anxiety, fear, worry, etc., during childhood. These are:

Emotional Reaction	*Percentage*
Sadness	31
Fear	8
Anger	19
Guilt/Shame	5
Shock	2
Helplessness	14
Disgust	7
Humiliation	3
Frustration	7
Confusion	2
Worry	2

Long-term Effects	*Percentage*
Hurt	48
Depression	19
Suicide attempt	2
Physical Problems	6
Intimacy	8
No long-term effect felt, learnt to handle situation	17

It is only very recently that a Delhi-based NGO, Centre of Concern for Child Labour (CCFCL) has made some inroads into the field. The CCFCL, in a study, has divided the girl child in the domestic sector into two categories—one, who did household tasks and the other, who was engaged in outdoors-economic work. The study revealed those middle or upper middle class families with small children preferred to employ young girls as domestic help because the help in that case not only came 'cheap' but was also considered 'safe'. The study further observed that like all other women workers in the informal sector, the child domestic workers were subjected to the sword of false allegations ever hanging over them. The Delhi Police, for example, arrested a domestic girl some time ago on a complaint lodged by her employer that she had stolen gold ornaments. It later came out that the girl wanted to quit and had asked for her rightful wages, the charges were just a plot to restrain her. Thus, it is very clear that even though a number of legislative measures have been passed in India for the welfare of children, they have failed to make any impact on life of the girl child because of lack of social and cultural support.

Prospects

1. Nowadays just like 'Help-Line' services, there are many 'Child-Line' organisations coming up. But we need to go further and

make sure that everyone consciously promotes 'childhood' for all children whatever family or community they belong to. But many, who profess to be friends of children, are the ones who violate her innocence and dignity. Hence, a VICTIM-ASSISTANCE SHOP may be created at state level initially and gradually district level and in the rural areas of different states. Functions of such a shop will be to propagate the curse of childhood and to get rid of such curse. They will have direct link with judiciary system and police authority. Local residents will be selected to run such shops and local police chief will be responsible to communicate with local citizens-in-charge of such shops. Modalities are to be prepared by the local police, citizens and local Government as per local demands and problems.

2. The question of children's rights is a very big one covering all aspects of their livelihood and, therefore, it has to be dealt with in a 'holistic' manner remembering that rights are indivisible and interdependent. We have to deal with many categories of 'problem' children or those with 'problems' such as children of nomads, of victims of terrorism, of sex workers, of women in jail, of immigrants or aliens and of consanguineous marriages. There are juvenile delinquents, children with disease or children with physical handicaps and children who belong to poor families. From the 'womb' to the 'tomb', children's rights have to be defined and safeguards provided.

3. The government decision to establish a National Commission for Children is to be welcomed so that it can help to implement their rights. A mere advisory and re-commission is not only unnecessary but will also be positively harmful to the interest of children. Therefore, a commission with power and accountability for implementation is needed for justice to children to become real and accessible.

4. The child-abuse is a national problem and so the responsibility for the welfare of children does not only lie on the government

alone, it is the function of the parents, family and the community. In fact, it is their failure and inability, which invites government intervention. Hence, since the 'morning shows the day', the parents have important duty to shoulder the future of child, protection of child from any severe consequences. Some tips are mentioned here for parents which may help to prevent physical, emotional and sexual abuse of children.

- Do listen to the explanation of the child before taking the stick to the child. Children can have problems too.
- Do encourage the child to participate in decision-making matters that concern them. This may help you to become less authoritarian.
- Do listen seriously when your child complains of seniors or teachers in school or elder children in the playground bullying him. It may be necessary for you to intervene.
- If sexual abuse is suspected, support acknowledge and accept what the child is saying and feeling. Disbelief and rejection by adults increases the helplessness and the self-blaming tendency of the child.
- When the child conveys unexplained aversion to adults, try to get to the root of the problem. The child may not know exactly what is wrong but the feeling will exhibit itself in aversion.
- Do be careful while entertaining your child to adults even if he be a trusted servant. Question and educate about the possibility of abuse.

5. The illegal abortion mainly in the private nursing homes should be looked into seriously. Although number of abortions are neither reported nor registered, it is sure that a survey in this respect will increase the statistical data shown by the NCRB. Rather, this may reflect as one of the important problems of

our country. In this regard, policy should be enacted which may help in eradicating such illegal abortion.

6. If government feels that merely by legislating a law to amend the conduct rules of civil servants prohibiting the employment of children below the age of 14 years as domestic servants by them is sufficient, it would be a major setback on the part of government to the concern and the plight of millions of child workers in the country. The government should look into its proper implementation. Senior politicians also expressed that the presence of twenty million child labourers in the country is a great concern for our country. The darkest aspect of this is the prevailing child prostitution. According to one estimate, about 7000 new cases of child trafficking are reported in India every year. If it is multiplied, one cannot imagine its severe consequences. The government should be cautious of such possibility and accordingly, it should take preventive measures to tackle the situation.

7. Last but not least, the task of making public aware of the dark side of the problem of foeticide and infanticide is to be taken seriously by the society and the government. NGOs, in this regard, should play a pivotal role in the society and they should enter into the remotest corner of villages and propagate against such crime.

References

From Crime Policing to Victim Policing by Ezzaf A Fallah St. Martin'sPress, New York.

Report of *The Times of India* New Delhi on "Courts need to protect Victimsof Crime" July 1999.

News published in *The Hindu* 'On the Child Domestic—a Life of Mute Sufferings'—23rd Oct. 1997.

News published in *The Hindu* August 18, 1999 under the caption 'The right to Childhood'.

'Crime in India - 1997' by National Crime Records Bureau, Government of India.

Article published in *The Hindu* by N.R. Madhava Menon entitled 'The Rights of Children'.

News item published in the *Tribune* on No. 1, 1997- 'Is Your Child Really Safe'.

'Dismal Fate of the Girl Child' by Ms. Uma Joshi.

9

Female Child—Victim of Gender Bias and Crime

Latha Krishnamurthy

Gender bias is a part of the social value system which has its roots in the society in general and in family in particular. The tradition bound Indian society, even today, is heavily tilted in favour of men giving them all the authority and prestige and reducing women to the lowest status. Traditional values and behaviour norms, bred through thousands of years, inhibit women from asserting themselves as independent individuals.

Independence brought with it the Constitution, with equality and social justice as its basic fundamental tenets. Constitutional mandates for equality and justice have considerably been diluted by a parallel regime of personal laws which continue to prop discrimination against women in the fields of marriage, divorce, custody, inheritance and succession. The personal laws, based on traditional socio-religious customs, continue to uphold male dominance over female needs.

Women are socialised as 'breeders' and 'caretakers'. This constitutes the definition of a 'normal' woman, a woman who will protect that patriarchal social order. Any other role by definition would be deviant. In a patriarchal order, gender becomes a normative system through which female behaviour is controlled. Definitions of deviance tend to be imposed on the powerless by the powerful. Given modern complex and stratified societies, with acutely conflicting interests such as those existing between men and women—deviance and control apparatus are created to prevent the deviant, i.e., the powerless from pursuing their interests[1]. Social control mechanism becomes a tool for oppression, suppression, exploitation and discrimination of women—the powerless; by men—the powerful.

Socialisation for gender role begins from the moment of birth. Parents treat male and female children differently and have expectations based on cultural definition of sex differences. Parents characterise daughter as weak, less attentive and coordinated, softer and more fragile and son is characterised as more alert and stronger, more coordinated and firmer. This perception coloured by sex stereotyping influences parents' behaviour towards their children, which subsequently shapes the children's self-concept and gender role expectations. Sex differences in socialisation experiences make women weaker and men stronger resulting in exploitation of weaker by the stronger. Obviously, women become more prone to oppression, suppression and exploitation.

Criminal victimisation of women, young girls have been prevalent throughout the history of mankind. The problem is common to a particular time, place and culture. It is rather a worldwide phenomenon and has aroused much public opinion and concern. Female child has been victim of abuse, discrimination and exploitation at all the stages of her life. She is discriminated at every stage which affects her adversely physical, social and psychological development.

Victim of Gender Bias

In all patriarchal societies females whether kids, adolescents or adults are believed to be treated as being inferior to males.

Even parents discriminate between their sons and daughters. Psychologists are of the opinion that the personality of an individual is governed by early childhood experiences. Behaviours like dependency, passiveness and submissiveness in female children comes out of discriminatory child rearing practices. These behaviours nurtured over the years makes the female children victims of various crimes in different situations.

Gender discrimination, the age old system of inequality and stereotyping of the role of women, have resulted in the low valuation of a female child. The parents always favour a son. This perhaps is the attitude all over the country with a few honourable exceptions. Girls are expected to be docile, modest, less talkative and submissive thus closing the doors of creativity and innovation for them. Gender bias does not stop at childhood but also continues during adolescence, at the time of marriage, in the household of in-laws, in the process of decision making, emotional rehabilitation as a member of group; employment opportunities and participation in the political affairs. Traditionally, most of the parents inadvertently instill orthodox, traditional and patriarchal ideas into the minds of children.

Female child has been the victim of various forms of abuse, discrimination and exploitation at all the stages. She is discriminated at every step, affecting adversely her physical, social and psychological development. She is treated as inferior to a male child. She is deprived of nutritious food, proper education and other needs required for her growth and development.

Victim of Domestic Crime

The Indian family structure is patriarchal, patrilocal and patrilineal. Traditionally men dominated the social structures. The dominant forms of family organisations have been the joint family headed by a male. Even where the matrilineal system prevailed, the real authority vested with men—wife's brothers, father and uncles. Indian women have been the victims of deep-rooted traditional oppression and socio-economic inequality in a male dominated society. Even today women are subjected to various forms of discrimination, oppression and exploitation in spite of widely prevalent legislations safeguarding their rights. The various forms of domestic victimisation of women range from wife-battering, dowry-killing, desertion, rape, incest and sexual abuse, female infanticide to other varied forms.

Women are innocent victims of discrimination, torture and harassment in their own families. Crimes like incest and child rape are located within the home, out of the purview of public, invisible and inaudible. Incest, never spoken about openly, exists in all strata of society and is often the cause of lasting trauma that can mar the family life for the victim.

A great proportion of incest and child rape cases that have come to light involve father-daughter relationships. Damodar Kunalienkar, a psychiatrist attached to the Institute of Psychiatry and Human Behaviour, Goa related the case of 17-year-old Tara. She was forced into an intimate relationship with her father since the age of 15. The girl's mother was mentally deranged and her two brothers were too young to know what was happening. Fearful of telling to anybody Tara found a way out of her private hell by attempting suicide. After three unsuccessful attempts of suicide the girl was brought for psychiatric treatment[2].

Responses to incest are so radically varied, ranging from trauma to outrage to acceptance, denial to open admittance, depression, guilt, shame... and most startling of all... indifference. While some people argue that in a permissive society, child molestion has increased, a recent study in the U.S. revealed that almost 12 to 15 million female children are subjected to incestuous abuse every year[3].

Shrouded in myth, secrecy and taboos, sexual abuse of children or paedophilia continues to rise alarmingly in India, where three out of every ten rape victims are children below the age of 16.

According to the National Crime Research Bureau's latest report, the year 1996 witnessed a 34.6 per cent increase in the cases of sexual abuse of children between 10-16 years and a 14.3 per cent increase in the victims below 10 years, when compared to the figures in 1992. According to Dr. Achal Bhagat, seventy per cent of child sexual abuser target girls who fall prey to the lust of perverse adults.

There is no special and separate law for child sexual abuse/ incest in India, with the result that the victim gets a raw deal and being a child is all the more traumatic for him/her as he/she is unable to understand as to what has happened to him/her.

Victim of Child Prostitution

From the ancient temples of Delphi to the modern Hindu temples of India, the regular sexual abuse of young girls as temple prostitutes has been a way of obtaining religious merit. The term commonly used for these prostitutes is Jogini or Devdasi. Historically, the Devdasis served a God to which they were ritually 'married' by dancing and singing in that God's temple. Around 5,000 girls are dedicated every year into this system in Andhra Pradesh, Maharashtra and Karnataka. These dedication ceremonies given religious sanction to a family's decision to prostitute a daughter—who is initiated into flesh trade at puberty.

It cannot be denied that more than religious devotion, it is the economic considerations that are paramount in most families decision to push a daughter into prostitution via the Devdasi dedication ceremony. The initiation ceremony is celebrated with a feast which is paid for by an upper caste man who has purchased the right to her virginity. The economic benefits for the family are immediate.

There are some castes that have traditionally accepted prostitution as their profession. The Rajna tribe in Rajasthan is economically organised around a system of child prostitution. This tribe is only one of many such in Rajasthan. The system of prostitution practices by this tribe is inherently child prostitution, as the girls enter prostitution by puberty. The eldest daughter is raised, being fully aware that the tribe's survival depends on her labour as a prostitute. The tribe's economic and social organisation ensure that these girls do not question their fate. Other communities—Dehrehar, Gandharva, Bedias and Kanjuars—have traditionally accepted prostitution as a source of livelihood.

Surveys have claimed that fifty per cent of all the prostitutes in Maharashtra began as Devdasis. Girls from this system have been estimated to account for twenty per cent of the total girls in this illegal profession. About eighty-five per cent of the prostitutes in Delhi and Calcutta were compelled into the flesh trade when very young, entertaining about seven to eight clients in a day. Often during heavy menstrual periods, ice is used and they are forced to receive clients. Physical and psychological torture may be specifically employed to ensure compliance in many cases. The girl in prostitution is a victim of sexual slavery in the name of deep-rooted tradition, social custom, religion and culture—which is highly discriminative, exploitative, oppressive and suppressive for females from their childhood[4].

It is a sad commentary on the social values of modern society that we can permit more than one million children in prostitution in Asia alone to remain in a form of sexual slavery which is akin to a living death.

Conclusion

Traditional discrimination against women has not come to an end irrespective of statutory provisions to that effect. There is little awareness among them about the existing social legislations to protect their interests. Patriarchal conditions and discriminatory socialisation patterns isolate women from asserting themselves in changing and redefining the social order which prop up discrimination against them. Until equality for women is made a reality through social attitude and its change, until concrete solutions are found to various gender related problems, until men cease to consider women as their subjugated/suppressed property—women will continue to be the victim of gender bias, faulty socialisation process, domestic crime and sexual abuse of various forms.

Legal machinery can play only a limited role in the social and economic emancipation of women. Law is an instrument of social change and regulates the social relations between the state and society. Women need to be educated on various aspects of legislations concerning them in order to take the maximum benefits of such legislations by which social justice and freedom from gender bias for women can be achieved.

References

1. J.F. Mc Donough, and R.C. Saari (Eds.), *The Trapped Women: Catch 22 in Deviance and Control*, N.Y., Sage, 1987.
2. Femina, *Battered Dreams—Villent Reality*—Cover Story, Aug. 1994.
3. Femina, *Crossing Bloodlines-Incest: The Unspoken Trauma* Cover Story, June 1992.
4. UNICEF Report, *Child Prostitution: The Ultimate Abuse*, 1995.

10

Women—Victims of Violence from Womb to Tomb

K. Shanthi

"There is one rape every 54 minutes, one molestation every 26 minutes, one kidnapping/abduction every 43 minutes, one dowry death every one hour and 42 minutes, one act of cruelty every 33 minutes and one eve teasing every 51 minutes" (Government of India—Data Sheet on violence against women 1991).

Introduction

Violence against women in their different walks of life, i.e., at home, at workplace and in public sphere is persistently on the increase and has come to be accepted as a common phenomenon. Violence against women is the manifestation of a historically unequal power relationship between men and women. The forces of development have further weakened women's position making them all the more vulnerable to societal violence. In this article an attempt is made to understand the concept, its different forms, its magnitude and what could be done to mitigate the same. A bird's eye-view is provided and the complexities are untouched. The idea is to create an awareness on the need for a movement against violence as such and against those acts of crimes which are perpetrated only on women because they are women.

The Concept

As per the definition found in the Social Science Encyclopaedia violence entails inflicting emotional, psychological, sexual, physical and/or material danger. It involves the exercise of force[1]. The Country Report submitted to the fourth International Women's Conference at Beijing observes, "It is now widely accepted that violence against women is not an isolated phenomenon. Much of it is related to social changes accompanying the processes of development and modernisation."[2] This clearly indicates that the issue cannot be analysed in a vacuum but in the larger context of changing values and norms emanating from modernisation.

Incidence and Magnitude

It is very disheartening to note that till 1988 no data on crimes against women were collected. It was only from 1989 that data relating to crimes against women began to be collected which relate to (a) the incidence of crimes committed (b) number of persons arrested and (c) social background of victims. The crimes committed against women are broadly classified under two categories. They are (a) crimes identified under the Indian Penal Code (IPC) and (b) crimes identified under the Special Laws (SL). Rape (Section 376 IPC), kidnapping and abduction (Sections 363 and 373), dowry homicides (Sections 302 and 304 B), torture—physical and mental (Section 498 A), molestation (Section 354), eve teasing or sexual harassment (Section 509), importation trafficking (1956 Act), demanding dowry (1961 Act), Commission of Sati (1987 Act) and indecent representation of women (1986 Act) are the crimes covered under these two categories.

Of the total crimes committed in India under the IPC every year about six per cent are crimes against women. According to Government of India statistics the total number of crimes against women (under the IPC and the SL excluding murders) increased from 68,000 in 1990 to 1,06,000 in 1995. Thus crimes against women have increased by forty-five per cent in five years[3]. The types of crimes' list indicates that about twenty-nine per cent are torture cases, twenty-seven per cent molestation cases, eight per cent immoral traffic cases, five per cent dowry homicide cases and half a per cent are other cases. The magnitude of the problem can be well appreciated if we take data relating to one particular crime say rape. While 2,487 cases of rape were reported in 1971 the number increased to 13,754 in 1995 which works out to thirty-eight rapes every day or about three rapes every two hours[4]. Here it should be remembered that the actual number of cases that occur is many times higher than the number registered as many cases remain unreported. In cases like rape it may be even 15 to 20 times more.

There is found to be high inter-state variations in the crimes committed against women in India. The highest number of crimes are recorded in Maharashtra followed by Madhya Pradesh, Uttar Pradesh, Rajasthan, Andhra Pradesh, Tamil Nadu and West Bengal. In 1995 of the 1,06,471 cases recorded under IPC and SL 15.3 per cent were in Maharashtra, 14.4 per cent in Madhya Pradesh, 11.2 per cent in Uttar Pradesh, 8.8 per cent in Rajasthan, 8.9 per cent in Andhra Pradesh, 8.2 per cent in Tamil Nadu, 6 per cent in West Bengal and 27.6 per cent in other states.[5] In the nation's capital, Delhi, according to Delhi State Commission for Women the rate of crimes against women is far higher, i.e., 34.1 per lakh of population against the national average of 9.5 which indicated that the problem goes far beyond policing and law and order.

The Life Cycle of Women and the Categories of Violence

Let us see how and what kind of violence is perpetrated against women from womb to tomb under various following headings.

(a) Female Foeticide

The right to be born is denied to a female child. Sex determination tests are widely resorted to even in the remotest rural areas to find out the sex of the baby only to kill, if it happens to be a female. It is learnt that about 4,000 female babies are aborted in Tamil Nadu alone every year. There is gross underestimation since all cases are unreported and there is no way of estimating such deaths in the absence of maintenance of records. A survey of 50 gynaecologists in Mumbai revealed that 84 per cent of these doctors were performing tests to determine the sex of the child.

The use of these services is not restricted to women from middle class but also include women from working class backgrounds. There is a clear nexus among physicians, sex determination clinics and abortion centres all operating as a network on the basis of commissions. The Registrar General of India has admitted that 3.6 lakh female foetuses were aborted in India in 1993-94, an estimate based on hospital births alone and a very large number of these are believed to have gone for sex determination test. Though data are hard to obtain private estimates put the number annually around two lakh. But an additional threat which causes much concern is the development of new pre-selection techniques such as electrophoresis, Ericesson's method, etc., which involve not detection but prior manipulation of the sex of the child. What is the future of the female race in such a context is the moot question which remains unanswered.

(b) Female Infanticide

In many families in the lower rung of the society if a female child is fortunate enough not to be aborted then a grim future awaits her soon after her birth in the form of deliberate forced killing by parents/kith and kin. Female infanticide is common in several parts of Tamil Nadu, Rajasthan, Orissa and in certain other parts of India. When a girl child is killed in Usilampatti, a village in Tamil Nadu people talk about the ignorance and poverty of the people that lead to this crime but what does not come to limelight is that this is happening in a community that has traditionally valued women as repositories of knowledge related to agricultural practices and seed cultivation and therefore were seen as an asset and not a liability. With the advent of green revolution and the dominance of cash crop economy this knowledge has become redundant and with it the women who possessed this knowledge. Sanskritisation process has added fuel to fire.

Every year twelve million girls are born in India and roughly three million or twenty-five per cent of them do not survive to see their fifteenth birthday. One million die in the first year itself. Little girls are allowed to die because of malnutrition and diseases and intentionally not treated. Acts of 'omission' and acts of 'commission' account for the lower survival rates of females.[6] Research studies very clearly indicate that gender discrimination and preference for a son have a growing negative impact on the sex ratio and life expectancy in a number of communities and geographical areas.

Female foeticide and infanticide are fundamental violation of the first and foremost right of the child—the right to survive and hence education of masses on this vital issue is a must. The materialism and consumerism projected through advertisements create a new value system wherein people are respected for what they posses than what they are. Children of economically weaker sections develop a poor self-esteem because of this. The Media has an important role to play in bringing about the desired changes. It should play conscious and responsible role in changing the status of the girl child through dissemination of information, balanced reporting, depiction of positive roles, avoidance of gender stereotypes, more development news and literature, films that portray girls equal to boys, etc.

Girl Child Labour and Violence Against Girl Child Workers

Poverty forces many families to send the girl children for work. They are denied the right to education. At the workplace they are subjected to physical and mental torture of varying degrees. The International Confederation of Free Trade Unions (ICFTU) in its report "Child Labour: World's Best Kept Secrets" points out that there are an estimated fifty-five million children who are workers.[7] Female working children out-number males in both rural and urban areas. For every 1000 male working children in India there are 1,193 female working children. The very denial of childhood is an offence or violence against children. When girls of seven to ten years are forced to act as surrogate mothers it is nothing but violence of a subtle nature.

The problems experienced by girl child workers in beedi (cigar) industry in North Arcot and Tirunelveli districts of Tamil Nadu are worth considering here. More than fifty per cent of the workers in the beedi industry are girls. Girls are pledged for a paltry sum of Rs. 1,000 or Rs. 2,000 borrowed from the employers by the parents. These children are forced to work 12-14 hours a day. The supervisor has a long whip and sits at the entrance and if any child gossips or is found to be slack in work the whip is used to beat the child. The rooms are cramped and ill-ventilated. Sexual assault of girls of 12-14 years is common. At the age of 15-16 the girls are withdrawn for marrying them off and employers also do not want grown up girls since they believe that by that age they become slack in their work. Most of the children suffer respiratory diseases and the incidence of tuberculosis is high among the beedi workers in general. In Tirunelveli beedi rolling is the occupation of one particular caste and for a girl to get married, knowledge of beedi rolling is a must. For beedi rolling the dust is supplied by the employers for prescribed number of beedies (normally 100) and there is always a shortfall of dust supplied. To make up the shortage girls borrow beedies for an interest, i.e., for every ten beedies borrowed twelve beedies are to be returned, the other two being the interest (popularly known in vernacular as 'vatti beedi' system). In the case of three girls such vatti beedi accumulated to such a huge number that unable to repay they committed suicide according to this case study.[8]

Child Prostitution

Child prostitution is another worrying factor. About fifteen per cent of the nearly two million prostitutes are believed to be children. Minor girls are preferred in the sex trade since they pose a lesser AIDS (Acquired Immune Deficiency Syndrome) risk to their clients. Young girls are purchased or kidnapped and then tortured and sold in various red light areas.[9] A hospital based study in New Delhi has shown that out of the 362 patients who were suffering from STD (Sexually Transmitted Diseases), 58 were below 14 years of age. A majority of the children below seven years were girls. Since below seven is not a sexually active age, the only inference is that they were all victims of sexual abuse[10]. In 1990 out of 9,863 reported rapes, 394 were committed on children below the age of ten and

2,090 on children between the age of 10-16 years. Almost one-third of rape crimes were against minors. It is also clear from the same records that 194 suspicious persons were arrested for rape in Delhi in 1988 in which only four were convicted. One hundred twenty-seven cases of dowry deaths were registered in 1990 in which only one was convicted. A study on the profile of prostitutes in India reveals that at the time of entry fifteen per cent of the women were children and twenty-five per cent of the women were minors between 16-18. The scheduled caste women constituted thirty-six per cent, the backward class women twenty-four per cent, illiterate women seventy-one per cent unmarried women 84.4 per cent, married women 10.6 per cent and divorced, deserted or widowed women five per cent. Among the causes for entry, economy distress (44 per cent), desertion by spouse (24.5 per cent), deception (11.9 per cent), social custom and family tradition (10.5 per cent) and abduction and kidnapping (2.25 per cent). On their earnings the profile reveals that sixty per cent of the women earn less than Rs. 3,000 per month and the actual earnings retained by them works out to Rs. 500-600 after the brothel keepers and pimps have taken their cuts and maintenance of the women's families. The average indebtedness ranges from Rs. 10,000 to Rs. 15,000 thus keeping the women under perpetual bondage.

Trafficking in Children

At the adolescent age women are subjected to lot of cruelty. Their free movement and mobility in search of better avenues of employment are highly restricted in view of increasing social violence against them such as eve-teasing, sexual abuse, rape, kidnapping, molestation, etc. Trafficking in women is consistently on the increase. Utter poverty urges many women of the Third World countries to migrate thus making them an easy prey for traffickers. Since several Third World governments are promoting export of personnel among which women constitute a significant portion, it becomes imperative to monitor the practices of traffickers in women such as mail order brides, fake marriages via domestic work, entertainment etc. Tourism as a way of economic development has now increased the possibilities for further malpractices.

Abuses Against Married Women

Then comes the next stage in women's lives—the married life stage—wherein they are subjected to maximum domestic violence like dowry harassment/dowry death, physical violence, maximum workload both at home and outside, the discarded harmful reproductive technologies being tried out on them in the name of birth control, etc. Hazardous contraceptives such as Depo Provera, Norplant, Net-en are freely available or administered without any thought to informed consent. They have very serious consequences to the health of women. Women are used as guinea pigs.

The torture meted out to widows is mental rather than physical in nature. Because of the social stigma attached to re-marriage young widows are forced to remain single only to feel insecure, face humiliation and fight a tough battle for livelihood. The mental torture caused to them by denying them participation in functions and ceremonies cannot be described in words. Certain other social practices which accord humiliating status to widows are to be condemned very severely. The social institution of absorption of widows by the natal families is dying very fast and they are left uncared to fend for themselves. No doubt female headed households are on the increase at an alarming rate. It is a pity that the very same society which denies higher education and employment in the name of culture to women, leaves them high and dry with no alternative livelihood strategy. It is never realised that it is one form of violence against women.

Communal Violence

The worst form of violence that anyone could think of is the communal violence. The lower caste women are invariably the victims of caste politics. Any mass agitation by agricultural labourers for higher wages or better working conditions is suppressed by mass rape of women of these labourers by the rich landlords. Again one of the war crimes is rape of women of the captives or refugees by the soldiers irrespective of which country they belong to. Sometimes the very protectors of law indulge in crimes and stories of custodial rapes are common news in the modern days. In the name of religion the violence perpetrated on women has come to be accepted as a socially approved normal behaviour.

Causes for Concern

The causes for concern are quite simple to understand. They are:

(a) increasing incidence and variety of violence against women,

(b) girl children of 5-15 becoming the victims in increasing numbers,

(c) growing proportion of children in flesh trade, and

(d) large scale trafficking of women at intra and international level.

The United Nations Conference held at Vienna in 1993 upheld for the first time the concept of women's rights as human rights and any form of violence against women is violation of human rights. The conference recognised that "The Human Rights of women are unalienable, integral and indivisible part of universal human rights which meant that the full and equal participation of women in political, civil, economic, social and cultural life at the national, regional, international levels and the eradication of all forms of discrimination on grounds of sex" are the priority of the international community. Human rights cover a whole range of rights relating to life, liberty, equality and dignity of the individual as guaranteed by the constitution or embodied in International covenants. But unfortunately in India both private and public violence against women is on the increase. The mass media continues to depict women as sex objects thereby degrading and dehumanising their life and encourages acts of violence against women and also reinforces traditional stereotyped roles.

Conclusion

Though the causes for violence against women are cited as many ranging from inability to support the family to insanity, one main reason that stands out predominantly is the continuation of patriarchy and unjust social order. Women's subordinate status and dependency are the major causes. Empowerment of women—economic, social, legal, political and cultural, i.e., a multi-pronged strategy to emancipate and empower women will go a long way in reducing the incidence of violence against women both at home and in society. Egalitarian outlook and equal sharing of power, work load, resources and fruits of labour is a must. The responsibility lies not only with the government but with each and every segment of the society.

It is a pity that in our country the need for counselling to victims of violence is not appreciated at all. Temporary shelter homes and rehabilitation strategies are other important requirements. But unfortunately the victims of violence are looked down upon with social stigma, further accentuating their misery. The outlook should change and this requires awareness among public at large on issues relating to violence against women. On the one hand efforts should be directed to reduce the incidence of violence against women and on the other hand public should be enlightened on the need for after-care of victims and their legitimate right to claim justice. This calls for sea-change in social values and norms relating to humans lives.

References

1. Elisabeth A. Stando, 'Violence' Adam Kuper and Jessoca Kuper (ed.) '*The Social Science Encyclopaedia' Routledge*, London, 1996, p. 186.

2. Government of India, Ministry of HRD, Department of WCD—Fourth World Conference on Women, Beijing, 1995, Country Report p. 49.

3. *Crimes in India*, 1995, p. 223.

4. *Ibid.*, 1995, p. 222.

5. *Ibid.*, 1995, pp. 224 and 231.

6. UNICEF's Gender Equity: Towards Women's Empowerment in '*The Progress of Indian States*', Nov. 1995, pp. 57-59.

7. *Economic Times*, 16.6.1994.

8. Karunanidhi, Child Labour in the Beedi Industry, Unpublished-Manonmaniam, Sundaranar University, Tirunelveli.

9. CBCI, Women's Commission Newsletter, Vol. IV, No. 3, May-June, 1997, p. 7.

10. *The Hindustan Times*, 4.3.1994.

11

Traumas of Child Victim of Rape

S. Sanyal

It is rightly being said that the reason why we have not been able to prevent child abuse is that we deal with the symptoms and rarely attack the root causes embedded in the society. Many of the propelling factors leading to child abuse are already known to us, *e.g.*, poverty, illiteracy, broken homes, overwhelming mothers, social isolation, interaction between the social class and social stress. There are no concerted and co-ordinated efforts to tackle these roots of problems. Although great studies have been made in dealing with the problem of child abuse, it is still pandemic. It is clear that the problem is more widespread than previously thought. The number of cases of child abuse are reported increasingly by the media.

The true incidents of child abuse culminating in sexual abuse often go unreported. It is a well-known phenomenon that unlike other crimes, sexual crime creates immense sensitivity in the society. People still do not like to discuss sex openly, and even today it is unthinkable in many sections that children can be sexually abused. Family plays a determinant role either as a contributor or defender of the act by undermining it and not reporting to the police in due time. Preference is given to the protection of the family as a unit rather than to the individual child. In an illiterate, underprivileged poor family, a mother may be a constant witness to the sexual abuse of her child by her husband but she hesitates to disclose the affair to any person including her own family members for fear of incurring the wrath of her husband and bringing shame to her family. She fails to realise that after effects of this act is not only traumatic for her daughter, but also will continue to have permanent effect on her behaviour.

Myths about Child Rape

Before a diagnose is made of rape of small children, it is necessary to discuss the myths and fantasies that enshrined the act so as to clear all misconceptions and handle the matter systematically. It is believed that children who are raped are primarily older ten-aged children. It has been proved wrong by reports in the media of incidences of child rape of even below 3-years of age, well-supported by researches at microscopic level within the country and outside. It has been assessed universally that the mean age of sexually abused children tends to be around eleven years. Second false belief is that children who are raped are retarded. Though it is true that retarded children are more prone to a sexual abuse than a normal one but that does not deny the fact that any child can be a potential victim, given the right set of circumstances regardless of the child's age, race, intelligence, social class or neighbourhood.

It is also wrong to assume that child rape victims come mainly from the lower socio-economic family. Family income and social status both are unrelated to child abuse. The difference is that while a raped victim in a lower socio-economic home gets exposed to public scrutiny and comments, it is generally hushed and kept silent in an established esteemed family for fear of social shame.

The likelihood of children becoming victims of rape is not higher outside because the offender is often the own kith or kin or some friend of the family. In fact, she is in more danger not only in her own home but also in the homes of her family friends. It is claimed with the support of various studies that three-fourths of child rapes occur indoors and only few are there which occur outside the child's home. There are many more myths, but they are gradually waning away with the people becoming more conscious towards this offences terming it not only barbaric and heinous but also demanding that the offender needs to be given life imprisonment.

To many people the rape of a child is a terrible incident, yet somewhere there is a belief that since the child is small and is unconscious of the act she will overcome the shock quicker than her elder counterparts, and this is the biggest myth because the trauma left by the offence remains unexpressed at the same time causing severe mental damage and a blockage of healthy emotional stability which continues till old age.

Symptoms of Rape: Sexual abuse such as rape is not often identified through physical indications alone. Physical signs such as difficulty in walking or sitting, torn stained or bloody under-clothes, complaints of pain or itching, bruises or bleeding, veneral diseases and pregnancy are there but there are also indications of behavioural change which may add to the traumas of Rape Syndrome. Several arguments can be made in support of a trauma specific approach. Studies have shown that sexually abused children as a group exhibit a greater prevalence of at least some problems than other clinical and non-clinical samples. Some logically related outcomes such as sexual behaviour problems constantly discriminate sexually abused children according to Friedrich 1993.

Rape is an outcome of an internal crisis in the psyche of the offender, and results in the external crisis in the life of the victims. Rape Trauma Syndrome is a label given to a collection of syndroms identified as past rape indicators in the victim and divide the rape trauma syndrome with two effects, one is the immediate disruption and disorganisation in the life-style of the victim in general and the second phase is the long-term effect in which some victims have nurtured suppressed feelings throughout the life while some attempt to reorganise their lives.

Studies have been done from time to time to assess the traumas of rape and Peter (1976) is one of them who comprehensively described the child victims of his study. He found eleven per cent of child victims did not feel safe any longer at their place of stay while thirty-two per cent showed more negative feelings for men they knew. Some of the children are less than usual and thirty-one per cent reported difficulty in sleeping. Nightmares were often seen and they cried out in sleep. Likewise Burgess and Holmstorm (1978) reported in their study that most of the children reported mild or moderate to severe symptoms. Very few children escaped with no symptoms.

It can be assessed from these studies that behavioural symptoms are many and they include general irritability, behavioural problems at school, acute withdrawal, depressive symptoms, running away from home and expressive of delinquent behaviour.

The long-term effect of minor rape is more harmful since it has detrimental effect on the self-concept and personality of the individual. A child who had shown little or no affect during the commission of crime stores up psychological dynamite that may explode during crucial point in her psycho-sexual development in later life. Among them can be courtship, marriage and child-birth. Sexual disorientation or psychoses were found by Peter (1976) to be related to childhood rape, who labelled this abuse as a *Psychological Time Bomb*. Moreover it has been observed that victims of early rapes had an extremely low self-esteem. They felt worthless, rarely achieved anything satisfying to adults and could not succeed in their lives. Amy Katan a psycho-analyst while studying a number of women who were raped in their childhood found her patients complaining of never feeling that they were complete women. They projected a displaced feeling of helplessness and pain of early childhood by turning aggressive against themselves or others.

Aggression turned towards self had been found to be continuously displayed in the form of exhibiting delinquent or criminal behaviour in engaging in sexuality or in other self-defeating behaviour. When the aggression was directed against others it resulted in an inability to get close to men because of suspiciousness, anger, rigidity, sexual unresponsiveness or need to be in control.

While justifying therapeutic treatment for rape victims, it must be acknowledged that rape raises certain critical issues for the victim especially when the victim is a child and for her family as well. The lives of the victim and her family members are disrupted by these issues. Parents find difficult to accept the fact that the child is no longer sexually innocent. Their attitude towards the child starts changing which becomes all the more shattering for the victim's mental equilibrium and unfortunately they bitterly fail to realise that their over-concern not only brings a guilt feeling in the child that she has done something wrong and she is a bad girl, but it also withdraws her into social isolation. Parents therefore need to know what happens after a sexual attack and attempt to understand the expressionless feelings of the child. They must encourage the child to discuss her problems with them, failing which, with a professional and seek counselling to regain a healthy and normal life. Unfortunately in many circumstances this does not happen. Parents besides being hysterical, urge the child to forget the unpleasant experiences and refuse to talk about it with her. This attitude aggravates the problem and children continuously feel that they have done something terribly bad, for which the parents are extremely disappointed with them. Therefore what is required is to make the incident less frightening so that the traumas are also less sever in nature.

According to such situations where child victims had experienced less traumas mentioned that if the attack was only once and the attacker was a stranger then the psychological injury is less. Also if the child received emotional support and understanding from elders and parents, and did not counter the ordeal of police questioning then the recovery from the emotional shock was quicker and easier than in other circumstances, facilitated further with counselling and psychiatric help. Feelings of fear, outrage, anger and guilt affect both victim and family and they are mitigated with proper intervention from a counsellor.

So far it is alright that therapeutic treatment is necessary for a rape victim, particularly a child, but what about the parents who are also thrown into a setback and undergo experiences which may be different in nature. They begin to feel guilty that they failed to protect their child. Some even lose confidence in their abilities to deal with future life crises. The feeling of powerlessness also engulfs them. Parents feel that they and their children are completely at the mercy of outside forces; helpless to protect themselves. Besides any sexual offence, be it is a rape or molestation of a child or of an adult in the family, becomes an issue of embarrassment for both victim and parents. Parents may not want neighbours, friends or other family members to know what happened to their child exactly in the same manner the child starts avoiding her peer-group in school, to the extent that she develops school phobia. There may be many other reactions emanating from rape, but it is conclusive that rape, especially of a child precipitates an emotional crisis in the victim and the family. The reaction to this stress can impair the mental health and functioning of both victim and the family. Timely crises intervention can help in preventing future emotional distress.

Incest: Many prefer not to think about incest. The public reacts with horror and disgust to any account of incest. Yet in spite of a strong taboo and legal sanction against it, incest occurs every day, to a great degree than most of the people would imagine. Incest is also a sexual abuse leading to rape, the only difference is that while other rapes occur outside the house, incest is committed within the house and the offender is none other than the victims's own kith and kin, be it her father, cousin, uncle or even father-in-law. The other deplorable fact about incest is that while rape by a stranger is an incident happening once with the victim, incest continues over days and years like a scorpion gradually eating into the mental and physical condition of the victim. She silently bears the shameful act much to her tolerance. Only when her tolerance crumbles does she revolt and people come to know about her plight. With the overwhelming impact of the traumas of rape, she has to remain in that environment maintaining the infamous relationship with the offender who can be her own father. This not only makes her terribly let down but also ruins her normal relationship with any other male-folk. Her life is coloured by violations. There is otherwise some opinion that the child victim sees the incest as a way of saving the family. She takes the guilt upon herself and endures the behaviour in an effort to keep the parents together. When the relationship is discovered, the child's guilt may centre more strongly on her failure to keep the family from breaking up.

The Profile of the Offender

While understanding the vulnerability of victimization and the traumas of a victim, the villain of the drama or the contributor of the tragedy should not be overlooked. Men who molest children are described as not only inept in their sexual lives but are also unsuccessful in other aspects also. Intermittent studies have revealed factors like social violation, unsatisfactory marital-sexual relationship, wife being mentally ill, passive, powerless or dependent, and marital discord, contribute making the individual rapist. Even then it cannot be generalized in all circumstances. In cases of incest some of the problems the offender faces are quite subtle, like power struggle with a child, boredom when not working or annoyance that a spouse has gone to work. The whole family involvement becomes an important precipitating factor to crime. These are however non-sexual problems and all child sexual abuse cannot be explained on the basis of the number or type of non-sexual problems. However, when designing a pragmatic treatment programme for offenders non-sexual problems have to be focused to enable the offenders to get an insight and learn to solve the problems directly. In certain studies paedophiles have not only been discussed but also classified. Geiser (1979) had mentioned about fixated offender whose psychosexual development was disturbed in childhood and who was mainly paedophile. He is the *paedophile*, lover of children and he will repeatedly attack on this target group without remorse, but this is not so in the case of those rapists who turn to children for sex when their adult relationship gets disturbed. For any reason whether it is marital discord or his passivity and dependency on his wife, this type of person regresses and develops intimacy with children and after winning their confidence rapes them. Child rapists are rarely mentally ill. They may be having emotional disorders but not to the extent that it impairs their judgement and rationality. To support this hypothesis, Geiser quoted a study where adult rapists were compared with child-molesters and incidences of psychosis among paedophile was low. The study concluded that psychoses were not associated with sexual offenders. So to say that the child rapists do not show any particular psychiatric disorders other than sexual deviation. All do not agree with this finding assumption and Joseph Peter was one of them. In his sample of 224 probationer male adult sex offender, he reported that all groups of sex offenders reported more symptoms of illness on a medical index than comparable groups of normals. The paedophiles in particular showed considerable immaturity, strong dependency needs, overall regression and a feeling of phallic inadequacy. Unable to attract adult women because of feeling of inferiority they turned to little girls for affection and sexual gratification. Unlike the other rapists, the paedophile under stress was found to be withdrawn and isolated. They were also more passive than rapists.

The vulnerability and the helplessness of the child make it all the more easier for the rapist to overpower her through treat, bribe or mild force since children rarely put up strong physical resistance.

Therefore extreme force is invisible in such incidents as with adult and adolescent rapes. Extreme is the mark of sadistic offender who intends to harm the child.

Judicial Implication of Child Rape in India

There is no separate law for the act of sexual assaults on a child except that according to Clause Sixth of Sec 375 IPC (1996). This particular section states that if rape is committed on a child who is not in a position to offer any substantial resistance, the mandatory sentence could be life transportation and if the act of sexual assault is followed with a murder the mandatory sentence could be death sentence.

It is seriously being thought in the judicial section that to minimize the incidence of child rape there is a need for modification in procedural law for the trial and investigation of cases related to child rape.

The Committee of National Federation for Indian Women had focused on lengthy procedure and questioning by the police which is prohibited in the existing laws of the minors. Rectification of the trials and amendments of laws to make the punishment rigid to the utmost are what every normal person in the society will desire.

Treatment of the Victim and the Offender

Group treatment for sexually abused children has frequently been recommended. Many researchers feel that child victim of rape will find it extremely difficult to disclose her experience to a therapist while she is alone than when she is in a group. It reduces isolation and facilitates peer-relationship in a manner impossible in individual therapy. This is, however, sometimes possible because of the limitation of the number of cases coming for treatment, particularly in the younger age group.

Counsellor while talking to a sexually abused child has to give extra concern to the dynamics of sexual abuse and the syndromes that children exhibit. In the foremost exists the child's perception of safety, as to whether she feels safe. Secondly, she must be persuaded to give vent to her feelings thereby creating a congenial environment where she feels secure. Children of incestuous cases often put up a rigid resistance to any treatment. Fear of loss of family image and the relationship with the members of the family inhibit the child from stating her experiences. To get the cooperation of the victim a therapist or a trained counsellor must use expressive therapy such as painting, drawing, writing or playing with dolls, particularly male dolls, enabling her to project her suppressed feelings mingled with shock and aggression on the external objects. The child through this process learns to communicate what has happened, thus reducing her isolation and provides an opportunity for sex education. Children have little knowledge of molestation and have trouble making sense of it. A child particularly needs to know that she is not the only one and that this has happened to other children also. This reduces her loneliness. Also, she can be explained that it is not she but the adult who is responsible for the act. This way she does not feel guiltier for the crime. In order to mentally as well as emotionally rehabilitate the sexually abused, the victim needs to know that while sexual abuse may make her feel different it does not make her look different from other children.

It is not enough to treat the victim alone. Incidences of sexual offence will remain unchecked as long as offenders remain unattended. While one victim gets treatment another may become vulnerable, as the rapist is always lurking somewhere. In circumstances where the crime has been committed intentionally and the child victim has died due to the injury of rape, there undoubtedly the offender should be given rigorous punishment including death penalty, but where the criminal feels guilty and regrets for his act therapeutic treatment can be offered to him. Sometimes, dissatisfaction of normal sexual life or rejection by the wife also leads to these types of deviant behaviour. Treating the offender alone in such cases will not help him to reform himself. It is necessary that family counselling be done and the individual is helped to reintegrate himself in the family fold. It is both difficult and critical when there is an incestuous relationship in the family and the therapist has to rebuild the normal relationship between the members of that house. This is possible only with the cooperation of the whole family and the offender is being made to realize the consequences of his act. We must not, however, mingle the treatment programme of this particular type with psychopathic criminals and with those who are mentally sick. Paedophilic falls in this category. In order to prevent them from offending again it is necessary that they are exposed to long series of clinical treatment.

Measures to Prevent Sexual Offences

(1) Uniform state laws are needed that define sexual abuse in detail, and penalties and treatment of offenders need to be standardized.

(2) There is a need for national forums for the reporting of child sexual abuse.

(3) There is a need for a broad public educational programme on child sexual abuse. Public awareness and discussion of the problem in seminars and media must be promoted, beginning with the education of the public with stress on the need to report cases of child sexual abuse. The largest single obstacle in doing something about child sexual abuse is the public's attitude of secrecy. It prevents victims and families from seeking and obtaining help. Child sexual abuse will not magically disappear if we do not talk about it. Rather, child sexual abuse thrives on secrecy.

(4) A public educational programme should also include information about the nature and incidence of child sexual abuse, and the community resources available to help children, parents, and offenders. As part of the programme, specific information about the needs of children and "how to parent" adequately should be made available. Courses in

parenting and child care should be an essential part of the public school curriculum.

Few young children have had an adequate sex education. It is still commonplace for parents to postpone discussions and to avoid mentioning sexual activities until children are in late middle childhood or early adolescence, by which time the information is seldom needed. Younger children who have been sexually assaulted are thus left in a confusing situation. Quite often, they do not understand exactly what happened to whom.

(5) To guarantee psychiatric treatment of all identified child victims of sexual abuse, communities need to institute treatment programmes specifically geared to treat the families and victims of sexual abuse.

(6) Many experts agree that the real trauma of child rape begins when it is discovered. This remark usually refers to the insensitive handling of the victim and family by the social and legal systems courts. Some people go so far as to claim that the child's contact with the police, courts and lawyers is often more traumatic than the original sexual assault, and advise against exposing the child to this process.

(7) In order to help the child rape victim, all agencies and individuals dealing with child sexual abuse cases must coordinate their efforts. The people involved must come to understand the needs of the victims, family and offender. They must be helped so that their own feelings don't get in the way of rational, helpful action.

(8) Professionals as well as the general public need help with their feelings about child sexual abuse. The usual reaction in most people is an emotional and punitive one. In such a climate it is difficult to find much support for preventive treatment and rehabilitation programmes.

(9) Prevention of sexual abuse of children is part of a larger need for developing healthier attitudes toward sex. Some experts have suggested that the most important thing in preventing sexual abuse is teaching children that they have a right to say "no".

(10) Part of preventing sexual abuse of children must necessarily involve general programmes to strengthen families. Obvious examples are day care centres, homemaker services, family counselling services, and parent education courses.

(11) The handling of rape cases and the relevant laws should be re-thought. Instead of the legal response being based upon our emotional horror about the crime, the more serious crimes should be those, which involve force or violence, those that are repetitive in nature, or those which contain an exploitative profit element.

Suggestions

No raped victim should be treated in an undignified manner, particularly if the victim is a child. The consequences of the sexual offence traumatize the child throughout her childhood and even continue to create imbalances in her emotions when she enters the adulthood. It is often seen that a sexually abused individual either propels or commits sexual offence as a sadistic pleasure. If the whole incident is dealt at the right time and in an appropriate manner then a child rape victim can easily be rehabilitated. She can enjoy life like any normal person.

References

Anna C. Salter, *Treating Child Sex Offenders and Victims*, p. 211, Sage Publications, The International Professional Publishers, Newbury Park, London, New Delhi, p. 211, 1988.

Amy Katan, p. 28, *Sexual Misuse of Female Children in Hidden Victims—The Sexual Abuse of Children* by Robert and Geiser 1979.

Burgers Ann W, *Rape Victims of Crises,* R.J. and Holmstrom-LL Brady Co. 1974.

Friedrich, W.N. Urquiza, (1986), Behaviour problems in Sexually abused young children, *Journal of Pediatric Psychology* 11 [1] 47-57, 1986.

K. Kumar and Punam Rani, 1996, Offences Against Children—Socio-Legal Perspectives, Chap. 7, p. 72-73. Regency Publications, New Delhi.

Robert and Geiser, 1979, Hidden Victims, The Sexual Abuse of Children, Boston Press, Boston.

12

A Spatio-Temporal Analysis of Child Rape in India

Tahir Hussain and Mary Tahir

A major chunk of the crime in the country's ascending crime graph is accounted by crime against children. Further, It has been observed that the proportion and number of crimes against children is constantly on the rise specially in the past decade. Child rape below 16 years of age accounted for 28.79 per cent of the total rape cases reported in 1997. Further out of total crime against children, child rape alone accounted for 73.8 per cent (1997). Between 1993 and 1997 alone child rape registered 30 per cent increase.

Needless to say minors have always been vulnerable to lustful eyes. Rape itself is inhuman, but the rape of tiny tots is much brutal and heinous because of its detrimental effects on them. The rape of children is unforgivable as it causes physiological, mental and emotional injuries. Many a time such acts deprive the child of motherhood and even lead to death. In several instances such children take to prostitution at a later stage because they are treated as outcasts even by their families. This alarming situation has awakened various social organisations who along with government support have been collectively addressing this menace. Thus, efforts are on to prevent and save children from the vulnerabilities and exploitations to which they are subjected. Although such crimes are viewed as social evils, but the reported incidence of such crimes continues to rise in magnitude. It is to be noted in passing that in the Indian situation majority of such crimes are not even reported. According to one estimate for every sexual offence reported, at least three go unreported because of the fear of further trauma and embarrassment to the child as also to the family.

Child abuse is a gift of 'Uncle Culture'. It is very shocking, but true that most of the rapists are either family members or family friends. According to a study conducted in Bangalore and its adjacent villages reveals that about fifty-five per cent of men responsible for the abuse of girl children were family members—uncles, fathers, brothers, cousins, or relatives. Fifteen per cent of the 348 girls who put down their experience had in fact been seriously abused or raped before their tenth birthday.

In the present study a spatio-temporal analysis of child rape in India is analysed. Firstly, the incidence of various crimes committed against children in India between 1993 and 1997 is observed. Secondly, the child rape pattern in various States, Union Territories and metropolitan cities between 1992 and 1997 is analysed. Lastly, an attempt has been made to understand the increasing rate of child rape as also to raise some pertinent questions related to the spatial aspect of child rape.

The data for this study is purely derived from a secondary source, namely, Crime in India—a Government of India publication.

Incidence of Crimes Committed Against Children in India—1993-97

The general penal code of this country and the various protective and preventive 'special and local laws' specifically mention the offences wherein children are known to be victims.

Thus the cases in which the children are victimised and abused are categorised under two broad heads:

1. Crimes committed against children which are punishable under Indian Penal Code (IPC).
2. Crimes reported against children which are punishable under Special and Local Laws (SLL).

Among the various crimes against children in India, child rape (up to 16 years) accounted for the highest number in 1993—3,393 cases. By 1997 there was a spurt in such cases 4,414. It is clear that there is an alarming increase in child rape cases—30 per cent in just five years. (Table 1). Kidnapping and abduction accounted for 485 cases in 1993 and 620 cases in 1997, showing an overall increase of 27.8 per cent. Another crime which is on the increase and is a cause of much concern is foeticide which has increased from 45 cases in 1993 to 57 cases in 1997. This crime is committed in large numbers in various hospitals, clinics and dispensaries in all cities and towns of India. But the data is very much under reported and is not at all a true picture of the actual situation. The incidence of abetment to suicide and selling of girls for prostitution went up by 18.2 per cent and 50 per cent respectively during 1996-97.

Child Rape in India (1993-97)

It is unfortunate and sad to note that of all the victims in rape cases during 1997, children alone accounted for 28.8 per cent share. The cases of rape of children below 10 years were on a rise every year in the country except in 1996 since 1993. From Table 2 it is clear that child rape cases increased from 634 in 1993 to 770 in 1997, below 10 years of age. A similar increase is found in 10 to 16 years age group wherein the number increased from 2,759 cases in 1993 to 3,644 in 1997. When compared to the figures of 1993, the victims in the age group of 10 years increased by 21.4 per cent while those in the age group of 10-16 years increased significantly by 32.1 per cent.

TABLE 1

Crimes Against Children in India (1993-1997)

		Year (Number of cases)					*Percentage of variation*	
Sl. No.	*Crime Head*	*1993*	*1994*	*1995*	*1996*	*1997*	*1997 over 1993*	*1997 over 1996*
(1)	(2)	(3)	(4)	(5)	(6)	(7)	(8)	(9)
1.	Child rape (upto 16 years)	3,393	3,986	4,067	4,083	4,414	30.0	8.1
2.	Kidnapping and Abduction	485	864	726	571	620	27.8	8.6
3.	Procuration of minor girls	-	206	107	94	87	-	-7.4
4.	Selling of girls for prostitution	-	34	17	6	9	-	50.0
5.	Buying of girls for prostitution	-	4	19	22	13	-	-40.9
6.	Abetment of suicide	-	7	9	11	13	-	18.2
7.	Exposure and Abandonment	-	491	570	554	582	-	5.1
8.	Infanticide	-	131	139	113	107	-	-5.3
9.	Foeticide	-	45	38	39	57	-	46.2
10.	Child Marriage Restraint Act	-	53	57	89	78	-	-12.3

Source: Crime in India (1992-97), NCRB, Government of India.

TABLE 2

Victims of Child Rape (1993-1997)

Sl. No.	*Year*	*Age Group*		*Percentage share of child rape victims to total rape victims*
		0-10 years	*10-16 years*	
(1)	(2)	(3)	(4)	(5)
1.	1993	634	2,759	27.8
2.	1994	727	3,259	30.2
3.	1995	747	3,320	29.5
4.	1996	608	3,475	27.5
5.	1997	770	3,644	28.8
6.	% change in 1997 over 1996	26.6	4.9	
7.	% change in 1997 over 1993	21.4	32.1	

Source: Crime in India (1992-97), NCRB, Government of India.

Statewise Incidence of Child Rape (1992-97)

A total of 2,928 cases were reported from all the states in 1992 and 4,107 cases in 1997. (Table 3) In 1992 and in 1997 Madhya Pradesh accounted for more than 20 per cent of all rape cases followed by Maharashtra and Uttar Pradesh accounting for more than ten per cent of total cases. More than five per cent cases were reported each from Bihar, West Bengal, Assam and Delhi in 1992 and West Bengal, Andhra Pradesh and Delhi in 1997. Bihar and Assam individually accounted for almost five per cent of child rape. Further, it is to be noted that the central part of India extending from Delhi and Uttar Pradesh in the north to Andhra Pradesh in the south, Bihar in the east and Maharashtra in the west, is much prone not only to child rape, but also to other crimes against children. (Table 4).

TABLE 3

Victims of Child Rape in 1992 and 1997

States and Union Territory-wise

States/UT	*1992*		*1997*	
	I	*P*	*I*	*P*
States				
Andhra Pradesh	313	9.73	347	7.9
Arunachal Pradesh	12	0.39	27	0.6
Assam	148	4.75	195	4.4
Bihar	249	8.00	198	4.5
Goa	4	0.13	8	0.2
Gujarat	112	3.60	130	2.9
Haryana	85	2.73	1156	3.5
Himachal Pradesh	33	1.06	48	1.1
Jammu & Kashmir	14	0.45	0	0.0
Karnataka	46	1.48	71	1.6
Kerala	73	2.35	167	3.8
Madhya Pradesh	635	20.40	1018	23.1
Maharashtra	407	13.07	501	11.4
Manipur	4	0.13	3	0.1
Meghalaya	5	0.16	4	0.1
Mizoram	24	0.77	11	0.2
Nagaland	4	0.13	3	0.1
Orissa	27	0.87	122	2.8
Punjab	19	0.61	75	1.7
Rajasthan	96	3.08	143	3.2
Sikkim	7	0.22	4	0.1
Tamil Nadu	38	1.22	108	2.4
Tripura	12	0.39	23	0.4
Uttar Pradesh	412	13.23	472	10.7
West Bengal	159	5.11	273	6.2
Total	2928	94.06	4107	93.0

States/UT	1992		1997	
	I	*P*	*I*	*P*
A & N Islands	2	0.06	6	0.1
Chandigarh	8	0.26	3	0.1
D & N Haveli	0	0.00	1	0.0
Daman & Diu	0	0.00	0	0.0
Delhi	172	5.52	295	6.7
Lakshadweep	0	0.00	0	0.0
Pondicherry	3	0.10	2	0.0
Total	185	5.94	307	7.0
Total (all India)	3113	100.0	4414	100.0

I = Incidence of child rape.
P = Percentage contribution to all India.
Source: Crime In India (1992-97) NCRB, Government of India.

TABLE 4
Statewise percentage of Total Crime against Children in 1997

States	*Percentage of crime*
Madhya Pradesh	20.8
Maharashtra	15.3
Uttar Pradesh	8.8
West Bengal	6.5
Gujarat	6.5
Bihar	6.2
Andhra Pradesh	6.1
Delhi	5.7
Others	24.7

Source: Crime in India (1992-97) NCRB, Government of India.

TABLE 5
Victims of Child Rape in 1992 and 1997 Metro-Cities of India

Cities	*1992*	*1997*
Ahmedabad	10	3
Bangalore	12	20
Bhopal	26	20
Mumbai	70	80
Kolkata	17	12
Coimbatore	1	2
Delhi	163	269
Hyderabad	2	23
Indore	16	12
Jaipur	13	21
Kanpur	8	11
Kochi	4	8
Lucknow	14	4
Ludhiana	2	3
Chennai	0	3
Madurai	0	0
Nagpur	16	16
Patna	15	0
Pune	18	18
Surat	5	9
Vadodara	1	5
Varanasi	1	3
Visakhapatnam	0	6

Source: Crime in India (1992-97) NCRB, Government of India.

Incidence of Child Rape in Union Territories (1992-97)

On the one hand Delhi reported 172 rape cases accounting for 93 per cent of total child rape cases among the Union Territories in 1992, and on the other hand not a single case was reported from Dadar and Nagar Haveli, Daman and Diu and Lakshadweep. A similar picture emerged in 1997 with Delhi alone accounting for 97 per cent of cases. Lakshadweep, Daman and Diu continued to have no case reported and Chandigarh and Pondicherry accounted for only 3 and 2 cases respectively. (Table 3).

Incidence of Child Rape in the Metro-cities of India

On observing Table 5 it is evident that Delhi, Bombay, Bhopal, Nagpur and Pune had consistently high incidence of child rape cases in 1992 as well as in 1997. On the other hand, not a single case was reported from Madras, Madurai and Visakhapatnam in 1992, whereas in 1997 only 3 cases each were reported from Madras, Ludhiana and Ahmedabad and no case was reported from Madurai and Patna. So it is unnecessarily true that urban areas are more prone to child rape as is evident from varying crime rate in the metropolitan cities. But, it is evident that some urban areas are more prone to such crimes than others.

A Framework for a Geography of Crimes with Special Emphasis on Child Rape

Crime is basically an urban phenomenon not only as an outcome of combination of various factors, but also a chain reaction of circumstances arising one after the other as a result of increasing urbanisation. Poverty and various forms of social disparities in some form or the other can be perceived as common in both urban as well as rural areas. However, in the rural context a relatively homogeneous set up with strong social bond in a close-knit society where everybody knows everybody else, deter many people from committing various types of crimes. On the other hand, the heterogeneous set up in urban areas leading to lack of social cohesion and increasing impersonality may tempt many people to commit various types of crimes. This explanation holds true as far as property crimes are concerned. In fact most of the crimes (murder, attempt to murder, kidnapping and abduction, etc.) against persons are also one way or the other connected to property matters. But what about rape?

At this juncture the most pertinent question to be answered is why people commit such heinous crime like child rape? Every crime is related to the motive behind it but what can be the motive behind child rape? To answer this question it is necessary to analyse the geography of this crime in a historical and socio-cultural context. From this study it has been found that the central States of India are more prone to such crimes, thus excluding the mountainous north, the coastal south, hilly and rainy east and the arid west. From time immemorial various scholars such as Hippocrates, Aristotle, Herodotus, Strabo, Al-Masudi, Kant, Ritter, Ratzel, Huntington and others have emphasized the important role played by the environment on man's mental and economic well-being. As such enormous and gigantic mountains enveloped with clouds, the mighty oceans and the unending desert landscape have as soothing influence on the mental state of its inhabitants. Thus, does nature play an important role in the reduction of various crimes including child rape in certain areas as against the others?

Historically the Indo-Gangetic plain has been prone to plunder and rape by the foreign invaders from the West many of whom settled down in India and many left their illegitimate progeny behind; and their violent nature being perpetuated by the succeeding generations. In a recent article in the *Sunday Review* of *Times of India* (21st Nov. '99) Mrs. Le Bon, a socialite, accepted the fact that she has a wild spirit because of her being half Persian. Due to continuous upheaval in the political and socio-economic set-up in north and central India many people took to crime as a way of life. After independence with better transportation network and peaceful political environment with adequate police protection, many of these professional criminals gave up crime and devoted themselves to sedentary occupations such as farming, but they have not been able to rid themselves of the inherent violent character in them. An outlet for it being child rape in appropriate opportunities in the environment. In fact people still continue to threat one another in terms of rape of the opponent's daughters, sisters and even mother, without even realising the magnitude of their loose talk. Does history play an important role in the occurrence of child rape in India?

The social set up of India prior to Independence was based on the Zamindari system wherein the Zamindar who only owns the land in actuality, but considers himself to be the master of the peasants tilling his land and thus rape of young children and women was a common day to day phenomena. After partition of India and abolition of the Zamindari system, although the Zamindars gave up their land somewhat readily, but continue to consider themselves the masters of the peasants and thus rape of young women and children still continues. Is this pre-independence social set-up responsible for perpetuating child rape?

References

M. Tahir, *Crime in Delhi*, NBO, New Delhi, 1996.

M. Tahir, Rape scenario in India; *Police Research and Development*, Quarter 4, 1995.

T. Hussain and M. Tahir, The Ugly Face of Rape, *Link*, August. 28, 1994.

T. Hussain and M. Tahir, Increasing Rape Incidents, *Link*, March 22, 1992.

T. Hussain and M. Tahir, Impact of Policing on Crime, *Social Welfare*, Vol. 42, No. 1, 1995.

M. Ponnian, *Criminology*, Neelam, Delhi, 1990.

13

Judicial Scrutiny for Protecting the Child as a Victim from Sexual Abuse

Raghunath Patnaik

Scriptures may proclaim *God* manifests in the innocent smile of a child, a philosopher may gaze at the sparkling eyes of a growing child to feel the quintessence of the universe and a poet laureate may announce with divine solemnity that a child is the father of the nation. But in recent times there has been unpleasant and unfortunate incidents against the female children, and it becomes a nostalgia, when she succumbs to become a victim of the most inferior bestial propensities of lowly human nature. Besmirched, she is forced to expose before a perverse impulse of a ravishing man. Unknowingly she shatters her serene innocence which deprives her from the life time privilege of cherishment of the childhood. She remains to recollect them in memory in poised tranquillity which compels her to embrace despair and forces her to bear the brunt of an incurable stigma.

In the recent past the subject of sexual abuse against the girl child has received considerable attention due to increase in the number of incidents. At one time it was felt that the law relating to sexual offences did not contain adequate provisions for protection of victims. The victim of sexual abuse who has undergone the trauma will have to live with the tragedy. Her nightmarish experience shakes her foundation of living a life worth of any kind. Further, suffer from it's effect for a long term and impair her capacity to build relationship or remould their behaviour for a virtuous living and in the process generate endless fear for anything around her. In addition to the trauma of being a victim of sexual abuse, the victims have to suffer further agony during the legal proceedings.

The antiquated laws governing the cases of sexual abuse, particularly rape[1] remained unchanged since 1860 for quite some time.[2] The law was amended as a result of sustained campaign against an infamous Supreme Court judgment in the Mathura case.[3] Incidentally, Mathura, a 16-year-old tribal girl was raped by policemen within a police compound. The trial court held that since the victim eloped with her boy friend and was habituated to sexual intercourse, the charges of rape against the policemen could not be sustained. On appeal, the High Court held differently that mere passive or helpless surrender, induced by threat or fear cannot be equated to desire or will and held the policemen guilty of offence. But the Supreme Court adjudicated that as the victim did not raise any alarm at the time of commission of offence, the allegations of rape were considered to be untrue and accordingly acquitted the policemen.

Such a judgment triggered off a campaign for the changes of the rape law as it became extremely difficult for a rape victim to prove 'beyond all reasonable doubts' that she did not consent for the sexual abuse. The Law Commission accordingly recommended that not only the onus of proof about the allegation should lie on the accused, but also the past sexual history of the victim should be ignored in all such trials. In response to the feelings of public, the government introduced necessary changes in the Indian Penal Code,[4] Criminal Procedure Code[5] as well as in the Indian Evidence

Act.[6] In the Indian Penal Code new provisions were added which made sexual intercourse by persons in custodial situations, such as policemen, public servants, managers of public hospitals and remand homes, etc., would amount to rape even if it was with the consent of the victim.[7]

Judicial Scrutiny

The Supreme Court held that rape is not only a crime against the victim but it is a crime against the entire society. It destroys the entire psychology of the victim and pushes her into deep emotional crisis. It is her sheer will power which helps her to rehabilitate in spite of the fact that the society looks down upon her in decision and contempt. Therefore in all cases of rape, law should take care about the social aspect of the matter.[8]

In *Delhi Domestic Working Women's Forum v. Union*,[9] the Supreme Court recognised the right of the victim for compensation and even to the extent of payment of interim compencation[10] in certain cases.

The Supreme Court held that in cases of sexual abuse, supposed considerations, which have no material effect on the veracity of the prosecution case or where there are discrepancies in the testimony of the prosecution, it should not be ordinarily disallowed by the courts unless such discrepancies are fatal in nature or are based on compelling reasons which necessitate looking for corroboration,[11] as corroborative evidence is not an imperative component of judicial credence in every case of rape. It may be stated that corroboration is a condition for judicial reliance on the testimony of the victim and is not a requirement of law but a guidance of prudence under a given circumstance.

In *Prem Chand v. State of Haryana*[12] the apex court neither characterised the victim as a woman of questionable character nor a person of easy virtue. Thus the character or reputation of the victim has no bearing or relevance in the matter of adjudging the guilt of the accused or imposing the punishment.[13]

In *Lankeswar v. State of Orissa.*[14] The Orissa High Court held that a woman cannot be treated as an object of pleasure. Therefore no man should entertain the idea that a woman has to depend on man at every stage of life for protection of her dignity and self-respect. Every man conceiving the notion of sexual assault must remember that in the bodily frame of a woman remains the soul of a mother and the essence of purity. Therefore no man has a right to indignify a woman.

Following such an idealism, the Orissa High Court in another case, where a minor girl of eight year old, while grazing bullocks in an open field, having gone to a little distance to bring stray bullocks, was lifted forcibly and raped, held that the accused having offended the dignity of the victim had to undergo punishment.[15]

In another case, it was a sordid tale of extreme brutality and raw unleashed sexuality of a teacher to satisfy his lust upon a thirteen year old girl student who having called her to his room undressed and raped her.[16] The court following the Supreme Court judgment in *Bharwada v. State of* Gujarat,[17] held that there is no tenebrosity in the position of law that the testimony of a victim of sexual assault should not inspire confidence and found to be unreliable, and accordingly the accused was sentenced.

In *Bansilal V. State of MP*,[18] the victim was eight years old and was not only raped at the air strip but also was subjected to unnatural sexual offence by putting the male organ into her mouth and also into her rectum, the court declined to intervene into the punishment inflicted upon the accused.

In *Surendra Kumar Patra v. State of Orissa,*[19] the victim was a minor girl of ten years and at the time of occurrence she was watching *Pala* [Night Opera] and was asked by the accused, a known villager, to accompany him to bring *Prasad [Puja offerings]*, who on the way took her to a secluded place and raped her. The court while convicting the accused did not pay credence to the medical report.

Significance of Judicial Scrutiny

In Indian setting, refusal to act on the testimony of a victim of sexual abuse, in the absence of corroboration, was considered to be an insult to the injury already sustained by the victim. There has been a significant judicial observation that the courts in India should no more examine the evidence of a girl or woman, subjected to sexual abuse and view the same with the aid of spectacles fitted with lenses tinged with doubt, disbelief or suspicion. In all such cases, the judiciary is of the opinion that the support for the need for corroboration and the relentless or remorseless cross-examinations must be made with a logical mind and not with an opinionated eye. This is for the simple reason that Indian culture is not swept off by westernisation, rather it depends upon its own social values or its own code of living a moral life.

The judiciary also have held that much importance should not be attached with the minor discrepancies for the reason that, by and large a witness cannot be expected to possess a photographic memory or recall the details of an incidence.

Therefore absence of corroboration notwithstanding the limitations imposed by prudence, the victim's evidence is entitled to great weightage in cases of sexual abuse. It was also considered not to put premiums on such defects as they would amount to usurpation upon justice based on defective investigation.

Suggestions and Conclusion

It is suggested that in cases of sexual abuse wherever corroboration is necessary, it should be from an independent source but not necessarily that every part of the evidence of the victim should be confirmed in every detail by an independent witness. In most of the cases such evidence could also be sought from either direct or circumstantial evidence or from both and from the totality of the background of the case. It is also suggested that society should come forward to rescue the victims of sexual abuse. Even law expects them to come forward to help the helpless victim. Although payment of compensation is but a poor solace to a victim of sexual abuse, unless people come forward to rescue the victim's human dignity, the victims of sexual abuse will continue to remain under erosion of societal values.

References

1. Secs. 375 and 376 IPC.
2. Criminal Law (Amendment) Act, 1983.
3. *Tukaram* v. *`State of Maharashtra*, AIR 1979 SC 185.
4. Changes in Secs. 376, 376A, 376B, 376C and 376D were introduced by Amendment Act, 43 of 1983.
5. Section 114A was introduced in the Indian Evidence Act, 1982.
6. Amended Sub-section 327(2) says trial of rape cases could be held in camera, likewise Sub-Section(3) prohibits/regulates publication of names of victims and proceedings; and the consequential Ist Schedule changes. See, Amendment Act 43 of 1983.
7. *Bodhisattwa Gautam v. Subhra Chakravarti*, AIR 1996 SC 922.
8. A presumption was allowed to the courts as to the absence of consent in certain rape cases under Sec. 376 Sub-Clauses (a), (b), (c), (d), (e) and (g) of IPC.
9. [1995] 1 SCC 14.
10. *Supra fn. 8.*
11. *State of Punjab* v. *Gurmit Singh*, AIR 1996 SC 1393.
12. AIR 1989 SC 937.
13. *State of Haryana* v. *Prem Chand*, AIR 1991 SC 538.
14. Jail Criminal Appeal No. 332 of 1994 disposed on Dt. 26.11.1996. [Unreported].
15. *Budhia Murmu* v. *State of Orissa*, 1997 (1) OLR 47.
16. *Bhikari Panda* v. *State of Orissa*, 1997 (1) OLR 338.
17. AIR 1983 SC 753.
18. 1999 (1) Crimes 275.
19. 1997 (II) OLR 49.

14

Child Labour Problem in India

Malay Dewanji

Child labour has always existed but it was only in the 19th Century in industrialised countries that it came to be seen as a social problem. Industrialisation led to a growing separation between home and the place of work. Production that had formerly been carried out within the family was now done in workshops and factories. In the early workshops it was still possible to maintain family and group ties. Children accompanied their parents to the workshop or factory where they acted as helpers. In the absence of technical education centres, this was a useful way of teaching the children a trade.

The women and children employed in these early workshops were always paid lower wages than men, so when mechanization reduced the number of operations requiring a lot of muscle power they became an attractive source of labour.

The 20th Century is sometimes referred to as the *Century of the Child*. For the first time in history the rights of the child were put on the international agenda. As far back as 1919 the International Labour Organisation (ILO) drew up a convention aimed at restricting child labour in industry by setting a minimum age

(ILO Convention 5). It was followed by various other conventions on the minimum employment age for different sectors, including shipping, agriculture and non-industrial occupations. In 1973, the ILO drew up a universal convention on the minimum employment age, applicable to virtually all sectors (ILO Convention 138). India has ratified this convention.

India has the largest number of working children in the world. The government itself acknowledges that at least 17.5 million children are working. An Indian research institute often cited by the ILO—the Operations Research Group, Baroda—estimates the number of working children at 44 million.

It is impossible to collect correct figure of the children employed in mines, factories, fireworks, brickfield, poultry, bidi-factory, building-construction, hotels and sweet-meat shops or as domestic servants or in polishing works and many other less hazardous works like agro or non-agro industries. In 1987, laws were made to ban child-labourers in hazardous works. Still out of 3 child labourers of the world, two live in India and the larger number of them are engaged in non-organised sectors, agro-industries and private industries based on low capital where the industrial environment is prone to cancer, of liver, nerve and eye. According to survey of WHO one- third of the children of the world suffer from the diseases caused due to poisonous effect of pesticides in our country.

The ICFTU's regional organisation in Asia—APRO—puts the figure of working children at 50 million. One private institution in India, however—the Centre for Concern for Working Children—which has carried out an inquiry into the number of children not attending schools, estimates the number of working children in India at 100 million.

In the absence of agreed criteria and reliable data, several agencies have computed the figure on the basis of people below the poverty line and children not enrolled in schools. For example, the Balai Data Bank, Manila considers that the number of children is likely to be over 100 million. The Campaign against Child Labour (CACL), an umbrella organisation covering about 1,000 NGOs (non-government organisations), estimates that "there are 70-80 million child labourers, based on the number of non-school going children and families living in destitution".

According to the 1991 census, there are about 11.20 million full time and 10.70 million part time child labourers in India. This excludes the unorganised sector and the self-employed children in which there are about another 20 to 25 million children. About a quarter of the working children in the metropolitan areas suffer from over work, inadequate pay and physical abuse. They soon fall victim to the street culture of drug abuse, smoking, gambling, drinking, vagrancy, stealing and prostitution. Most of these remain untouched by social welfare programmes.

According to the Asian Labour Monitor, every third household in India has a working child. Further, according to the same journal, the extent of child labour can be gauged by the fact that in the age group of 5-15, every fourth child is employed, 20 per cent of all children in the age group of 10-14 years are employed in one form or the other, and over 20 per cent of the Gross National Product (GNP) of India is contributed by child labour.

According to a study conducted by the All India Guild of Law Graduates, 6.7 per cent of the work force consists of children, below fourteen years of age. A study conducted by the National Institute of Public Co-operation and Child Development revealed that 24.7 per cent, child labour surveyed in Mumbai started work between the ages of six and nine, 48.4 per cent between ten and twelve and 26.9 per cent between the ages of thirteen and fifteen.

Children Working in Different Areas of Employment in India According to the Censuses of 1971 and 1981

Sl. No.	Nature of Activity	1971 Census		1981 Census	
		No. of child workers in age groups 0-14 years. (in thousands)	Percentage	No. of child workers in age groups 0-14 years. (in thousands)	Percentage
1.	Cultivators	3,870	36.05	4,013	35.95
2.	Agricultural labourers	4,586	42.72	4,774	42.76
3.	Livestock, forestry, fishing, hunting, plantations etc.	885	8.25	704	6.30
4.	Mining and quarrying	24	0.22	27	0.23
5.	Manufacturing, processing, servicing, repairs, etc.	653	6.08	965	8.63
	(a) Housing industry	338	3.15	525	3.79
	(b) Others	315	2.93	540	4.84
6.	Construction	59	0.55	79	0.72
7.	Transport, storage and communication	42	0.39	34	0.29
8.	Trade and commerce	211	1.97	246	2.20
9.	Other Services	405	3.77	3926	2.92
	Total	10,739	100.00	11,168	100.00

From the above table, we find that about 85 per cent of working children are to be found in the agricultural sector and that the overwhelming chunk in any sector are from the scheduled castes and tribes.

Agricultural Sector: Child labour has always been common in the agricultural sector, especially in small family farms. Generally speaking, Indian rural families have a strong sense of community and it is taken for granted that every member will contribute to family resources. It is impressed upon children from a very early age that they must show their solidarity by contributing to the family income. Many children, therefore, consider it quite normal that they should start working from a very early age and this situation is reinforced if the schools are a long way from where the children live or if the parents do not have the money to send their children to school. Moreover, while in many farming castes and communities education is no guarantee for a better future, the contribution in work and income made by children is often essential to the survival of impoverished rural families.

Traditional rural customs often persist after the family has migrated to urban area. All too many parents take off their children from school at an early age and send them out to earn their living as domestic servants, street traders or factory workers.

Service Sector: Due to migration from the countryside to the city, increasing unemployment and a lack of social security, a growing section of the population in India is obliged to generate its own employment in the "informal" sector.

Our children are often found working in small factories, motor garages, food stalls, doing shoeshining, as domestic helps, rag pickers and even as beggars. No education policy could make the parents interested to send their children to schools as earning by them is more lucrative for a poor family than education. The wages paid to children are normally lower than the prevalent rate while the exploitation is abnormally high to turn them into bonded labourers or child prostitutes. Sex tourism is another factor that is contributing to increasing child prostitution in India too.

In the match and fireworks factories at Sivakasi (Tamil Nadu), 40,000 children (out of a total workforce of 70,000) are employed. In other industries as well, such as bidi-manufacturing, diamond-polishing, handicrafts, agriculture, rag-picking and the hotel industry, children form a major portion of the total labour employed.

The Gurupadaswamy Committee Report in 1979 identified sectors of the economy where there were substantial numbers of working children, namely, bidi-factories, glass factories, the carpet industry, the handloom industry, in jari making and embroidery, in polishing precious stones, in match and fireworks, foundries and repair shops, in hospitals, restaurants, canteens, tea stalls, shops and establishments, service stations, construction sites, as rag pickers and as casual labourers.

The prevalent gender bias of the society is naturally reflected in this world too. In the field of child labour, girls have outnumbered the boys and consequently, in illiteracy, their number is double to that of the boys. The girls are engaged in work at an earlier age and deprived of literacy. They are thrust into unpaid or unproductive activities from their very tender age and made easy prey to physical violence and sexual abuse, in addition. As these child labourers come mostly from the poor families, the combined effect of impoverishment, lack of access to education and health, physical labour and their social condition bring them to accept poverty and violence in their later lives.

It is traditional for very young girls from poor families to be sent to work in the homes of wealthier families in return for boarding and lodging. Many impoverished parents prefer their daughters to work in some other family's household rather than in a workshop, factory or as a street vendor, because they imagine that it is safer for them. Maidservants work long hours, have little or no leisure and receive little or no pay. There is virtually no official inspection of the conditions under which these domestic slaves work.

The number of children—especially girls—working as domestic servants has risen over the past few decades. As more and more girls from the lower middle classes go out to work, the demand for cheap domestic labour keeps rising. In metropolitan cities like Delhi and Mumbai, for example, this has led to the emergence of a new category of middlemen who ruthlessly recruit children for domestic work. In addition to this, all too many child refugees end up in host families where they are treated as domestic slaves.

Other types of service where child labour is on the increase occur in the informal tourist and entertainment industry, for instance in restaurants, guest houses and brothels. Poverty, war and violence expose children to new dangers and new forms of exploitations.

Industry and Mining: Only a small percentage of child labour is accounted for by large, export-oriented enterprises in mining and industry. This is related to the fact that these enterprises are subject to more government control and that trade union influence is often greater there. Child labour mostly occurs in unorganised and small sectors such as in the match and carpet industries in India.

There are few statistics on child labour among children under the age of ten. In the first instance, this is because work by very young children is rarely recognized as such or because it is simply overlooked by census-takers. Such young "domestic helpers" are either recorded as adoptees or uncounted because they are unpaid. A second reason for the inadequate registration has to do with the fact that labour by very young children is illegal in all countries and as such is hushed up or deliberately concealed.

Most of the children work in the so-called informal economy—both in the cities and in the countryside—where protective labour laws and regulations regarding working hours, pay, social security and working conditions are generally absent. Children usually work in situations where it is difficult, if not impossible, to offer them any protection, such as, on the streets, in unregistered enterprises, workplaces, small factories, guest houses, cafes, restaurants, eating-houses, shops, family businesses, clothing workshops, buildings sites, small private mines and in remote farming areas.

It is estimated that only a small percentage of working children—roughly five per cent work directly in export-oriented industries. Examples can be found in the production of clothing, carpets and shoes, in the diamond industry, the food processing industry, in tanneries and furniture makers. On the other hand, the practice of contracting work out via middlemen makes it difficult to estimate how many children are indirectly involved in production for the world market.

In India and many other developing countries, poverty has risen sharply in recent decades as a result of the Structural Adjustment Programmes (SAPs) imposed by the International Monetary Fund (IMF) and the World Bank. These have led to privatization, a decrease in government expenditure on social services (including education and health), a deterioration in social security, promotion of export-oriented production, deregulation and flexibilization of industrial relations, and a dilution of trade union rights. The percentage of Indian Union Government's expenditures (1990-97) allocated only 1 per cent in health, 2 per cent in education and 13 per cent on defence.

United Nations International Children's Emergency Fund [now United Nations Children's Fund] (UNICEF) warned as early as 1984 that SAPs were having a devastating effect on poor families in general, and on the welfare of children, in particular. Experts in various countries have shown that the increase in child labour is one of the direct consequences of economic crisis and structural adjustment. Much of the social costs of SAPs is passed on to women in poor families, a process that is sometimes described as the "faminization of poverty". The sectors hardest hit by privatization and government cut-backs are also those sectors which employ a lot of women, such as, education and health care, child care, telephone and postal services. For most of the women, there is no alternative employment available except in the informal sector which is where many laid-off women workers end up.

Growing unemployment and rising prices lead to a reduction in spending power and an increase in women's workload. Families affected by unemployment generally have no financial reserves to fall back on. Impoverished families who can no longer afford the rising cost of education and child care find themselves obliged either to keep their children home or to send them out to earn some money so as to at least keep the family unit afloat. Poverty and despair lead to an increase in violence within the family. When their own income proves inadequate men tend to force women and children out to work. The number of deserted women with children is on the increase, partly owing to the growing number of migrating men going in search of work, elsewhere. In 30 per cent of the families, according to the United Nations, women have to bear the burden of looking after their families alone. The majority of such families are among the poorest in the world. Women caught in these situations tend to be physically and mentally exhausted and in the absence of alternative resources they often have no choice but to let the children work for the sake of their families as a whole. Children from poor families run a high risk of ending up as street children. Child workers in Calcutta do a variety of jobs ranging from self-employment to employment in the service sector.

Discussions with NGOs reveal that children who are just four to five years old do manual labour several hours each day in Calcutta. The kids break apart batteries with rocks and hammers, separating the acid and lead for re-sale, often poisoning themselves in the process. There are other child workers who make flip-flop sandals with scissors, sometimes as long as their arms, or work in light bulb factories where they breathe in fine glass dust particles that can scar their lungs. Many do not appear in the records and become invisible in statistics. A large number of girl children are surrogate mothers to their siblings while also helping their mothers in domestic or piece rate work.

There are others, who look after cars, shine shoes, sell newspapers, etc., and the average earning of a child labour in Calcutta is less than US $ three in a month. Sometimes, they stay out on the streets and meet up with youth gangs or groups of children who live on the streets. The worse the child's home situation, the greater the chance that it will join these street children instead of returning home. Such children all too often end up in the criminal circuit.

The unloading of the social costs of the SAPs onto families is referred to in a UNICEF study as "invisible adjustment". This invisible exploitation of individuals affects not only the socio-economic rights of the women, but also the living conditions and future prospects of their children, a process that is further reinforced by the inequality between men and women.

While on one hand the supply of child workers is rising as a result of poverty, on the other hand, changes in the production process are leading to an increased demand for child labour. The growth in subcontracting, flexibilization and deregulation, the emergence of free trade zones and the informalization of labour appear to have made child labour more attractive and easier for employers.

Many sectors are increasingly contracting out parts of the production process. This saves larger companies high labour costs and enables them to make use of the cheapest employees, which include children. The client firm and the actual workers are often separated by a long chain of middlemen and subcontractors. Multinationals contract local firms in India to fill orders. These local firms compete fiercely with one another to land the limited number of multinational orders; they look for the cheapest labour and where possible they use child labour in their own factories or contract out work to informal workshops or to home workers, who in turn enlist children in order to boost the family income. It is often difficult to discover who is really employing the children working in grimy workshops or at home, pressured to work for eight to eleven hours a day to reach the production norm and often paid a pittance for their efforts. In a number of industries, such as shoe and cloth manufacturing, a few specific parts of the end product are made by children. These are then exported to the big factories for further processing by adult employees before being finally exported to Europe and the United States.

Most of the children work for over 12 hours a day under inhuman conditions, on starvation wages. Child labour is cheap and unorganised. Since child workers have no legal status, even unions are also helpless. They suffer from severe mental and physical retardation. In case of accidents employers easily get away by paying a pittance by way of compensation.

In almost all cases, there is extreme exploitation of working children. There are laws to protect them, but no proper enforcement agency. Punitive measures are laughably flimsy. In 1986, the Supreme Court released 800 children from Palamau in Bihar, from where they were taken as slaves to work in the carpet weaving industry in the Mirzapur belt. They had been branded, tortured and made to work 20 hours a day. The local magistrate reportedly fined the exploiting employers a mere Rs. 40 a head.

It is Irony of the Fact that Article 24 of the Indian Constitution Reads:

"No child below the age of 14 years shall be employed to work in any factory or mine or engaged in any other hazardous employment."

India has stood for constitutional, statutory and developmental measures that are required to eliminate child labour. India has ratified six ILO Conventions relating to the child labour and three of them as early as in the first quarter of the 20th Century. Following the directions of the Constitution, the Child Labour (Prohibition and Regulation) Act, 1986 was formulated to encounter the magnitudious problem of increasing child labour. This act bans employment of children below the age of fourteen in certain fields such as port, railways, transport, fireworks, etc., and in other cases, if a child is engaged, cannot be made to work for more than six hours a day. The violator of this act shall be punishable with imprisonment for a term of three months to one year or with fine which may extend from Rs.10,000 to Rs. 20,000 or with both. But the pathetic side of this act is that if nowhere declares child labour illegal and the provisions for monitoring over the proper implementation of the act is very poor. Result is the frequent violation of childhood prerogatives.

It has been pointed out time and again that there is no need for child labour in a country where there is large scale adult unemployment. In many cases, industries employ children as cheap labour while their parents sit idle because from the employers' point of view, little children spell big profits. Children are more amenable to discipline and can be ruthlessly bullied by adult supervisors without fear of protest; they cost less, are more active, agile and quick; further, since in certain industrial sectors child labour is illegal, no laws apply; and finally, most children work in the unorganised sector in any case and hence find it doubly difficult to organise and fight for their rights.

The UN Convention on the Rights of the Child is the most frequently ratified international human rights treaty. It was passed by the General Assembly of the United Nations on 20 November 1989 and by October 1993, it had been ratified by 152 countries including India. This universal acceptance makes the convention an important instrument in improving the situation of children and adolescents.

The central message of the UN Convention is that children may demand their own rights. It thereby gives expression to a new perception of childhood, one that has been almost universally accepted during the course of the 20th century—the Century of the Child. Children are no longer seen as a "possession" which parents, educators and other adults can dispose of at their own discretion, but as having their own individual and socio-economic rights. Children have a right to life, to their own name and nationality, to well-being, love and care, as well as a right to free expression, a right to freedom of association and assembly, a right to access to information, a right to the best possible health and care, a right to free and compulsory primary schooling, and a right to harmonious development, recreation, art and culture. These are just some of the rights that are dealt with in the UN Convention.

Article 45 of the Indian Constitution Says that:

> "The State shall endeavour to provide, within a period of ten years from the commencement of this Constitution, for free and compulsory education for all children until they complete the age of fourteen years."

The absence of adequate, competent and affordable educational facilities is often a major contributing factor to the existence of child labour. In India, the simple fact is that children who are not at school are mostly at workplace.

The largest number of illiterates live in our country. Academic atmosphere, infrastructure, the teacher and the taught and the teaching-system are entirely pathetic. There is no teacher in 2,624 primary schools, there is only one teacher in each of 1,48,033. There are only two teachers in each of 28.5 per cent, there is no building for 7 per cent schools. The schools are run under open sky. Twenty per cent schools are run in thatched huts or in tents. There are 6 lakhs primary schools and number of students are 110 million. The number of drop-outs are thirty-six per cent before they are promoted to Class V and fifty-two percent students leave school before they are promoted to Class VII. Six and a half crore children are out of the periphery of academic institution and out of three such children, two are females. The spectacle is more pitiful than of Pakistan and Sri Lanka. Notwithstanding, the allocation of money in national budget for education is gradually decreasing: 1990-91—4 per cent, 1992-93—3.6 per cent 1993-94—3.5 per cent.

According to the *State of World's Children 1999 Report,* in India, over 80 per cent of children in urban areas are enrolled in school, but in rural areas, the rate is about 60 per cent. But there is great variation between the states. Though Kerala is not a rich state of India, nine out of ten primary school age children go to school, while in Bihar only half do.

Nearly fifty-three per cent population of India lives in severe poverty, earning less than one dollar a day. Child labour is a persistent problem, a cause and consequence of low enrolment and high dropout rates. Students-teacher ratio is very high (greater than 60 to 1 in India), particularly in the primary schools. There are many single teacher primary schools, in which at least four different classes of students from standard I to standard IV are to be taken at the same time by one teacher.

According to *Mahbub Ul Haq,* the noted economist, "Education is the true essence of human development. Without education development can be neither broad based nor sustained". But the educational situation is so much worse in India that the percentage of primary school entrants reaching grade V (1990-95) is 62 % and secondary school enrolment ratio is as follows:

Sl. No.	*Particulars*	*Year*	*Male*	*Female*
1.	Secondary School Enrolment Ratio (Gross)	1990-96	59	38
2.	Adult Literacy Rate	1995	66	38

However, educational participation statistics are sometimes an accurate guide to the extent of child labour. Child workers, such as many child newspaper sellers, tea stall workers, particularly in the cities, often do manage to attend school. Indeed, they sometimes work in order to able to pay for their education. Often, children work eight or more hours a day in addition to the hours they spend at school, a practice that ends in mental and/or physical exhaustion.

A major factor influencing the extent of child labour is the introduction of compulsory education: without it, government will find it difficult to enforce child labour legislation. According to the American Professor Myron Werner, no country has succeeded in putting an end to child labour without first introducing and enforcing compulsory education. It is very important that the upper age limit for compulsory education should correspond to the minimum age limit for employment.

The extent of child labour is partly influenced by the way in which the Indian society reacts to the problem. In India, marked indifference or lack of conviction stands in the way of tackling the problem effectively. Therefore, the Government confines itself to enacting legislation without providing the instruments for enforcing the laws nor are trade unions always as interested in the problem as they might be, because their members often work for large companies where child labour is less prevalent. Even parents from backward communities display indifference to the importance of education, as educational opportunities were denied to all the backward communities in India for thousands of years, preferring to let their children work rather than "waste their time at school". The media pays little attention to the problem because where child labour is regarded as normal, it is not newsworthy. In India the initiatives to expose the problem and to demand actions are mostly coming from some committed individuals and NGOs.

The importance of political will can be illustrated by the example of Kerala. The government there decided to give priority to education. By spending more than double the national average in education, Kerala has succeeded in providing virtually all children with primary education and almost 90 per cent with secondary schooling. The upshot is that only about three per cent of children in Kerala work while in other Indian states the figure can be as much as ten times higher.

In Order to Tackle the Child Labour Problem the Following Recommendations have been Passed by the State Education Ministers Committee:

- Fundamental duty of all parents is to ensure that their children upto fourteen years of age attend school. Punishment for "defaulting" parents.
- Establishment of primary schools within a distance of one to one and half km from rural habitations.
- Set up upper primary schools within a distance of three km from a village with a population of 500 people.
- "Deserving private schools should be given adequate opportunity" to help them operate in remote and inaccessible areas.

The government considers Child Labour a "*necessary evil*" and the Child Labour Act, 1986 does not completely ban, but only seeks to "protect" working children. But the question remains—if earlier laws could not protect children from exploitation, what is the guarantee that new ones will. And where is the will or the machinery to enforce such laws?

The argument given in favour of not banning child labour is that such a ban would affect industries employing child labour. The authorities talk in terms of profits, and foreign exchange earned by industries (carpet, gun polishing) employing child labour. No wonder there is reluctance to face the issue head on. But no one cares about the effect of such exploitative and dangerous working conditions on the children.

So, the 1986 Act was drafted with the view that child labour cannot be banned. Social activists immediately attacked it as regressive. The Act covered only ten per cent of the total working children.

Those working in an unorganised sector are not protected. The Ministry of Labour did not find it necessary to include the glass industry among the list of occupations hazardous to children even though there is enough evidence to prove that glass works are dangerous for children (high temperature, burn injuries, toxic fumes). The slate pencil industry, where workers succumb to silicosis and other respiratory ailments before they even reach middle age was excluded from the purview of the Bill. However, after prolonged movements, these industries are now included in the list of hazardous industries, prohibiting children's employment.

Considering the Magnitude of the Problem of Working Children the Government of India has Formulated the National Policy on Child Labour in 1987 and has Committed to Undertake the following Measures for the Welfare of the Children:

1. Comprehensive health programme for all children.
2. Programme to provide nutrition services for removing deficiencies in the diet of the children.
3. Free and compulsory education for all children upto the age of 14.
4. Physical education, games, sports and other types of recreational as well as cultural and scientific activities in schools, community centres and such other institutions.
5. Special assistance to children belonging to weaker sections of the society.
6. Special attention to children who have become delinquent or have been forced to take to begging or are otherwise, in distress. Facilities for education, training and rehabilitation shall be provided so that such children are helped to become useful citizens.
7. Protection of the children against cruelty, neglect and exploitation.

8. No child under the age of 14 years shall be permitted to be engaged in any hazardous occupation or be made to undertake heavy work.

9. Facilities for special treatment, education, rehabilitation and care of children who are physically handicapped.

10. Priority to children in relief operations in times of distress or natural calamities.

The celebrated Child Labour (Prohibition and Regulation) Act, which was passed on December 23, 1986, is today fifteen years old. Even a cursory assessment presents a dismal picture. The Central Advisory Board on Child Labour set up a Task Force under senior advocate L.M. Sanghvi to implement the Act. The report of the Task Force submitted in December 1989 highlighted that the Act had lowered the age for a child's entry into certain types of employment and had not prohibited night employment of children below the age of 17 years as had the earlier Employment of Children Act, 1938. Most important, the report pointed out that children working in the agricultural sector and in homes and home-based industries were left outside the purview of the Act. The list of "hazardous" industries was badly defined and that the only yardstick of harm used was physical harm, claimed the report.

CACL reports that between 1986 and 1993, there were only 3,488 prosecutions under the Act with 1,426 convictions all over the country. Not one employer has been put behind bars in the entire history.

Apart from requiring enforcement of legal provisions to protect the interest of children, the National Policy envisages focussing on general development programmes for the benefit of child labour and project-based plan of action in areas of high concentration of child labourers. Under the project action plan of the policy, National Child Labour Programme (NCLP) have been undertaken in different areas to rehabilitate child labour. A major activity undertaken under the NCLP is the establishment of special schools to provide non-formal education, vocational training, supplementary nutrition etc. to children withdrawn from employment. At present, it has 2528 schools in 76 districts and covers about 1.5 million children only.

On August 15, 1994, the then Prime Minister P.V. Narsimha Rao had proclaimed with much fanfare that child labour would be eliminated from hazardous industries by the year 2000. Subsequently, a sum of Rs. 850 crore was announced for the purpose; a National Authority for the Elimination of Child Labour was set up to provide educational and nutritional support to children withdrawn from hazardous industries. They were to be given vocational training to enable them to become productive adults. However, for the year 1995-96 a meager sum of 34.4 crore was spent covering 140 districts and 12 States; this was spent on awareness generation, surveys and direct action programmes.

India has also been participating in the International Programme for Elimination of Child Labour (IPEC) launched by International Labour Organisation (ILO) since 1991. However, according to Government reports, the total number of children covered by all these projects is about two lakh (0.2 million) only. Now the question arises, when do we reach the target of rehabilitating all the working children of India?

The grey areas of enforcement of the child labour laws as well as the slow progress in the implementation of special welfare measures for working children are a clear indication of the lack of concern at the official level for the plight of these children. Even the money spent so far has not resulted in any substantial change in the condition of the children who are "covered" by these welfare projects.

For example, most of the special schools set up for the working children are inefficiently run, and studies have demonstrated that non-formal education for working children has very little impact in the rehabilitation process, unless an integrated approach is undertaken in this regard.

The Chairperson of the government-appointed Commission on Labour Standards and International Trade, Subramaniam Swamy, asserted in September 1995 that child labour was growing at the rate of four per cent per annum as opposed to the population growth rate of two per cent per annum. "He also put forward a forceful plea for a National Labour Standards Act, superseding all existing disparate laws, in this context, to arrest, reverse and eliminate its growth." (*The Pioneer,* September 2, 1996).

Further, the Commission estimated that to meet the avowed target of eliminating child labour from hazardous industries by 2010 would cost a whopping Rs. 15,000 crore. If a "shorter target" was to be met, i.e., by the year 2004 then the bill would climb to Rs. 45,000 crore! The figures have been arrived at by taking into account factors like payment of salaries of child labourers to their families and the cost of educating them, claims Swamy. Now for the punch line: "India seeks international cost-sharing through a Global Social Facility and Fund located in the ILO and UNESCO." Bandying words and shopping for finance are the trademarks of our politicians as is the setting-up of committees and commissions a substitute for action.

The Supreme Court judgment in M.C. Mehta vs. State of Tamil Nadu [1996 SCC 756] delivered on December 10, 1996 brought the issue of child labour under the spotlight for a few weeks. Hailed as a major victory for the cause of child labourers, the judgment directs the setting-up of a fund called "the Child Rehabilitation-cum-Welfare Fund" to which offending employers of child labour in hazardous industries are to contribute Rs. 20,000 and the appropriate state government is to contribute Rs. 5,000 per child; the child's family is to be paid a monthly amount from the interest accruing on the corpus of Rs. 25,000. The Court also directed the State governments to complete surveys and report to the court within a period of six months. The judgment adheres to the distinction between hazardous and non-hazardous work that is the bane of the Child Labour (Prohibition and Regulation) Act, 1986 and does not address the issue of agricultural child workers at all.

On December 10, 1996 a three-judge Bench of the Supreme Court comprising Justice Kuldip Singh, Justice B.L. Hansaria and Justice S.B. Majumdar delivered a judgment in writ petition No. 465 of 1986 M.C. Mehta v/s State of Tamil Nadu [(1996 6 SCC 756] which falls in the category of the much-worked phrase, "landmark" or "path-breaking" where child labour has been recognised as a "national problem."

Despite several constitutional provisions, both Fundamental Rights and Directive Principles of State Policy, several National Policies and Plans of Action and ratification of the Convention of the Rights of the Child in 1992, children are being forced to work in sub-human conditions and at wages well below par.

Poverty is no excuse for denying a child the basic rights to survival, protection, development and participation. In fact, the Supreme Court judges have rightly pointed out that poverty as such has not stood in the way of other developing countries such as Zambia, Ghana, Ivory Coast, Libya and Zimbabwe from taking care of child labour.

The Court has also asked the state to ensure that an adult member of the working child's family gets a job in place of the child. In case this was possible Rs. 5,000 be contributed to the rehabilitation fund for each child. In view of the magnitude of the task, a separate cell in the Labour Department of the appropriate government would also be created. Nine major industries have also been identified as hazardous. Some of these are match-making at Sivakasi, diamond polishing at Surat, Ferozabad's glass industry, previous stone polishing industry at Jaipur, brassware industry at Moradabad, handmade carpet at Mirzapur, lock-making industry at Aligarh, slate industry at Markapur, slate industry at Mandsaur, etc.

The issue of child labour is a very sensitive one and apt to provoke an emotional response. The question is not so much whether child labour is permissible or not. Child labour is almost universally rejected and regarded as reprehensible, as is witnessed by the widespread ratification of the UN Convention on the Rights of the Child.

A purposeful and coherent national policy is of overriding importance in the fight against child labour. In the last instance, it is up to the government and people of India to give priority to the abolition of child labour. If we lack the necessary political will, all action from outside is doomed to fail. Nevertheless that political will can be stimulated by the international community, both by government and by the trade union movements and NGOs.

Child labour is a complex problem demanding a multifaceted approach. What is needed is a mix of policies in different areas, policies which complement and reinforce one another. Measures are particularly needed in the following areas:

Effective legislation: Improved legislation on the minimum age for employment and for monitoring its observation is an essential requirement for combating child labour.

Creative and effective education: A second element in a coherent approach to child labour is creative and effective education. Education is the most important instrument in preventing children from entering the job market at an early age. Millions of children never even complete primary education. In India, the drop-out rates are extremely high. *Compulsory education* is, therefore, of vital importance. There should be however, one provision: primary education and school meals must be free, otherwise, children from poorer families will simply be kept at home.

Improved status of Women: A third element concerns improving the socio-economic status of women from poor families. The campaign to abolish child labour cannot be separated from women's struggle for recognition, decision-making power, autonomy, equality with men, a fair division of paid and unpaid work, and from structural measures to combat poverty and violence.

Research has shown that the social welfare of children is closely related to the status of women. Throughout the world, it is women who spend more time looking after and raising children. Women who have an income of their own give priority to expenditure that contributes to the welfare of the children. Not that this should be allowed to release men from their obligations as fathers. Men and women must be made aware of their responsibility for future generations. Special attention must be given to reinforcing the status of women from poor families via trade union organisations, education, vocational training, the promotion of equal opportunities for employment and income and the creation of facilities that make it possible to combine paid work with family responsibilities, for an increasing number of women in India and all the developing countries, good quality child care is vitally important for both their own position and that of the child.

Consciousness-raising campaigns: The fourth element consists of consciousness-raising campaigns. Because child labour is regarded as a "fact of life" in India, increasing public awareness is of vital importance. The media are a particularly important target in this context but also employers, employees, parents and the children themselves.

Replacing children with adults: Very often, children have to work while their parents or older relations remain unemployed. The latter would often by only too happy to take the place of a child if only the employer would agree. An anti-child labour campaign by the LAMP of West Bengal has achieved some positive results with this approach. Some firms have replaced children with adults from the same family so that the family is ensured of a steady income. LAMP believes that special government incentives and trade union campaigns should be used to persuade employers to co-operate in such a programme to replace child workers with adults from the same family.

Promoting the interests of child workers: It is important to establish and support local programmes concerned with improving the lot of child workers. Sometimes, these programmes are initiated by the children themselves, sometimes by other organisations.

Abolition of work under extreme conditions and by young children: Finally, strict measures are needed to ban all child labour that is in any way—physically, mentally or morally—hazardous for the child.

It goes without saying that the trade union movement has an important role to play in combating child labour. After all, trade unions represent workers' interests and that includes the interests of child workers. Despite this, the trade union movement has been less directly involved with specific anti-child labour actions than might be expected. One major reason for this is that trade union representation in India is strongest in the larger enterprises where, partly as a result of the union presence, there is relatively little child labour. Most child labour occurs in the informal sector, agriculture and at the family level where the trade union movement has less influence. The result has been fewer specific activities and more attention to general measures against child labour.

In coming years, trade unions in India and all other developing countries should concentrate on sectors with a low rate of organisation where extreme forms of child labour occur. Collaboration should be sought with NGOs, women's organisations, etc., already active in this area.

From our experiences what is urgently needed is a commitment to protect all young children and provide compulsory schooling for every child under the age of 14. Tackling adult unemployment is also an urgent necessity. It is also obvious that poverty, unemployment, bonded labour, rural indebtedness and women's low status are directly linked to the exploitation of child labour. These larger issues have to be dealt with on a priority basis in order to restore happy childhood to all children including working children of India.

References

The Census of India, 1971, Office of the Registrar General and Census Commissioner, Government of India, New Delhi.

The Census of India, 1981, Office of the Registrar General and Census Commissioner, Government of India, New Delhi.

The Census of India, 1991, Office of the Register General and Census Commissioner, Government of India, New Delhi.

State of World's Children 1999 Report, UNICEF.

Child Labour, published by Legal Education and AID Society, Madras, 1991.

Eliminating Child Labour—Stichting FNV, Amsterdam, The Netherlands.

The Lawyers Collective—Vol. 12, No. 4, April, 1997.

National Policy on Child Labour, 1987, Government of India.

Constitution of India, Government of India Publication.

The Pioneer, September 2, 1996.

15

Child Labour in Beedi Industries: A Case Study

S. Ramdoss • A. Mathan Raj

Introduction

Child labour is a complex social problem whose roots are deeply embedded in cultural, social and economic structures and traditions. Having to labour as a child and most children who work do not have the privilege of free choice—can have an immense impact on the child's physical and mental development. Child labour as understood by international conventions and national legislation is a violation of human rights so fundamental that it must be outlawed without compromise.

Debt bondage, which involves children becoming sort of human collateral for the debts incurred by their parents, is a common form of child slavery in some countries. Even though national laws ban it, it is proving to be exceedingly difficult to enforce such laws because the problem is deeply rooted in poverty, in local traditions as well as in local power structures.

Children are certainly an asset for any country as they are future citizens. It is the duty of the parents and also the state to meet the physical, emotional, educational and other needs of children. It is estimated that 250 million child labourers around the world are forced to work and abandon school at an early age[1]. Growth rate of child labour in different states of India, varies from 7 per cent in Uttar Pradesh to 0.7 per cent in Tamil Nadu. At the national level the growth between 1981 and 1991 was 1.2 per cent[2]. The results of the United Nations estimate brought out that, of every five working children in the world one is from India. Children below the age of 14 years form about forty per cent of the population and 17 per cent of them are workers. The government reported that in 1993, 17.4 million Indian children below the age of 15 work in labour force, constituting 68 per cent of the rural population and 24 per cent of the urban labour force[3].

More than 325,000 child labourers are in the beedi industry, most in Tamil Nadu[4]. Other States with beedi production are Madhya Pradesh, Maharashtra, West Bengal, Andhra Pradesh, Karnataka, Kerala and Uttar Pradesh. Beedi rolling is a stationary work, the children sit cross-legged on the ground or floor all day, with a large and smoothly woven shallow basket in their laps. The basket holds a pile of tobacco and stack cf rectangular rolling papers cut from the large leaves of the *Tendu* plant. Children take a paper, sprink tobacoo into it, roll it up tightly, and tie it with string. The tips are closed either by the roller or by their colleagues. Typically four to severn years old children often begin their careers by working as tip closers.

The Extent of Child Labour and Bonded Child Labour

Beedi rolling is an important economic activity and a major source of income for over 7.5 lakh workers in Tamil Nadu. Tirunelveli and North Arcot districts alone employ more than 70 per cent of the total workers. Of the total workers children form a significant proportion. Though beedi rolling is spread out in several districts of Tamil Nadu, the system of bondage is widely prevalent in North Arcot district. Children are bonded to the beedi agents who give advance money to the child workers. In many cases, entire families are in bondage to the contractors[5].

In North Arcot district alone, a study conducted by Arivoli Iyakkam, quoted in a Government report, estimates around 50,000 bonded labourers working in beedi manufacturing spread over one hundred beedi factories. Pledging of children as pawns for borrowing money is a common practice in this district and it has been continuing for several decades now and highlighted in the press. Worst form of child bondage is witnessed as far as beedi industry is concerned in this district. The element of bondage being debt. The debt amount ranges from Rs. 1000 to Rs. 5,000 and the bonded children are forced to work for long hours without any statutory benefits allowed in the Beedi and Cigar Workers (Conditions of Employment) Act, 1966[6].

The North Arcot district of Tamil Nadu is home to some of the worst and most extensive bondage of child beedi rollers in the country. Entire clusters of villagers are to see evidence of the industry everywhere. Children sit rolling beedi under trees and in doorways, to catch the light. Large, baskets stuffed full of bundles of beedis are piled up near agents doors. Stacks of uncut *tendu* leaves and piles of tobacco in the morning becomes a box full of thousands of beedis by the night. It appears that every second person on the street, from the very young to the very old, has the tips of his or her fingers stained a deep orange brown. Beedi is a way of life in these towns of North Arcot and so is bondage[7].

A survey on child labour conducted by CLASS (Child Labour Abolition Support Scheme) in North Arcot district found the existence of child labour and bonded child labour. Kassikuttai, one of the villages surveyed had 159 of 174 families engaged in beedi industry; 66 of these families had children under the age of 14 working in the production of beedi and of these 102 child beedi workers, 41 were in bondage.

According to the parents, while the children worked up to 16 hours (from 6 a.m. to 10 p.m.) a day, rolling, tying and packing beedis, they were neither fed nor clothed adequately. Bonded child workers are old in North Arcot, especially in the exploitative beedi industry which employs some two lakh of them[8].

Objectives of the Study

1. To find out the prevalence of child bonded labour in North Arcot district.
2. To study the nature and extent of child labour and bonded child labour in the beedi industries.
3. To analyse the causes for victimisation of children in beedi industries.

METHOD OF INVESTIGATION

Sample and Sampling Procedure

Thirty children working in the beedi industries in the North Arcot district were taken as sample for the purpose of the present study. Structured interview schedule was used to collect the data and the data collected was analysed by using simple statistics. Purposive sampling method was adopted to choose the sample from the areas selected for the study. Since studies on working children of beedi industries show the prevalence of bonded child labour the place was chosen to study the problem.

Tool of Investigation

An Interview-Schedule constructed for the purpose of the study was used as the tool of investigation. The tool consisted of 23 items comprising of the following: Bio-demographic variables such as age, sex, education and income of the subjects and occupation, education and income of their parents (1-7). Variables relating to loan, loan amount, reasons for taking loan, rate of interest, period of working and working hours, etc. item (8-18). Variables pertaining to abuse such as verbal abuse and physical abuse, willingness to continue the work and willingness to study (Item 19-23).

Data Collection

The primary data was collected from the sample selected for the present study by the researchers. The present study was undertaken in the few villages of Vaniyambadi Taluk in the North Arcot district of Tamil Nadu.

TABLE 1
Age, Sex and Education of the Respondents

		Frequency (N=30)	*Percentage*
Age	8-10 years	6	20
	11-14 years	24	80
Sex	Male	16	53.3
	Female	14	46.7
Education	Illiterates	14	46.7
	Primary	8	26.7
	Middle	8	26.7

It is evident from the findings that children below the age of 14 years were employed in beedi industries of North Arcot district. Of the total sample 53.3 per cent were males. While 26.7 per cent had middle school education and another 26.7 per cent had primary school education and 46.7 per cent were illiterates.

TABLE 2
Occupation, Education and Income of the Parents

		Frequency (N=30)	*Percentage*
Occupation	Beedi workers	28	93.3
	Others	2	6.7
Education	Illiterates	24	80
	Primary	3	10
	Middle	2	6.7
	High School	1	3.3
Income	Rs. 15-20	6	20
	Rs. 25-30	24	80

It is clear from the findings that 93.3 per cent of the subject's parents were beedi workers and 80 per cent were illiterates and the income of 80 per cent parents was Rs. 25-30 per day.

It can be established from the findings that with having this little amount of money to feed their children and to provide them education are beyond their capacities, in this line they are forced to force their children to meet the economic necessity arising out of their family situation into beedi rolling.

TABLE 3

Period of Work, Type of Employer and Loan Procurement

		Frequency (N=30)	*Percentage*
Period of work	1-4 years	11	36.7
	5-8 years	19	63.3
Type of employer	Sub-contractor	20	66.7
	Contractor	10	33.3
Loan procurement	Yes	30	100
	No	0	0

The findings shown in Table 3 reveal that 63.3 per cent of children were working in the beedi industries for 5-8 years. It is clear from this that they were working from their childhood.

More than 66 per cent of children were working under sub-contractors whereas 33.3 per cent were working under contractors. Those who were working under contractors were under bonded labour system and working in the premises of contractors. Whereas, those working under sub-contractors were working with their parents at their premises.

Invariably, parents of all the subjects had obtained loans from the contractors and sub-contractors. Hence, all the parents were under bonded labour. Only those who obtained loan from the contractors had pledged their children to them, whereas those who obtained loan from sub-contractors had not pledged their children, though they were rolling beedis.

TABLE 4
Loan Amount, Reasons for Procurement, Periodicity, its Repayment and the Interest Rate

		Frequency (N=30)	*Percentage*
Loan amount	Rs. 1000-2000	15	50.0
	Rs. 2001-4000	8	26.7
	Rs. 4001-6000	7	23.3
Reasons for Procurement	Marriage	3	10.0
	Medical Assistance	3	10.0
	Festivals	9	30.0
	Repair/Construction of House	10	33.3
	Others	5	16.7
Periodicity	1-3 years	8	26.7
	4-6 years	12	40.0
	7-9 years	10	33.3
Repayment	Not sure	30	100
Interest rate	20%	10	33.3
	10%	9	30.0
	5%	8	26.7
	Not sure	3	10.0

It is evident from the findings that 50 per cent of the families of the child workers had obtained a loan of Rs. 1 000 to Rs. 2,000. It is clear from the results that the most cited reason for taking loan was construction or repair of houses (33.3%); the next reason was to meet festival expenses (30%); 16.7 per cent constitute others, i.e., to meet day to day needs like buying provisions and other miscellaneous items.

It is found that 40 per cent of the children's parents had obtained loan between 4 and 6 years. More than 33 per cent (33.3) of the families obtained loan between 7 and 9 years. It is also found that none of the respondents were sure about when the loan can be repaid.

It is evident from the findings that rate of interest on 33.3 per cent families of child beedi workers was 20 per cent and 30 per cent child workers' interest was 10 per cent and 5 per cent interest was on 26.7 per cent families of the children. Those who were having 20 per cent interest were bonded child labourers.

It can be perceived from the above findings that due to economic necessity the parents are forced to take loan from the employers. The more they take loan, the more they are forced to pledge their children to the employers and the rate of interest on the loan they take is exorbitant and they never come out of bondage unless they pay the full amount of loan which is unlikely.

TABLE 5

Wage, Freedom to Work Anywhere and Hours of Work

		Frequency (N=30)	*Percentage*
Wage per day	Rs. 5	10	33.3
	Rs. 6	8	26.7
	Rs. 7	10	33.3
	Rs. 8	2	6.7
Freedom to work anywhere	Yes	20	66.7
	No	10	33.3
Hours of work per day	10 hours	20	66.7
	12 hours	10	33.3

As shown in Table 5, it is found that 33.3 per cent of beedi rolling child workers were earning Rs. 5 a day and the same per cent of child workers were earning Rs. 7 a day, the maximum wage they were earning was Rs. 8 a day (6.7 per cent). It is clear from the findings that reveal 33.3 per cent child workers had no freedom hence they were bonded child labourers. It is evident from the findings that 66.7 per cent of the children were working for 10 hours a day whereas 33.3 per cent of the children were working for 12 hours a day.

From the findings shown in Table 5 it can be established that the child workers who were earning Rs. 5 a day and had no freedom to work anywhere and were working for 12 hours a day were bonded child labourers.

TABLE 6

Abused, Abuser and Forms of Abuse

		Frequency (N=30)	*Percentage*
Abused (N=30)	Yes	27	90
	No	3	10
Abuser (N=27)	Parents	17	63
	Contractors	10	37
Forms of abuse (N=27)	Verbal	19	70.4
	Verbal and Physical	8	29.6

It is evident from the findings (Table 6) that 90 per cent of the children were abused. Of them 63 per cent were abused by their parents and 37 per cent were abused by the contractors at workplace. A great percentage (70.4) of the children were abused verbally whereas 29.6 per cent of the children experienced both verbal and physical abuse.

From the above findings it is clear that those who were working with their parents at home are also as abused as those who were working under the contractor's house. Those who were abused by contractors were child bonded labourers and they only experienced both forms of abuse, i.e., verbal and physical.

Since they are children they cannot show any resistance against the exploitation of their being at workplace. Taking advantage of this, both the parents and the employers abuse the children.

Major Findings of the Study Are:

- 46.7 per cent had no education at all.
- 93.3 per cent of the subjects parents were beedi workers and 80 per cent were illiterates and the income of 80 per cent parents was a meagre Rs. 25-30 a day.

- 63.3 per cent of children were working in the beedi industries for 5-8 years.
- 66.7 per cent children were working with their parents at their homes.
- Those who were working under contractors (33.3 per cent) were under bonded labour. The bonded child labourers were forced to work for twelve hours a day.
- 50 per cent of the families of the child workers had obtained a loan of Rs. 1,000 to Rs. 2,000.
- The most cited reason for taking loan was construction or repair of houses (33.3 per cent) and to meet festival expenses (30 per cent); 16.7 per cent constitute others, i.e., to meet day to day needs like buying provisions and other miscellaneous items.
- 66.7 per cent of the children's families had obtained loan 6 years before; 33.3 per cent of the families obtained loan nine years before. None of the respondents was sure about when the loan can be repaid.
- The rate of interest varied from 5 per cent to 20 per cent, worker's interest was 10 per cent and 5 per cent was for 26.7 per cent families of the children. Those who were having 20 per cent interest rate were bonded child labourers. The bonded child labourers had no freedom to move anywhere.
- 33.3 per cent of beedi rolling children were earning Rs. 5 per day.
- 90 per cent of the children were abused. Of them 63 per cent were abused by their parents and 37 per cent were abused by the contractors at workplace.
- 70.4 per cent of the children were abused verbally and 29.6 per cent of the children experienced both types of abuse, i.e., verbal and physical.

Conclusion

The exploitation of these innocent children is increasing day by day even though there are constitutional and legislative safeguards to protect children from such exploitation. The government machinery had so far failed miserably in implementing the provisions and Directive Principles of State Policy of the Constitution of India. At least in the days to come, the government, the employers and the parents should understand the great harm that is being done to millions of future adults. The magnitude of this problem needs to be recognised and serious steps to be taken.

This study recommends

1. Concrete plans should be evolved at the grass root levels to provide free and compulsory education to the children up to the age of 14 years. For this, Village Panchayats and other local bodies may be entrusted with more powers (including financial power).
2. Economic position of the families should be raised so that they will not send their children for work.
3. Both financial and technical assistance to be rendered for the purpose of self-employment including cottage industry.
4. Strict enforcement of Child Labour (Abolition and Regulation Act, 1986) and Bonded Labour System (Abolition) Act, 1976.
5. The parents of the children should be educated on the ill effects of the child labour and bonded child labour.

References

1. Jaspreet Kaur , "Tending the Toiling hands—Child Labour", Labour file, January—April 1999, 1998.
2. Gani and Shah, "Child Labour in Carpet Industry of Kashmir", *Indian Journal of Industrial Relations*, Vol. 33, pp. 349-65, 1998.
3. Archana Sinha, "Child Labour and Health", Social Action, Vol. 48, No.1, pp. 35-46, 1998.
4. Neera Burra, "Child Labour in India", Oxford University Press, Delhi, 1995.

5. Siraj Sait, "Report of the Commission on Bonded Labour in Tamil Nadu", October 31, 1995.

6. *Ibid.*

7. R. Vidyasagar, "Child Labour in North Arcot Ambedkar District—A Pioneering Survey", Human Rights Watch/Asia, 1995.

8. Asha Krishna Kumar, "Bonded Labour: Reprehensible by Any Name Children in Beedi Industry" *Front Line*, Nov. 17, 1995.

16

Deviant Behaviour as a Consequence of Child Abuse and Neglect Among Street Children in Chennai

R. Thilagaraj and Prasanna Poornachandra

Street children are a symptom of a deep and disturbing trend in society. They encompass a wide section of children in distress such as those who have been abandoned, abused and neglected and the missing children. Literally, they are children who live on the streets and have been categorised by the UNICEF into three groups based on contact with their families as: children who have regular contact with the family, 'children on the street'—who have occasional family contact and 'children of the street'—who do not have any family contact.

These children often live on the street and try and earn a livelihood to support their families and in the process become vulnerable to exploitation by others and to a variety of physical and moral dangers. They are exploited and victimized at various stages of their lives irrespective of the place, that is, the home, the school or the workplace. The most disturbing fact is that while being exposed and victimized by various factors besides poverty, these children are forced to become deviants.

Magnitude of the Problem

To give a short statistical picture on the magnitude of the

problem of street children in India—in 1991 it was estimated that there were nearly four lakh street children in India and 17 lakh children had been identified in the 'high-risk' category. In Chennai, there was an estimated figure of 27,000 street children in the year 1994.

The Present Study

The present study aims at understanding various forms of exploitation leading to the neglect and abuse of street children by parents, employees and police and the deviant behaviour as a consequence of these abuses.

Methodology

For selecting the sample, the classification of Chennai as per the corporation divisions has been adopted. Chennai has been divided into 10 circles which are further subdivided into 150 divisions. Those areas which are commercial and mixed residential in nature have been identified. This has been done on the basic assumption that street children are more likely to be concentrated in these areas because of their specific advantages such as easy access to facilities and employment opportunities as compared to other areas. Using the non-probability technique of purposive sampling, street children living in these areas have been selected to constitute the sample. By this strategy a sample of 706 street children in different parts of Chennai have been selected for conducting interview and collecting data through an interview schedule designed for this purpose.

Family Victimization

Wholesome food, clothing, shelter, opportunities for education and recreation, health care and economic stability are certainly essential for the healthy growth of children. Functionally inadequate home is one which cannot or does not meet the basic needs of the child. It is either incapable of or too maladjusted to perform the functions necessary for the development of healthy and well-adjusted personality of the children.

Among the 706 street children included in the sample of this study, 42.78 per cent do not have access to basic facilities like food, clothing and shelter, 86.9 per cent of them state that the amount of food is inadequate while 60.53 per cent are unsatisfied with both food and clothing facilities. Very few have access to all the basic necessities such as food, cothing and shelter. 55 per cent of them do not have sufficient clothes.

The availability of these basic needs and facilities to the street children varies depending on whether they live with their families or not. A significant number of children in this sample do not live with their families and there are children who have to undergo a great deal of hardship to secure their basic needs. They have no one to provide them with food when they are hungry and sometimes starve. They live in the same clothes for days or even months for lack of a safe place to keep their belongings in. Shelter for these children is just a corner of a building, a park or under the bridge and if no space is available, the pavement itself. This is not the case of children who live with their families. They are provided with basic facilities to a certain extent although the adequacy of these facilities does not satisfy the children.

This is a serious problem for the street children posing a threat to their daily existence. They have to find some means of feeding and, clothing themselves and a place to sleep. This is a day-to-day problem since the children do not have sufficient money for their meals. Their victimization by their parents forces them to seek alternate sources for survival and when it crosses the limits of endurance they do not hesitate to steal or resort to illegal means of satisfying their needs. The children are, in other words, pushed into deviance due to the situation of inadequate and feeling of frustration which they are unable to overcome. When the family is unable to offer the basic necessities and protection, it is but natural that the children have to learn means of fending for themselves and this they do, ignoring the morality of their actions.

The street children are abused by their family members physically (25.5 per cent). It is unfortunate but true that the perpetrators of such ill-treatment are the children's parents themselves in majority of the cases (89.44 per cent) besides the siblings (7.2 per cent). The children are subjected to sexual abuse too in some cases but most of them are harassed physically (98.3 per cent). The forms of such physical harassment or abuse include beating, scolding, starving and the like.

Another form of victimization of the street children by their parents is that they are made to work beyond their capacity in their homes. A big chunk of the sample (29.75 per cent) have admitted to working in their homes. They are assigned work such as looking after siblings and working, fetching wood and water. More than one of these duties is allotted to one-half of the sample (50 per cent) which they feel is beyond their abilities. This is an unfortunate practice among these lower sections of the society which only value the source other than anything else. Therefore, the children are deprived of the opportunity to educate themselves. However, the victimization of children who live with their families is different from that of children not living with their families. Those living with their families have a greater risk of being victimized. These children are exploited by their parents/step-parents who expect them to look after the domestic responsibilities while they are at work. These children are denied the opportunity of attending school and of recreation. Instead of spending their childhood in the routine of household chores, they should be given ample opportunity to play and indulge in healthy pastimes—thereby facilitating their development as well-adjusted individuals.

The type of treatment meted out to the children by their families also varies significantly. As the analysis indicates, majority of these children are not living with their families at present and among these children, very few have been ill-treated in their homes. Their running away has been precipitated by other reasons. However, it is significant to note that these children who are living with their families have reported the ill-treatment they are subjected to by the family members themselves.

Victimization by Employers

The common modes of exploitation adopted by employers of child labourers are, unjustified payment of wages for the extraction of profits, hazardous conditions of work that jeopardise their physical and mental well-being.

A major problem faced by those children who are working under employers is payment of low wages (24.48 per cent) for the long hours of work they are engaged in. Not only that, the workload assigned to the children is excessive (11.11 per cent) in some cases equal to that of adults. Fourteen per cent of the children have admitted to being physically abused by their employers. More than one form of exploitation is adopted by the employers in the case of 42.49 per cent of the street children.

This ill-treatment at work is one of the reasons why street children hesitate to work under employers. More than 19 per cent (19.6) of the children have stated that they have been subjected to punishment by their employers. Physical abuse of these children is most common involving measures like beating, scolding, starving or denial of other facilities. Verbal abuse of children (20 per cent) is also one form of punishment that psychologically affects the children. Reduction of payment and suspension from work are other punitive methods resorted to by the employers (6.6 per cent). The reason for punishing the children at the workplace is often petty to deserve such stringent treatment.

The nature of treatment of the street children by their employers is a factor that determines the attitude of children towards them. More than half of these children (52.94 per cent) do not have a healthy attitude towards their employers. Others are indifferent (54.10 per cent), neither friendly nor hostile. A few of these children (7.84 per cent) are hostile towards their employers. The negative attitude of these children is probably influenced by the treatment they are subjected to at the workplace.

Work Hazards

Besides the harassment by their employers, the hazardous conditions of work is another major problem faced by the street children. According to the street children, they have been physically injured and affected by diseases and accidents at the workplace. Most of the time physical injuries (20.8 per cent) are caused by handling sharp, heavy tools or articles at work. This is common among rag-pickers who use their unprotected hands and also among children working in factories and workshops. Diseases are common among children working in proximity to toxic fumes, chemicals and contaminated articles. Some of them have been victims of accidents in the workplace. Instances of amputated fingers and serious injuries have been reported during this study.

Thus, street children face exploitation at every sphere of their lives, the most serious being exploitation of child labour. This is a disturbing situation in our country where the health and safety of the children are placed at stake for the sake of a pittance offered as wages. Poverty and unemployment both are the reasons for the employers' exploitation of children. Physically the children are unsuited for long hours of work. Their bodies suffer the effects of fatigue more quickly than adults because of the strenuous work they are engaged in. It is a compulsion for these children to resort to deviant means of supplementing their income. This is a vicious cycle from which children have to be rescued.

Police Harassment

Among the 706 street children 50.4 per cent have been to the police station at one time or the other during their street life. These children are mainly arrested on ground of suspicion (65.5 per cent) and sometimes as offenders (15.8 per cent). This is evident from the harassment of street children by the police who take advantage of these children because of their vulnerable situation and bypass the departmental procedure while apprehending them. Street children have also been arrested for gambling, violence and selling illicit substance. Majority of these children are older than 12 years (62.08 per cent) and have been subjected to punishment. The most common form of punishment meted out to the street children is institutionalisation (59.9 per cent), or imprisonment (15.35 per cent).

The police arrest of the street children varies depending on whether they are living with their parents or not. This is one factor which makes them vulnerable to police harassment. Those children living with their families stand a lesser chance of being arrested because of the fact that the parents are responsible for them and may enquire the whereabouts of the child. The police are also restrained by the parents or the guardians of the child. Those who live on their own or with friends, however, are more vulnerable because there is no one to question their whereabouts even in the event of them being arrested by the police. A large section of the children (38.10 per cent) have pointed out that they are frequently harassed by the police on the streets. The harassment takes in the form of severe beating most of the times. To quote an instance of police ill-treatment of street children, one of the boys explains how he was arrested by the police on grounds of suspicion and beaten until he was forced to admit a crime that he had not committed. The beating was so severe on that occasion that the 'lathi' used by the police broke and the boy was unable to walk normally even after a week of his experience when interviewed for the study. The police are known to take away personal possessions of the street children or demand bribes from them if they wish to continue being in the same place or work in a particular place. A few of the street children have admitted that they were made to work in the police station. Works such as cleaning and washing of the premises, vehicles of officers and such similar works were assigned to them and then they were released. The police even resort to measures such as wrongly recording the higher age of children in order to register cases against them. It is a gross violation of the Constitutional rights of the children to be arrested, foisted cases upon and be ill-treated by the very officers of the society.

The harassment of the street children (below 13 years of age) of both sexes varies significantly. It is the boys who are targets of police. Living on the pavements, under the bridge and in the parks, the boys are more visible than girls. The police are familiar with the haunts of these children and when facing an acute shortage of cases find it easy to apprehend them and foist cases upon them in order to reduce the number of undetected crimes and to keep the record of crimes at a stable level. Similarly, the harassment of these children is more among older boys and girls than younger boys and girls. The reasons are easy to understand. These children are often living with their families and have not yet run away due to any reason while the older children have taken a decision to leave their homes and come to the streets. Their street life brings them into contact with the police thereby increasing the risk of harassment.

Other Forms of Harassment

Other forms of victimization of the street children include the loss of their belongings and physical injuries inflicted by the people on the street. Other forms of victimization by public are theft (13.3 per cent), assault (1 per cent) and rape/sodomy mostly committed at night. These incidents occur at the place of dwelling of street children (32.4 per cent), or at the workplace (21.6 per cent), or even in the institutions (11.7 per cent) where these children stay. In most of the cases (68.4 per cent) the street children lose their money while clothes are stolen in a fewer cases (44.4 per cent). Attacks and assaults are rarer (9.9 per cent) but there have been instances where street children have been severely injured by such assaults. Out of fear of being harassed by the police most of the children (65.38 per cent) do not complain to them of their victimization. Homosexuality is more among institutionalized children.

Thus, the perspectives on the deviance and victimization of street children reveal a new dimension of social problems in the present day. India, being in the infant stages of industrialization is at present undergoing a phase of concomitant social problems such as poverty, unemployment, slums, street children, etc. The children are forced into deviance or voluntarily choose a deviant way of life because of the perennial poverty that envelops them. They are unable to obtain even the minimum needs for survival due to this gross imbalance between their wants and the means of satisfaction. Their standard of living is one which is wrought with insufficiency draining them to the extent of illegal behaviour at an early age. This deprivation and inadequacy begins in the home, family members are incapable of avoiding any necessity. The children continue to live in a state of impoverishment which sooner or later precipitates the running away behaviour. Not only the unfulfillment of wants, there is also an unhealthy atmosphere in the front characterized by the perpetual need for money, lack of adequate privacy, unhealthy habits of parents and siblings, unemployment and neglect.

In most of these families, the parents are compelled to send their children to work and earn a livelihood because of the economic pressure. Outside the home the neglect and exploitation extends to the workplace where employers are the main exploiters. They take advantage of the children by paying them a pittance sometimes for long hours than a child is capable of working. These children are deprived of the schooling opportunity and are made to work for less than the minimum wages.

The conditions at work are also hazardous with no consideration being paid to the child's well-being. Child labour is profitable and the employers protect their own interests by extracting work from the children. The resulting retardation of their healthy development, education and recreation exerts a negative influence on the children. The children do not complain like adults and suffer their lot in silence. Some of them therefore, continually move from one job to another in search of better working conditions. They often do not remain in a job for long periods without shifting when they are dissatisfied with the terms of employment or due to some other factors. They are liable to abuse by the employers and the only alternative is to change the job. They do so but the difficulty in seeking employment without sufficient education and training is more acute among these children. They are absorbed only into jobs which do little to improve their situation. The situation is worse in the case of the unemployed.

Besides the harassment at work and neglect at home the children are taken advantage of by the police also. No special consideration is given to the child's age and even petty misconduct becomes an excuse for the police to lock them up. There have been cases of imprisonment of children despite the passing of special legislation. This is one of the reasons that the children seek places to reside which are safe from the reach of the police. These children are targets of harassment to aid the police fill up their quota of cases. False cases are registered against them and they are treated in the same manner as adult criminals.

Becoming Deviant

More than 50 per cent of street children take drugs and alcohol and indulge in gambling and prostitution. A major part of their earning is spent on these deviant activities. The average size of the gangs are 5-10 members and there is an intimate relationship between the members of the gangs. Parents neglect them initially and they run away from homes. Even children living with their parents are also ill-treated. Unable to find alternatives, they are forced to live on streets without any control on their behaviour. On the streets, they are looked down upon by the members of the society as the lowest of the low. They are forced to do certain menial jobs, where they are exploited to the hilt by the employees, paying low wages for long hours in hazardous working conditions. The police harass the street children unduly. Hence, they are not recognised as human beings, instead they are rejected and alienated in all walks of their lives, by all groups of society except the deviant subculture of street children. These children are recognised, accepted and given a status only by this subculture and thus they become an active members of the gangs of the street children and get involved in deviant activities.

Bibliography

Akers, Ronald L.: Deviant Behaviour: A Social Learning Approach, Wadsworth Publishing Co., USA, 1973.

Bartollas, Clemens, Miller, Stuart J., and Dinitz, Simon: Juvenile Victimization; The Institutional Paradox; Sage Publications, Inc., USA., 1976.

Bosco Institute of Social Work: Situational Analysis of Street Children in Madras City, Sacred Heart College, Tirupattur, 1989.

Children's Aid Society: Study of Kidnapped Children in the City of Bombay, Research Dept., Central Office, UNICEF 1973.

Clinard, Marshall B.. Sociology of Deviant Behaviour, Holt, Rinehart and Winston, Inc., New York, 1974.

Cohen, Albert K.: Deviance and Control, Prentice Hall of India Pvt. Ltd., New Delhi, 1970.

Dingwaney, Manjari et al: Children of Darkness—A Manual on Child Labour in India. Rural Labour Cell, New Age Printing Press, New Delhi, 1988.

Elkin, Fredericko: The Child and Society: The Process of socialization, Random House Inc., New Yorko, 1965.

Erikson, Richardson V.: Young Offenders and their social work, Saxon House, Lexington Books, Lexington, USA, 1975.

Goldmeier, J. and Dean, R.D.: The Runaway person, problem or situation. Crime and Delinquency 19, October 1973, pp. 539-44.

Knutsson, Karl-Eric: Responding to the Needs of Street Children, UNICEF Regional Director's Statement (South Central Asia) at the National Workshop on Street Children, New Delhi, August 29-30, 1988.

Koerin, Beverly B.: Child Abuse and Neglect: Changing Policies and Perspectives, Journal of Child Welfare, League of America, Vol. LIX, No. 9 November, 1980, pp. 542-50.

Pinto, Rita P. and Nangia, Parveen: Children in specially difficult circumstances in Delhi—Focus on working and street children, UNICEF Report, 1988.

Spergel, Irving: Street Gang Work—Theory and Practice. Addison—Wesley Publishing Co., Inc., Massachusetts, USA, 1966.

17

A Study on Child Beggars in the City of Chennai

S. Latha • S. Ramdoss • A. Mathan Raj

India is a highly populated country second only to communist China. Population experts in India and abroad have predicted that India's population at the present birth rate would exceed the population of China in another ten to fifteen years. This is a very alarming situation which India has to face. Equally alarming if not more is the problem of begging consequent to the increase in the population. It is said that begging is not a new phenomena and it has been there for hundreds of years all over the world and in India as well.

Categories of Beggars

There are several kinds of begging and the classification of beggars are also many. Many of these following categories deserve the consideration of all concerned and particularly the Government, the NGOs and the people at large.

There are:

1. Juvenile
2. Able-bodied
3. Diseased and old; and
4. Physically handicapped and mentally retarded.

Explanation about the categories of begging is not so very essential as is the manners and the gravity of begging.

Causes for Begging and Socio-economic Conditions of Beggars

There are several reasons for begging. Of them, generally identified are poverty, unemployment or underemployment, family background, lack of adequate income and inability to meet both ends, greed and neglect. These are true of the Indian societies in several ways. On one side there is unlimited income from several sources manifested in the affluence of a few privileged. On the other there is extreme poverty from which most people find it difficult to come out. In between these two extremes of haves and have nots, there is yet another section of population called the middle class. This section of population is patronized by the government and private agencies with decent jobs which are just sufficient for livelihood as honourable citizens. The third category of group belongs to the construction workers, industrial workers, factory labourers or agricultural labourers. The last mentioned category of the population has income just sufficient for ordinary living. Sometimes it is less than that. Besides these sections which have income there is yet another section of population which has no employment or no source of income and comes under the category of unorganized sector. It is generally believed that the larger the population the greater the source of labour. But in India the unemployment has reached a point where it is absolutely impossible for the government and other agencies to provide jobs.

Government Help and Inadequacy of Income

The Central as well as the State Government in India have been giving doles which are called as allowances for the unemployed persons who are registered with the employment exchanges of government.

The government whose responsibility is to provide the security to the life of its people has introduced several schemes which extend help to the poor and the needy. But it is marginal and several times less than what is required. With the available income of any sort the people who belong to the lower ranks of the society are unable to meet requirements their in performing their duty to the family vis-a-vis providing sufficient means of living, meet the expenditure towards social and religious functions and the long term needs of their families. So it is not surprising that people resort to several ways and means to earn their livelihood. Begging is also one of these means.

Objectives of the Present Study

This study looks into the plight of child beggars and their level of victimization in Chennai. Main objectives of the present study are to study the socio-economic conditions of the child beggars, the causes behind begging and to estimate the level of victimization they have experienced. Based on these, certain research questions were framed.

Chennai Corporation and its Role

Among the major cities of India Chennai is the fourth largest city with the population of roughly 35 lakhs. The city has Municipal Corporation which is divided into as many as 150 divisions or wards for administrative purposes. The administration the city is run by the Municipal Corporation consisting the Commissioner, Mayor and the Municipal Council. While the Commissioner is appointed by the Government of Tamil Nadu, the Mayor and the counsellors are directly elected by the voters of the Chennai. As in the case of the government at the Centre and in the State the Municipal Corporation is also taking several welfare measures to mitigate the poverty of its population. It is an enormous task which cannot be handled easily for the population is ever increasing. Naturally in spite of the best efforts of the corporation, authorities and voluntary agencies, begging has become a routine if not a profession for some people. Among the beggars the child beggars are a class in themselves. It is very difficult and sometimes baffling as to how the children come to beg. Whether they beg of their own freewill or forced to do so, is a matter to be studied carefully and in detail for arriving at useful conclusions.

Reasons for Child Begging

It cannot be said categorically or convincingly as to what exactly is the total number of beggars and in particular child beggars and why they resort to it. However, as stated earlier in the general causes, they apply very well to child beggars also. The chief reasons for the prevalence of child beggars are the poverty, the compulsion on the part either of the parents, guardians, neighbours and the neglect of the children.

It may be noted that among the beggars whether old or young there is a group whose members do not suffer from any physical strength or disability but have taken to habitual or professional begging. They evade work and remain as social parasites. Though one could be critical of this category of beggars it might at the same time be due to the non-availability of work and employment also.

Child begging generally and in most of the cases may be attributed to the parents at home compelling their wards to beg. The parents even inflict physical injuries on them so as to evoke public sympathy. These children are generally below the age of 14. They have been trained in the art of begging from the childhood itself. Women holding an infant is a common sight on the streets.

So it may be said that the children are trained and inducted into begging even from their birth. In certain other cases, begging is resorted to by children when they are treated unkindly and harshly by the parents and then they run away from their homes. This kind of beggary is not necessarily confined to the poor population alone. Even among the middle class people children who disobey the parents and elders for which they are criticised and severely dealt with and thus they also leave their homes and take to begging. Sometimes a few of these children land themselves as menial workers in ordinary hotels and roadside restaurants. Others who are not accommodated this way and who are accustomed to the easy way of living resort to begging at the bus stops, road junctions on the streets and the premises or places of worship like temples churches and mosques, theatres etc. Once they earn more than what is required for their living they continue to beg throughout their lives. Very rarely they return to the fold of their families whom they had abandoned. Sometimes it may be the vice-versa when their parents locate their children after serious search, they appeal through mass media which enable both the children and the parents to reunite.

Sample of the Study and Methodology

Some of the observations and generalizations made hitherto in this chapter are strengthened by a sample study conducted and views obtained from 30 child beggars in the main arterial highway viz., Anna Salai (Mount Road) in Chennai. An interview schedule consisting of twenty questions was framed and used as the research tool. Faculty members, research scholars and students of the Department of Criminology were consulted to ensure the validity (face validity) of the tool. A pilot study was conducted to find the feasibility of the study and it was found feasible. The data were analysed using simple statistical methods and they are given in the table below:

TABLE 1

Socio-economic Background of the Child Beggars

S. No.	Socio-economic factors		Frequency (N)	Percentage
1.	Sex	Male	21	70.0
		Female	9	30.0
		Total	30	100.0
2.	Parent's Education	Illiterates	28	93.3
		Literates	2	6.7
		Total	30	100.0
3.	Parent's Occupation	Beggars	20	66.7
		Flower Vendors	2	6.7
		Construction Workers	4	13.3
		Vaga bonds	4	13.3
		Total	30	100.0
4.	Children's Education	Illiterates	25	83.3
		Literates	5	16.7
		Total	30	100.0
5.	Residence	Platform Dwellers	24	80.0
		Huts	6	20.0
		Total	3 0	100.0

TABLE 2

Compulsion to Beg

	Number of children Forced	*Perpetrators*	
		Parents	*Guardians*
Frequency	20	15	5
Percentage	66.7	75.0	25.0

TABLE 3

Places of Begging

Places of begging	*Frequency*	*Percentage*
Mosques	20	66.7
Beach	15	50.0
Theatres	10	53.3
Bus Stand	23	76.7
Road Signals	20	66.7
Temples	18	60.0

TABLE 4

Types of Abuse Faced by Child Beggars by Parents/ Guardians

Types of abuse	*Frequency*	*Percentage*
Verbal	26	86.7
Both verbal and physical	4	13.3

TABLE 5

Abuse of Child Beggars by Public

Types of abuse	*Frequency*	*Percentage*
Verbal abuse	18	60.0
Both verbal and physical abuse	12	40.0

Findings

The findings of the study are as follows:

1. 93.3 per cent of the parents were illiterates and had no knowledge of what was happening around them.
2. Among the parents 66.7 per cent were beggars, 6.7 per cent were flower vendors, 13.3 per cent were construction workers and 13.3 per cent were vagabonds.
3. The child beggars were denied their rights to education, proper food and equal treatment. Their parents compelled them to beg. Of these 83.3 per cent were illiterates. However, a negligible number was drop-outs of schools.
4. 70.7 per cent of the child beggars were males in the age group of five to fourteen.
5. The percentage of child beggars who were abused verbally by their parents was 86.7 while both verbal and physical abuse accounted for 13.7.
6. Sixty per cent of public also abused these child beggars verbally while the percentage of physical and verbal abuse was forty.
7. 16.7 per cent of the child beggars were previously inmates of the juvenile homes.

Level of Victimization

From the findings given above, it may be said that the children are made victims by their parents and guardians by compulsions and other methods. As they are tender in age with no experience about life and matters pertaining to life they cannot adopt by and large an independent view about the need otherwise of begging. In other words, it is simply cruelty perpetrated on the young children by all concerned. It might be observed in this context even if the children wanted to leave begging at some stage they could not do so because of the vested interest who are the beneficiaries of the income fetched by these child beggars. They prevented and in some cases also brutally assaulted the child. For all that the child beggars though bring wealth to their masters they are not properly fed, given clothing and provided shelter. This is how most of the child beggars are ill-treated and exploited.

Constitutional Provisions

The Constitution of India provides care, protection and adequate facilities for proper development of its future citizens as it is evident from Articles 15, 24, 39, 42, 43 and 45. In pursuance of these Constitutional provisions, the Parliament adopted in August 1974 the National Policy for Children and resolved inter-alia that children "shall be protected against neglect, cruelty and exploitation" and that "no child under 14 years shall be permitted to be engaged in any hazardous occupation or be made to undertake heavy work".

The U.N. Convention on the Rights of a Child states the following rights to the children:

"Right to life which includes the highest attainable standard of health, nutrition and adequate standard of living; the right from birth to a name, to acquire a nationality as far as possible, the right to know and be cared by his or her parents.

Also includes freedom from all forms of exploitation, abuse, inhuman or degrading treatment and neglect including the rights to special protection in situations of emergency and armed conflicts.

Right to education, support for early childhood development and care, social security and the right to leisure, recreation and cultural activities.

Right to respect for the views of the child, freedom of expression, access to appropriate information and freedom of thought, conscience and religion".

"The 20th Century has witnessed worldwide efforts made to create an environment in which all the children are able to live securely and realize their full potential. As a result today there are more than eighty International laws, covenants and declarations setting out human rights of the children" (U.N. Convention, 1959).

Conclusion

All said and done the big question, probably the question for the 21st Century is, as to how to achieve the laudable and noble objectives enshrined in the documents mentioned above. The probable answer is that affluent nations of the East and West along with the efforts of the various agencies of the United Nations should set apart a sizable percentage of their resources. It is not simply a case of individual or a nation or a State. It can be tackled only by collective, sustained and co-ordinated efforts of all.

References

George, Report on the Beggar Survey in Madras City. The Madras School of Social Work, Madras, 1956, p. 9.

Gore, M.S., "The Beggar Problem in Metropolitan Delhi", Delhi School of Social Work, Delhi, 1959, pp. 143-44.

Government of India, "Towards Delinquency Control", National Institute of Social Defence, Ministry of Social Welfare, New Delhi, 1979, pp. 24-26.

John L. Gillin, "Begging" in Encyclopeadia of the Social Science, The Macmillon Co., New York, 1962, pp. 493-94.

Madhuri Kakal, YUVA, "Labouring Under Delusion: The Myths Underlying Child Labour", Facts against Myths Information Bulletin, Vikas Adhyayan Kendra, 1996, Vol. III, No. 8.

Bhatia, V.B. (1995), "Beggary: Cause and Consequences", Social Welfare, New Delhi, pp. 23-26.

UNICEF; Rights of the Child, New Delhi.

UNICEF; The State of the World's Children, 1995, New Delhi.

18

Preventing Child Victimisation—Some Strategies

Bharati Sharma

The period from birth to late adolescence is extremely important in the life of an individual. It is the formative and developmental period and experiences during this period shape one's personality and character. But, it is noticed that most incidents of victimisation take place during this period, as the children are unable to assert and are too innocent to understand that they are being victimised.

The concept of victim appears among the most ancient ones in humanity. Inextricably connected with the idea and the practice of sacrifice, the notion of victim belongs to all cultures. Most religions, for example, are fundamentally sacrificial. Early ritual literature from all religions offers abundant clues to the study of sacrifice and of its victims—human, divine, animal or inanimate. The epics and mythological sources provide sufficient evidence pointing to the existence of the different types of sacrifice and victim, and contain a wealth of symbolic elements connected to those rituals and practices.

Although interest on victim's role in a criminal situation is not very old, various facets of the victim's situation have come under scrutiny and have spurred people into action. Although victimisation as the form of human sacrifice is very rare these days, victimisation goes on nevertheless. Most common among them are child labour, child prostitution, child beggary, sexual abuse and child marriage.

An attempt is made in this article to deal with a few forms of child victimisation and suggest some strategies for its prevention. Emphasis is given on parental abuse and neglect, sexual child abuse and child labour. Some forms of victimisation such as parental abuse in the form of child battering and neglect has not been well-documented in India because of supports provided by the extended family. However, increasing media coverage, emergence of nuclear family have forced us to conclude that child abuse is varied and includes beating, emotional abuse, abandonment and sexual abuse. They are often connected with parental expectations, marital discord, divorce, and career families, poor housing, poor parental mental health, alcoholism and superstition.

Parental abuse and neglect had, till recently gone unnoticed in India. It is however a major form of victimisation of children. The social change, structure of modern family and inter generational relationship has brought it to the forefront. The concept of child abuse and neglect has gone considerable change over the years. In the beginning, baby-battering was in the foreground to which phenomenon of maltreatment was added. Neglect and violence are latest additions.

If we try to analyse the causes of child abuse and neglect we must first understand the characteristics of abused children and the type of individuals, who would harm their children. Secondly, we must understand the situational factors that lead to abuse. This will enable us to establish a link between the individual, societal and situational factors, which precipitate child abuse.

There are theories to suggest that child abuse is learned behaviour and transmitted from generation to generation. Parents treat their children the way they were treated by their parents. Although we cannot deny the concept of cycle of abuse we find that many children have survived neglected and abusive childhoods and become successful parents in spite of it all and well-cared-for children turn out to be parental monsters. So situation, rather than the cycle of abuse, seems more acceptable.

Parental authority and conquest for obedience is a major issue concerning child abuse and neglect by parents. Parents are heard saying that they would rather have dead children than disobedient ones. They rarely understand that no child is born disobedient. It is the relationship between the parents and children that make a child obedient or disobedient. Disobedience apart, lack of proper parental care due to broken homes often leads to serious delinquency. Children cannot be considered as sole property of parents anymore. They need to be considered, as human beings with a mind of their own. They must feel wanted, loved and trusted. Studies reveal that non-abusers manage to raise their families with relatively more success. What children need to grow to their full potential is support and guidance, not indulgence. This imbibes confidence in children and they are able to face the rough world gracefully. Parenting is not a power game where asymmetry of power should lead to child abuse.

Stress is one factor, which is widely accepted as the cause of child abuse. The origins of stress in such cases are jobs, finances, loneliness, isolation where children are made the scapegoat. What parents need to develop are coping skills for managing stress and not make the children victims of their stress, may it be related to job and economic issue or family matters. To combat stress, emphasis should be on a closer tie between family life and work life.

Parental screening, abused child therapy and parenting classes will help prevent child abuse. Counselling is needed for both parents and children which will help manage and solve many a problem arising out of parent-child conflict. Child protection strategies must aim at changing structural inequality of our families. Last strategy to protect child from neglect and abuse will be to have child protection services, which will be always available to protect the child. However, for the rural poor, only education and awareness programmes can help.

Sexual abuse during childhood is one of the worst forms of child victimisation. Children are innocent, timid and powerless in front of adults and adults take advantage of this helpless situation and victimise them sexually, i.e., use them for the sexual gratification. Child sexual victimisation may be termed as sexual abuse, sexual exploitation, sexual assault, sexual misuse, child molestation, sexual maltreatment and child rape.

Too often parents and other professionals believe that sexual abuse of children is committed by strangers. This is true in only about ten to fifteen per cent of the cases. Warning children to avoid unknown persons may be an unclear message to children. A manipulative person can easily win over a child, and before too long the new person is not a stranger but a friend. According to developmental theory only by age six a child can be taught the difference between the two forms. Yet, even if the word stranger has been clearly explained the child might not know why strangers should be sidestepped. The child might not understand what he or she should do if someone approaches him or her. This can create and generate feeling of anxiety for children. The irony of it is that in at least 85 per cent of the cases, the child sexual offender, is known to the child. In at least twenty-five per cent of the cases the offenders live in the child's home.

A variety of behaviour is encapsulated within child sexual abuse. The most common among them are non-contact sexual abuse such as sexual comments, exhibitionism, watching pornographic film and videos and contact sexual abuse such as kissing, handling or fondling, vaginal or anal intercourse, frottage (an adult rubbing against a child in a sexual manner) pornography and cyber sex. The child is never at fault if sexual abuse occurs. Most sexual abuse begin at an age when the child has no knowledge about what sexuality means. Sexually abusive situations are characterised by lack of consent, exploitation, secrecy and force.

Although every child has a potential to become a victim of child sexual abuse, persons who molest children have a tendency to look for children who can be easily controlled. Most molesters seek out children who they think will keep a secret. They will also look for children who are very respectful and cannot say no to adults. The children who live with their stepfathers, live away from their mothers, not close with mothers, fathers very dominating have more chances of being abused sexually.

People close to the child must look for some indicators, which is different for different age group of children of sexual abuse. Children most often will not talk directly about sexual abuse and thus determining if a child is sexually abused is a complicated procedure. They do not tell straightforward that they have been abused as they are threatened or made to feel as if the abuse was their fault.

Not all adults however can sexually abuse children. It is perversions some people have who are paedophiles. This kind of pervert sexual behaviour is thought to be a result of emotional, physical or sexual trauma. The individual may be emotionally underdeveloped. Due to retardation in development the individual may age in years but not emotionally.

Some behavioural theorists maintain that paedophilia is a learned behaviour where abusers become conditioned to responding to young, sexually underdeveloped bodies. In a patriarchal society male being dominant, controlling and powerful, connect with partners who are younger, smaller and weaker than themselves. Some people who engage in child abuse cannot get their sexual and emotional needs met in adult rélationships. They do not have any inhibition and are able to overcome the moral and legal sanction against performing sexual acts with children. Lowering inhibitions can be the result of alcohol usage, social isolation or senility.

Sexual child abuse may be extrafamilial as well as intrafamilial. Contrary to the common knowledge the abusers need not be always males. However sexual abuses by females with either male or female children are less harmful than abuse by adult males. Although the existence of female offenders is now beginning to be recognised, it is still met with great skepticism. Accepting the harsh reality that females can and do abuse children and adolescents in both gender groups, perhaps attacks one of the last remaining vestiges of cultural myth: the myth that mothers or females are always protective towards children and could not be abusive, violent, or sadistic, sexual offenders.

Almost common among the intrafamilial abuses is father-daughter incest; the most common sexual abuse. This incest is viewed as a result of internal and external forces in the family in which the father is seen as pathological and alcoholic and the mother as unassertive. Mother-son intrafamilial abuse although was non-existent till recently is now being reported although literature reference regarding it is very scant. Brother-sister incest, too, is a common form of child abuse, which is grossly underreported. One cause of incest between siblings could be sexual experimentation. It could also be as a result of family dysfunction, ill-defined and poor boundaries within the family. It is surprising to note that a small portion of grandparent population too is identified as being sexually abusive.

It is disheartening to note that child sexual abuse is on the increase. The latest police statistics show that three out of four rape victims in Delhi are minor girls. Worse, there is still no legal recognition of serious kind to sexual abuse like non-penile penetration and incest. Crime statistics reveal a gory picture. In the past decade the rape of minor below 16, accounts for more than 25 per cent of the total rape cases while cases of rape of children below the age of ten years increased by 26 per cent. The dismal rate of convictions is even more disheartening. Less than ten per cent of the reported rape cases in India result in convictions. Of the 284 reported rape cases in New Delhi in 1992 there were only three convictions by 1995. Of the 309 cases in 1994 there was not a single conviction.

Prevention of sexual child abuse must address three areas. First, all concerned with children such as parents, baby-sitters, pediatricians, psychologists must recognise the situations in which abuse has been occurring. They can come together and learn to be more protective towards children and learn what to do if abuse is suspected. Secondly, prevention must concentrate on societal elements that encourage child sexual abuse, such as advertisers exploiting children's sexuality to sell products and services. Thirdly, healthy parenting skills must be developed increasing child's self-esteem. Building self-esteem in children makes them less vulnerable of being abused. If a child feels positive about himself or herself and has his or her physical and emotional needs met, than he or she is less likely to be abused. Parents can teach their children some basic safety rules and make them tell a trusted adult (may be parents) about what happens outside home.

It is needless to say that parents are the best protectors of children. While protecting the child outside home, they should always hold the hands of the young child while shopping or walking on the road or parks. They should know the exact route the child takes to school and help the child identify restaurants, small business, and homes of friends where they know that the child could run if help was needed. They must make sure that child is not away from school during school time. Child should be protected at all the places such as religious meetings, public toilets, swimming pools, etc.

At home children should never answer a knock on the door. They should be taught to deal with all types of phones early in their lives, the parents must make a list of emergency telephone numbers. If alone they should not tell a strange caller that their parents are absent there but tell that they are unable to come to the phone and ask them to give the number so that they can ring back. If the child gets gifts, parents must find out who is giving the gift, what is in the gift and determine how the child exactly got the gift. One should never allow stranger to photograph his/her child.

Intrafamilial abusive situations are much more complex. Once the abuser is identified he must be sent out of home or the child must be kept away from the abuser. Help may be sought from some organisations, which have now developed to protect children.

Family members talking to the abuser about stopping the abuse will not be effective. If the father or the mother is the abuser due to whatever reason it is the duty of the other parent to protect the child. Children must be taught that the adults are not always right. Above all, the children should be encouraged to build self-confidence from an early age.

Child labour is one of the worst form of victimisation where they are sent to work instead of their rightful place in school. Child labour is usually defined as participation of children between the ages of five and fourteen years in gainful activity. According to the latest International Labour Organization (ILO) report global child labour figure is 250 million and statistics show that India has the dubious distinction of having the largest child labour force in the world. Inspite of the constitutional directive (Article 45 of the Directive Principle of State Policy) to provide free and compulsory education for all children until they complete the age of fourteen years, this social problem has grown unabated.

Poverty coupled with population explosion and illiteracy are the basic causes of child labour. Income of the child becomes essential for the survival of the families, which are invariably large. Children's employment is preferred because they work for less remuneration than adult labourers, they can be pressurised easily into the exploitative tactics of the employers, children being amenable to discipline and control of child labour is trouble-free and not unionised.

The children working for long hours and sometimes even during the night in poor, polluted and hazardous conditions under constant mental and physical strain results in stunted growth. They suffer from lung and eye diseases, backaches and often become victims of fire accidents. Unable to participate in leisure and recreational activities, these children become drug-addicts, spend time in gambling and smuggling. It affects their physical and psychological growth, which finally degenerates the whole socio-economic structure.

While considering strategies to prevent child victimisation in the form of child labour we can first cite various legislations enacted from time to time. The obvious fact that in spite of these laws, child labour still prevails in contemporary society indicates that these legal measures are cleverly violated by the unscrupulous employers due to inadequate enforcing and monitoring machinery. Banning child labour altogether will be a long-term strategy. What can immediately be done is to combat exploitation. Children must be released from dangerous occupations and bondage. There is a need to build public opinion against child labour. Women and youth organisations must come forward and shoulder this responsibility. Many NGOs have the reputation of being able to get closer to the communities who resist any attempt to tackle the problem of child labour. Greater social awareness, low cost job-oriented education and encouraging more women to the work force will go a long way in eradicating child labour.

References

Ahmed, Iflikhar "Gelling Rid of Child Labour", *Economic and Political Weekly,* July 1999.

Emilio Viano, "Victimology: The Development of a New Perspective", *Victimology*, Vol. 8, 1983.

The *Hindustan Times*, November 19, 1999.

Julianu Whetsell—Mitchell, *"Rape of the Innocent"* Taylor Francis, USA 1995.

Segal, Uma A., "Child Abuse in India: A Theoretical Overview" *Indian Journal of Social Work,* July 1991.

Singh, S.P., "Child Labour Malady and the Remedy" *Yojana,* July 1997.

19
Child Protection

Jyotsna Chatterji

The Convention on the Rights of the Child recognizes the exceptional vulnerability of children and proclaims that childhood is entitled to special care and assistance. It obligates the state to respect and ensure that children get a fair and equitable deal in society. It emphasizes the importance of the family and the need to create an environment that is conducive to the healthy growth and development of children. It advocates public action by all individuals and agencies—government and non-governmental, local, regional, national and international—to promote the rights of the child.

The convention in a sense, is a means of empowering children and creating an environment in which all children are able to live securely and realize their full potential in life. It highlights four basic rights:

(1) the right to survival,
(2) the right to protection,
(3) the right to development,
(4) the right to participation.

The National Policy for Children, 1974 affirmed the Constitutional provisions—"it shall be the policy of the state to provide adequate services to children both before and after birth and through the period of growth to ensure their full physical, mental and social development".

With such excellent intentions and policies, children should have had a better deal but unfortunately this is not so. Article 39 of the Directive Principles of State Policy states "that the health and strength of workers, men and women, and the tender age of children are not abused and that citizens are not forced by economic necessity to enter vocations unsuited to their age or strength", "that children are given opportunities and facilities to develop in a healthy manner and in conditions of freedom and dignity and that childhood and youth are protected against exploitation and against moral and material abandonment". Similarly Article 24 stipulates that "no child below the age of fourteen years shall be employed to work in any factory or mine or engaged in any other hazardous employment".

These conventions, Constitutional provisions are for the empowerment and protection of all children. But in a society that is divided on the basis of caste, class, religion and sex, and where poor, marginalised parents and guardians are also discriminated against with the majority, powerful on top of the social ladder taking away most of the benefits, children on the lowest rung of the ladder face four times more discrimination and exploitation. It is these children we need to focus upon. These are the children of weaker sections, especially the scheduled castes and scheduled tribes, who are almost 35 per cent of the total child population of India and among them the girl children.

Children of the Marginalised Sections

While all children need their rights to be recognised and ensured—their right to survival, good health and adequate standard of living:

- their right to development, education, leisure, recreation and proper and balanced development.
- their right to participation, freedom of expression and thought, access to information.
- their right to protection from exploitation, abuse, inhuman and degrading treatment, special protection in times of emergency and armed conflict, children of the marginalised

> sections need protection from all kinds of exploitation and violence prevalent in society. It is these children who are bonded labourers in various jobs, domestic workers, street children, child prostitutes, beggars, rag-pickers and the deserted. Of them the girl child is further exploited because of her sex.

How do we protect these children? Laws are there but social awareness about the plight of these children is missing and also ignored. These are the same children who are denied all other facilities with regard to health, education, freedom to choose and participate, and abused by the existing socio-cultural structure of society.

Who is a Child?

According to the Convention on the Rights of a Child "...a child means every human being below the age of 18 years unless, under the law applicable to the child, majority is attained earlier".

(Article 1)

The legal conception of a child varies depending upon the purpose: whether it is for imposing legal disabilities (e.g., in the political rights sphere), for spelling out duties and obligations (e.g., in juvenile justice systems), for affording protection (e.g., from exploitative or hazardous employment), or for establishing eligibility to receive benefits or special services (e.g., health, education and maintenance benefits). Underlying these alternative definitions are also very different conceptions of the child. These include viewing children as a burden which invoke rights to maintenance and support; regarding children as undergoing temporary disabilities making for rights to special treatment and discrimination; treating children as specially vulnerable for ensuring rights of protection; and recognizing children as resources for the country's development, giving rise to rights of nurturing and advancement. Under different economic and socio-cultural circumstances, the child has also been regarded as a commodity, as an insurance, as a source of labour, and as a social burden.

In India too, the definition of a child varies with the purpose. The Census of India treats persons below the age of fourteen as "children". While making use of standard demographic data, social scientists include females in the age group of 15-19 years under the category of the "girl child". According to the Constitution, no child below the age of fourteen years shall be employed to work in any factory or mine or engaged in any other hazardous employment (Article 23). The legal definition of a "child" depends very much upon the specific legislation.

Definition of a Child: Illustrations from the Law in India

Criminal Law	: Nothing is an offence which is done by a child under seven years of age (Section 82).
Indian Penal Code, 1860	: Nothing is an offence which is done by a child above seven years of age under twelve, who has not attained sufficient maturity of understanding to judge the nature and consequence of his conduct on that occasion. (Section 83).
Juvenile Law The Juvenile Justice Act, 1986	: "Juvenile" is a boy who has not attained the age of sixteen years, and a girl who has not attained the age of eighteen years.
Family Law Child Marriage Restraint Act, 1929	: "Child" means a person who, if a male, has not completed twenty-one years of age, and if a female has not completed eighteen years of age.
Labour Laws Apprentices Act, 1951	: A person shall not be qualified to be engaged as an apprentice... unless he is not less than fourteen years of age.
Factories Act, 1948	: No child who has not completed his fourteen years shall be required or allowed to work in any factory.

Mines (Amendment) Act, 1983	: No person below eighteen years of age shall be allowed to work in any mine or part thereof.
The Child Labour (Prohibition and Regulation) Act, 1986	: "Child" means a person who has not completed his fourteen years of age.
Immoral Traffic Prevention Act, 1986	: "Child" means a person who has not yet completed sixteen years.
Indian Penal Code, 1860 (Rape Law)	: "Child" means a person who has not yet completed sixteen years, if she is a wife. Age of consent sixteen years if not wife.

Some Existing Laws related to the Child

I. ***Child Labour***

Factories Act, 1948
Mines Act, 1952
Motor Transport Workers Act, 1957
Plantations Labour Act, 1951
Beedi & Cigar Workers Act, 1966
Apprentices Act, 1961
Minimum Age Convention, 1973
Child Labour Prohibition and Regulation Act, 1986

II. ***Social Laws***

Immoral Traffic Prevention Act, 1986
Child Marriage Restraint Act, 1929
Prevention of Vagrancy and Beggary Act
Children Act, 1960
Indian Penal Code—Rape Law, 1860
Juvenile Justice Act, 1986
Guardians & Wards Act, 1956
Compulsory Free Primary Education under the Directive Principles of State Policy, Article 45
Right against exploitation—Article 24

The Ways to Protect these Children Must be:

1. Recognition of the fact that the socio-cultural structure has marginalised them, we need to promote attitudinal changes among people so that unconstitutional, cultural, traditional factors are challenged and unaccepted and practised.
2. Poverty and ignorance need to be combated through policies that specifically address these issues.
3. Restructuring of development policies so that rural areas are economically developed and poverty alleviation programmes become possible.
4. Free compulsory primary education with necessary infrastructure—buildings, study material, uniforms and food be immediately implemented through legal measures.
5. Child Marriage Restraint Act be changed to Child Marriage Abolition Act and measures for the punishment for those who violate the law be made more stringent.
6. Registration of all marriages to prevent child marriage and false marriages which are one of the means of recruitment into prostitution.
7. Immediate action be made possible in cases of child abuse, assault, rape of children, especially of the marginalised. The law and order machinery be especially trained and advised to take up their cases. A special cell to handle cases of child abuse to be set-up at police stations.
8. What we demand is—complete control of trafficking of children and young women into prostitution; and rehabilitation to those children in prostitution and children of prostitutes, and women, young and old who can be weaned out of this system.
9. Change in existing legislation providing for new laws is a must, along with coordination among all existing laws J.J. Act, IPTA, Police Act, Cr. P.C. and IPC is necessary, especially in their applications.

10. Setting up of more educational boarding schools, vocational training centres, where they can be accommodated along with others so that they are not isolated as criminals carrying a stigma.

11. Activate anganwadi workers, gram panchayat and other rural and grassroots functionaries like schoolteachers, medical workers, police, etc. to take up their job seriously and thus protect the children from harm.

12. Networking of NGOs and relationship with all law and order agencies for suitable joint action.

13. Participation of society in the form of watchdog committees in rural and urban areas to identify people, areas, and families that indulge in the business of forcing children into labour and prostitution, and break the existing laws. Take immediate action with law enforcement agencies against them.

14. Other facilities for health, nutrition, counselling be provided.

15. Role of the media be more sensitive and responsive. Need for general awareness and sensitization programmes for media professionals so that they can evolve healthy media campaigns to sensitize the public.

There is a need for concerted effort to develop a new set of a social norms and cultural practices which will enable equitable distribution of wealth, rural regeneration, eradication of poverty, removal of illiteracy, sex and caste bias and promotion legal reform and law enforcement. Only then can all children be protected and developed as responsible citizens.

20

Protecting Child from Victimisation: Strategies and Innovations

Pradeep Kumar Bhardwaj

Our criminal justice system is tilted in favour of the accused and the real victims of crime have by and large remained out of focus of the welfare agencies, government and judicial system. An overview of the plight of crime victims reveals that while the criminal justice system in west is getting geared unto espousing the cause of crime victims, in India the victims of crime remain neglected at every stage, i.e.—investigation, trial, prosecution and most importantly their own rehabilitation. The victim is perceived merely as an object, a piece of evidence in the conviction of the offender. Our system provides little succour to alleviate the trauma and pathetic living conditions of crime victims.

It is mostly seen that the child victims are the most ignored category. For every horrendous tale of abuse and violence against young children that gets reported in the news columns, there are thousands others who shed silent tears, their cries for help unheard and their pain unnoticed. The increasing incidence of assaults on children, whether physical, emotional or sexual, is symptomatic of the violence that is pervading our society across all sections and classes. Child victimisation may range from the milder cases of neglect, deprivation, verbal or emotional abuse, to the extremes of physical battering, maiming or even appalling sexual crimes like rape and incest. Victimisation of child has often been thought as the sickness of an industrialised and/or developed society. However, recent literature in India, though sparse and frequently subjective, has indicated that we have little to congratulate ourselves. Child victimisation evokes societal responses that are sharp and emotional. We need to consider this phenomenon dispassionately and objectively.

In this article, we attempt to discuss the phenomenon in the light of experience and information gathered by *Pratidhi* in the course of its intervention with victims of child abuse. We begin by discussing the concepts interrelated to child abuse and its various manifestations. Finally, we end by describing some of the issues associated in intervention. Based on the experiences of *Pratidhi*, we feel, some generalisations may be made about possible professional and informed interventions in such cases and the factors which may be borne in mind while doing so.

Clarification, Definition and Categories

Any attempt to define and clarify the concept of child abuse runs into several difficulties. Firstly, the concept has largely been clarified in western contexts where it has been extensively studied. Secondly, there is some lack of clarity and specificity in the use of the term. To some extent, this is because of the multidisciplinary nature of the issue. Consequently, medical writers refer to 'child battering' which focuses on the physical aspects, social workers to 'child neglect' which focuses on the need for intervention, psychiatrists/psychologists to 'child abuse' which connotes emotional aspects of the situation. Quite often, the terms 'child battering', 'child neglect', 'child abuse', 'child maltreatment', 'physical abuse', are used by different authors to refer to the same situation.

At the very outset, let us define 'child maltreatment' since this forms a starting point for our inquiry. Child maltreatment is a generic phrase that covers a whole range of behaviour. "...... It covers all behaviour patterns, whether or not sanctioned by law and custom, which are in some way injurious to the child's health or social, economic, emotional or moral well-being."

Child abuse and neglect comprises a wide range of behaviour distinguished conceptually as well as operationally. For analytical purposes, such behaviour has been categorised under broad categories. It is to be noted that these are not mutually exclusive categories. For example, child prostitution may be categorised as child exploitation as well as child sexual abuse. Some of the broad categories are as follows:

Child Neglect: This occurs when parents or guardians fail to perform their duties and obligations which fall under responsibility. This includes denial of food, shelter, clothing, medical care, education and toilet facilities or total abandonment.

Child Exploitation: This is a form of child abuse which yields some economic benefits to the perpetrator or someone else. Specifically, this occurs when a child is made to engage in economic activities which are harmful to its physical, social, psychological and moral development. This may take the form of employing children as servants, as street beggars, as child prostitutes, as hawkers, as apprentices, etc.

Child Battering: This occurs when, due to any physical abuse or non-accidental injury, the child requires medical attention and treatment. However, it has to be noted that physical punishment, as a disciplinary measure for bad behaviour, is accepted and often encouraged in many cultures.

However, punishment, physical or non-physical, becomes maltreatment when:

- it is too harsh for the child's age, or physical and emotional state;
- it runs against the community's norms and value orientations; and
- it is in any way detrimental to the child's well-being and proper development.

Child Abuse: This occurs when ".... a parent or guardian knowingly misuses a privileged position over the child to commit acts 'of non-economic nature' which are not in tune with the societal norms and which are detrimental to the child's health and well being." At a National Seminar on Child Abuse in India (1998, NIPCCD), the following was offered as a definition:

"Child Abuse and Neglect (CAN) is the intentional, non-accidental injury, maltreatment of children by parents, caretakers, employers or others including those individuals representing governmental/non-governmental bodies, which may lead to temporary or permanent impairment of their physical, mental and psycho-social development, disability or death."

Child abuse can take any of the following forms:

- Physical Abuse,
- Social Abuse,
- Emotional Abuse,
- Drug Abuse,
- Sexual Abuse.

Sexual abuse refers to any sexual act being misuse of the child by any care-taking or family related adult. This includes acts of incest, oral-genital contact, sodomy, molestation, etc. Sexual abuse can be physical, verbal or emotional and includes: fondling, exposing children to adult sexual activity or pornography, having children pose undressed or perform in a sexual fashion, 'peeping' into bathrooms or bedrooms to spy on children and attempting rape.

Thus, it is seen from the discussion above that child abuse and neglect incorporates a wide range of behaviour ranging from simple neglect to sexual abuse and even murder.

It is, thus, obvious that our discussion of child abuse would cover a wide range of behaviour. In view of this wide range, and for operational clarity, we shall focus on sexual abuse of children. However, the importance of inter agency co-operation and role of parents in protecting children has also been discussed. The foregoing discussion has been largely to emphasize that we are aware of other dimensions of child abuse and also to place our specific focus in a wider framework.

Some Facts about Child Sexual Abuse

Mostly child sexual abuse is committed by someone who knows the child. The offender is usually a family member, trusted friend, acquaintance, person who regularly comes into contact with the child or a relative.

Sexual abuse often starts with a long process where harmless touching gradually crosses over the line to fondling. The child may not realize that fondling has become inappropriate.

Physical force is seldom used because the child usually trusts or depends upon the offender. Physical evidence or injuries occur in only a small percentage of child sexual abuse cases.

Children who have been sexually abused feel many different and often overwhelming emotions. These can be put under following expression of feelings:

- Fear,
- Anger,
- Isolation,
- Sadness,
- Guilt,
- Shame,
- Confusion.

Protecting Children

Role of Agencies Involved in Child Protection

This section deals with the role of the agencies and other associated groups in relation to child protection and how their duties and functions should be organised in order to contribute to interagency co-operation for the protection of children. The responsibility for protecting children should not fall entirely to one agency: awareness and appreciation of another agency's role will contribute greatly to collaborative practices.

Social Services

The child protection work of social services departments should be considered in the wider context of all the department's work and more precisely in the context of its child care services. Field workers engaged in child protection work are also involved in a wide range of other child care work and they often work with other client groups. They are aware of the wide child care facilities provided and known to the department and can draw on these in order to provide support and treatment services for children who have been abused. These include day care facilities, residential accommodation and foster homes.

Police

It is usual for the police to dissuade the victim from lodging a report on many grounds. For the reason few cases get reported/ highlighted and the entire vicious circle of non-reporting results in increase of abuse cases. The importance of police action in child abuse cases is such that even if there is no clear scope for prosecution, the process of police action in itself is going to be of great value in deterring offenders.

The police involvement in cases of child abuse stems from their primary responsibility to protect the community and to bring offenders to justice. Their overriding consideration is the welfare of the child. In the spirit of working together, the police focus should determine whether a criminal offence has been committed, to identify the person or persons responsible and to secure the best possible evidence in order that appropriate consideration can be given as to whether criminal proceedings should be instituted. Failure to conduct child abuse investigations in the most effective manner may mean that the best possible protection cannot be provided for a child victim.

The decision whether or not criminal proceedings should be

initiated should be based on three main factors: whether or not there is sufficient substantial evidence to prosecute; whether it is in the public interest that proceedings should be initiated against a particular offender; and whether or not it is in the interests of the child victim that proceedings should be instituted.

The evidential requirement of the criminal courts is proof beyond reasonable doubt that the defendant committed the offence of which he/she stands indicted. The burden of proof rests with the prosecution, i.e., the defendant does not have to prove his innocence. It is usual for the police to decide that criminal proceedings cannot be initiated against a person.

In investigating an allegation of child victimisation the police should normally collect a considerable amount of information. Irrespective of their decision whether or not to institute criminal proceedings, the information they hold may be highly relevant to a decision about a child who may need protection from abuse, and should, where appropriate, be shared with other agencies.

Police/Social Services Consultation

Although in cases of child victimisation both the police and social services nave as their foremost objective the welfare of the child, their primary functions, powers and methods of working are entirely different. Whilst the police should focus on the investigation of alleged offences, the social services are concerned with the welfare of the child and other members of the family.

Difficulties will be encountered in joint inter-agency investigations but these can be minimised by the selection of specialist staff who undergo appropriate inter-agency training. However, it is essential that methods of joint working are established between the two agencies over and above the joint interviewing of child victims. There should be agreed procedures for the joint inter-agency investigation process which ensure that there is adequate planning and full consultation at all stages of any investigation. It is important that those engaged in child victimisation investigation and their supervisors fully understand the responsibilities of both agencies, the powers available to them and the different standards of proof that exist in relation to criminal and civil proceedings. This will assist to remove some of the tensions that can otherwise exist.

Health

All those working in the field of health have a commitment to protect children, and their participation in inter-agency support to social services departments is essential if the interests of children are to be safeguarded. Health professionals are major contributors to the inter-agency care of children which extends beyond the initial referral and assessment, participation in planning and the ongoing support of the child and family. There will always be a need for close co-operation with other agencies, including any other health professionals involved.

Probation Service

Probation officers may become involved in cases of child victimisation as a result either of their responsibility for the supervision of offenders, including those convicted of offences against children, or of their responsibility to the court for the supervision of children. They may be able to identify potential cases and bring in other agencies when, through their work, they become concerned about the safety of a child.

The Education Service

The education service does not constitute an investigation or intervention agency, but has an important role to play at the recognition and referral stage. Because of their day-to-day contact with individual children during school terms, teachers and other school staff are particularly well-placed to observe outward signs of abuse, changes in behaviour or failure to develop. Social workers and counsellors also have important roles because of their concern for the welfare and development of children.

Other Voluntary Organisations

A wide range of voluntary organisations provide services, including telephone helplines, to help parents, guardians under stress and children at risk. Some of these are national, such as

Childline, which provide counselling for children with problems and help children in distress. Authorities should be alert to the opportunities to promote voluntary efforts in their area, and ensure that there is good liaison with voluntary organisations. Staff in these and other voluntary services concerned with children and families can also help by bringing children who are thought to be in need of protection to the attention of the statutory agencies—such as, Juvenile Welfare Board, Department of Social Welfare, etc.

The Community

The community as a whole has a responsibility for the well-being of children. This means that all citizens should remain alert to circumstances in which children may be harmed. Individuals can assist the statutory authorities by bringing cases to their attention. Relatives, friends and neighbours of children are particularly well placed to do so, but they must know what to do if they are concerned, in addition to providing support for the family and children, which may include help with caring for children. They must also be confident, because of the difficult and sensitive nature of the situation, that any information they provide will be treated in a confidential way and used only to protect the interests of children. They should know too that early action on their part is often the best way of helping a family stay together as well as protecting of children.

The availability of self-help groups, telephone helplines and other counselling services, often provided by volunteers, can do much to help parents help themselves or to seek help from others when it is needed. Victim support schemes which are being set up in many areas may be in a position to offer help to young people who have been abused.

Role of Parents

Quite obviously, parents have a major and significant role in the prevention of sexual abuse of children. Their role cannot be balanced by any amount of professional intervention. Quite often, shameful incidents of sexual abuse take place because of parents taking the safety of their children for granted. However, this is not to imply that all incidents of sexual abuse are caused by the carelessness of parents. Such an assumption would lead to harmful feelings of guilt and all that those feelings may entail. Nevertheless, we list out here some elementary measures/responses that parents can adopt to prevent sexual abuse and also to respond in a helpful manner once the child indicates that she has been thus abused.

Sexual abusers can make the child extremely fearful of telling, and only a special effort can help the child to feel safe and talk freely.

As concerned adults, we want to prevent children from sexual abuse, but we cannot always be there to do that. We can, however, teach children about sexual abuse in order to increase their awareness and coping skills. Without frightening children, we can provide them with appropriate safety information and support at every stage of their development. We can provide personal safety information to children in a matter-of-fact way, with other routine safety discussions about fire, water, health, hygiene, etc. Although even the best educated child cannot always avoid sexual abuse, children who are well-prepared will be more likely to tell you if abuse has occurred. This is a child's best defence.

In this article, we have attempted to provide some basic information and leads for intervention. However, our focus here has not stressed professional intervention but rather intervention/ response by parents, state agencies and voluntary sectors.

References

Ackley, Dana C.: "A brief overview of child abuse"; *Social Casework*, Jan. 1997, pp. 21-24.

NIPCCD: *Report of National Seminar on Child Abuse in India*; New Delhi, NIPCCD, 1998.

Deblinger, E and Heflin, AH: *Treating Sexually Abused Children and Their Non-offending Parents*; New Delhi, Sage Publishing House, 1996.

Late Michigan S.E.: *Report on Sexual Abuse of Children*; Department of Social Work, Delhi University.

Wolfe, David A.: *Child Abuse: Implications for Child Development and Psychopathology;* New Delhi, Sage, Publishing House, 1987.

Home Office, Deptt. of Health, Department of Education and Science, Welsh Office: *Working Together—A Guide to arrangements for Co-operation for the Protection of Children from Abuse.* London, HMSO, 1991.

Hallet, C. and Stevenson, O.: *Child Abuse: Aspects of Interpersonal Cooperation;* London, George Allen and Unwin, 1980.

Tayley, Brain (Ed.): *Perspectives on Paedophilia;* (London, Batsford, 1981).

Bhan, Sushila: *Child Abuse: An Annotated Bibliography;* New Delhi, Northern, 1991.

21

Protecting Institutionalized Child from Victimisation: Strategies and Innovations

Sneh Lata Tandon

The future of any nation is largely determined by the parameters on how its children grow and develop. The National Policy for Children, 1974 envisages special facilities for socially handicapped children and for providing protection to children who are victims of neglect, cruelty, and exploitation. The Policy also recognizes the importance of family, neighbourhood, and community environment and states that efforts be directed towards strengthening of family ties. The UN Convention also mentions several rights of the children within the context of the family. Protection of Rights of the Children is an adult concern because children are not in a position to protect their rights themselves. The family no doubt is an important institution for protecting their rights. Under normal circumstances, family is the best institution for proper nurture of the child. However, when there is a conflict between the interests of the child and the parents that often result in abusive situations, then the welfare of the child becomes a matter of paramount consideration with the state. Accordingly the Juvenile Justice Act, 1986 was designed for the care, protection, development, and rehabilitation of the neglected and the delinquent juveniles. This responsibility, therefore, has been entrusted to the state. Institutions for their welfare were thus, established in various states for boys upto the age of 16 years and for girls upto the age of 18 years.

Categories of Children Who Come Into Care

According to the Juvenile Justice Act, 1986, the following categories of children come into institutional care. Children who have come in conflict with law and children who are considered as neglected. The neglected category covers a wide spectrum of children, i.e., the destitute, the abandoned, the orphaned, those abused either outside or within the family, children on the streets irrespective of whether or not they are working or are found begging, children found in vulnerable situations, and also destitute children who are mentally and physically handicapped. The main reason for the children for being in such situations is primarily their poverty.

Sondhi (1989) conducted a study to delineate the psycho-social factors influencing street children working as porters at the New Delhi railway station. A sample of 46 boys in the age group of 9-14 years was taken. Striking facts were revealed about their life on the streets. Life for children on the streets was fraught with physical and social insecurity. They not only experienced a harsh, rejecting and uncaring environment but were also uncertain of their future. They did not have any place to keep either their belongings or the money they could save from their earnings. They also worked under constant fear of being picked up by the police for being lodged in remand/observation home. The boys stated that they had left their homes because of variety of traumatic experiences at home. Most of the boys reported cruelty, extreme forms of physical punishment and parental neglect, which led them to severe the emotional bond with their parents. Data on child abuse and neglect is scarce but evidences suggest that it is a widespread phenomenon within families.

Although the institutions are established with the objectives of providing care, protection, and development to those children who are deprived of these in the family settings, the experiences of the children exposed to institutions set-up under the Juvenile Justice System are, however, very different. These highlight not only the ineffectiveness of the system, but also the discrimination, abuse and neglect that many a time occurs in these institutions. Ranga* aged 13 years reported that he was mercilessly beaten and mentally tortured. He was identified as a thief for ragpicking and both the police and the remand home staff treated him extremely shabbily for days together while he was there. "The food was bad, they made us bathe in cold water. I fell sick but they did not give me any medical care." It has been observed that very often, because of administrative inadequacies the individual needs of the children are either postponed or completely ignored. Situations such as non-availability of institutional vehicle; reluctance to avail of the local transport for taking the child to the hospital, inadequacy of staff, the caretaker entrusted with the responsibility being on leave, some function at the institution, or a visit of some dignitary, etc. many a time may result in depriving the child from getting immediate medical care. Another boy stated that "they would make all of us sleep in the same room where the older boys would beat the younger ones and indulge in dirty acts with them." Gopal* aged 15 years, caught while working at the railway station stated his experience as follows: "Behaviour of the staff was very bad. They used to beat up children. There were threats of sexual abuse and life threatening responses if anyone thought of running away." Iqbal* aged eight years reported that the staff appointed the older boys as their leaders and they were used to discipline the newcomers and the younger children. These older boys "harassed us and exploited us by taking away our belongings and even bargained on our food if we wanted to be spared of the punishment." The younger children had to part away a portion of their food if they were to be spared of beating by the older boys. It was also stated that the watchmen/caretakers bartered drugs and cigarettes for sexual favours. There is also a lot of sexual abuse between the older boys and the younger children. Sujeet* aged 10 years while reporting on the quality and quantity of food provided in the juvenile homes stated "In the children's jail they did not feed us properly. The pulses was watery, same vegetable was served for days together, and even the quantity served was insufficient especially for the older boys." The food was not given according to the age and requirement of the child. The result was that either the younger children wasted the food or they bargained it with the older boys. The older boys would also snatch the food from the younger lot that would often lead to fights, and some children even died in such situations.

Reactions of the inmates of a juvenile home in Delhi was reported in the *Times of India* dated 19 November 1999, p. 2. A child from Bihar stated that "there is extreme poverty in my house. Why do you have to send me back to my family? Does the government have any plans to look after my needs after sending me home?" Another boy narrated his experience with the police as follows "I used to work at the railway station and one day a policeman forcibly took me to the police station and asked me to clean up the place. After I had finished the work, they did not give me any thing. On the contrary, they took away whatever little money, I had earned that day."

In at least one instance, the author was shocked to note that the Superintendent of the 'home' made the children stand naked in a row while the doctor was examining them for scabies. This was in clear violation of the right to privacy and dignity. The superintendent, however, justified his action stating that checking the children individually takes too long and very often, some children are missed out.

Whilst institutional care was supposed to be used as a last measure, in the absence of suitable alternatives, it has become the main recourse of action. Further, children are being indiscriminately picked up and placed in such Homes without due regard to their circumstances. In such situations questions regarding the appropriateness of the current system must be asked. Is the approach of picking up children and placing them in institutions an appropriate strategy to respond to the needs of children and families living in poverty? Are these actions really in the best interest of the child? Considering the poor conditions and the exploitative situations prevailing even in the institutions in which the children are placed, one must examine if this is really a better alternative to the life on streets, or with their families? Far from being placed in an alternative setting which should be conducive to their care, protection, growth and development, these children feel that they are being incarcerated in jails where they are vulnerable to further neglect, and are prone to further physical, emotional, and sexual abuse. Developmental needs are also not ensured and their freedom of movement, expression and thought are curtailed. Further, once the child has been institutionalised, the whole issue of re-integration into the mainstream of the society, which needs to be addressed, is often sidelined and the net result is that the children keep rotating from one institution to another. After attaining the maximum permissible age, they are released from the juvenile home. No rehabilitation programmes are planned by the institutional staff for their re-integration into the mainstream of society. The juveniles on release having no other place to go, are back on the streets and are again exposed to the criminogenic and exploitative situations which force them to graduate into the life of a criminal even in adulthood. This is how many children of yesteryears have been inducted into the criminal justice system.

Children's Rights Perspective

Government of India became a signatory to the UN Convention on the Rights of the Child in 1992. It, therefore, accepted the obligation of bringing all state laws and policies in line with the main principles of children's rights namely, the right to survival, right to development, right to protection, and right to participation.

It is baffling to note that to-date, when we are advocating for protecting the rights of the child, the children in many institutions are still being addressed by their badge/entry numbers like *Billa No. x, y, z*. It may be pointed out that the right to survival includes not only right to life, health, nutrition, and adequate standards of living but also the right to a name and nationality.The institutional staff, especially, the caretakers consider these children as 'Naali Ka Keeda' (worms of the gutter) and flog them on petty issues, like, not telling their names, or their home addresses. This practice is in clear violation of the right to life and health of the child. (Some of these observations are based on eyewitness account of the author during field placements in children's institutions and during visits to such institutions for supervising students placed there).

Assuring children of the right to protection implies safeguarding them against all forms of exploitation, abuse, inhuman or degrading treatment, and neglect including the right to special protection in situations of emergency and armed conflicts. The extreme cases are where children are being used instrumentally for the profit of others and where conditions are hazardous for their health, e.g., child prostitutes, child labour, street children, etc. These children are abused, and exploited irrespective of whether they are in family settings, or on the streets, or in institutional set-up, because they are weak, voiceless and are dependent on adults. The question, therefore, arises as to who will protect their rights.

Institutional programmes do not even take adequate measures for ensuring the basic needs of the children. The rights to development of the children are not concerned only with protection, food, health, affection, and security. It is also concerned with providing opportunities for interaction that stimulates, learning through exploration, and discovery in an environment that is safe and nurturing. It is unfortunate that children's institutions are set-up without giving adequate thought to the layout and the architecture of the building that needs to be child friendly. Personnel are appointed without assessing their mental ability and capability to work with children. The love, affection and understanding which the children require calls for plenty of energy and patience on the part of the staff, which is rarely forthcoming. No thought is given to the quality of training required for the staff. Further, the emphasis on rehabilitation programmes is also lacking The result is that in these institutions interaction, stimulation and learning through exploration are un-thinkable.

Right to participation includes respect for views of the children, i.e., freedom of (expression, access to appropriate information, freedom of thought, conscience and religion. Unfortunately, children in institutions are deprived of even this right of theirs. They neither are involved in programme planning nor are their views invited on even simple matters like the colour or design of clothes meant for them, or in working out the menu for their meals. I recall one non-governmental institution that had made a very rigid programme for the children that was both impractical as well as impossible to execute. Only one hour was kept for their daily chores of toilet and bathing without having due regard to the fact that for two hundred children there were just four toilets and two bathrooms. Further, no time was provided for their recreation. Communication in institutions is always from top to bottom. The children were, therefore, not even given the opportunity for expressing their views regarding their basic problems and on the contrary were punished for not being able to follow the programme chalked out for them by the agency staff's.

There are two possible ways of solving such situations: (1) by enabling citizens to act as better spokespersons for children; and (2) by encouraging the children themselves to voice their concerns and allow them to participate actively in programmes designed to improve their own well-being. In India, participation of children in decision-making is relatively a new concept. It has to be recognized and accepted that children also have ideas and these need to be heeded, nurtured, and given space particularly regarding matters that concern them. (Ref.: Rights and Opportunities: The Situation of Children and Women in India, UNICEF, New Delhi, 1998).

Clearly, rights cannot be fulfilled through government actions alone. Government's role is important in setting standards, raising public awareness and in providing vision of what values and standards should be adopted as norms in the society. There is need for other parts of the civil society to be involved in reaching out to groups that have been outside the reach of conventional programmes, such as, adolescents, youth, etc.

In some states *Shishu* or *Bal Panchayats* have been established, inviting children representatives to debate, discuss and advise on how their own groups can respond better to the needs of the poor communities. In 24 Parganas, West Bengal a *shishu* panchayat carried out community surveys in an entire block, identifying weaknesses in government services and supplies of water, health care, education and general responsiveness to the people's needs. The adult panchayat deliberated on the suggestions of the *shishu* panchayats and with their collaboration they are now carrying out improvements in the government programmes. The CRC recognises the right to involvement of children in decisions affecting their lives according to their age, maturity and capabilities. Thus a rights approach obliges the state to respect, protect, facilitate and fulfil the rights of all children by adopting an approach that is both participatory and universal. This should be adopted in institutional care as well. Creative ways of communicating with children and involving them in programme planning and implementation should also be thought of.

In partnerships with NGO's and community groups, one of the areas of greatest potential is the involvement of adolescents, both boys and girls not only as beneficiaries but also as active participants in development. The outreach of the Nehru Yuvak Kendras (NYK), National Service Scheme (NSS), Scouts and

Guides, and National Volunteers Service (NVS) is unique and offers untapped opportunities for mobilisation in support of community development as well as empowerment of the young people so involved. The process of decentralisation of planning and implementation of national programmes and their adoption at the local level taking into account the ground realities are critical to the success of developmental efforts and for the realisation of the rights of every child.

Strategies and Innovations in Institutional Care

One important question that is often debated is whether or not the state should hand over all the institutions to the NGO's to run them. It is often believed/contented that the non-governmental organisations do a better job because of greater flexibility, commitment and motivation, which many a time is lacking in government run institutions. Undoubtedly, the NGO's can be made partners with the government in providing institutional care and can play a monitoring role but not at the cost of government abdicating its responsibility altogether. The principles enshrined in the Constitution and the International Conventions and covenants make the state responsible to ensure fulfilment of human rights. What is required is to make institutions manageable. Instead of one large institution, it may be more viable to have smaller set-ups similar to the night shelters developed for the street children. Such centres should preferably be established in each Municipal Ward. In order to improve the working environment of the existing institutions consideration of the following aspects are essential:

(1) Classification of inmates on the basis of age and the category of problem, i.e., destitute, orphan, handicapped, etc., should be made and programmes for them should be worked out accordingly.

(2) Periodic review of cases regarding their needs and progress in the areas of intervention.

(3) Involvement of children in the decision making with regard to especially those activities that directly concern them, like their daily routine, food, leisure time activities, discipline, and grievance committees, etc.

(4) Visitors Boards, comprising of three persons with a background in child psychology and voluntary work as per the provisions of the Juvenile Justice Act, 1986 should be made mandatory and functional. These boards should be responsible for making surprise checks periodically and must take appropriate action at the desired levels.

(5) It was observed that when the Juvenile Welfare Board had people with background in child psychology the admission of children was streamlined, the board members were approachable, and a working relationship could be established with them. The children also could express their problems with ease.

(6) The institutions should follow an open door policy and allow volunteers in the institutions to interact with the children.

(7) The provision of inducting two social workers, preferably having a background in the rights of the child, on the Advisory Board should be immediately executed.

(8) Release on license to maintain family contact should be resorted to more often. I recall a superintendent refusing the release of a child during Ganesh Puja, (this being his main festival) stating that the boy could not be trusted. How can one be sure whether he would come back after the license period was over? He in fact went to the extent of saying, "I don't care if he runs away from the institution because that will not be entirely my responsibility. I will just report the matter to the police." This kind of myopic and rigid attitude on the part of the institutional heads is unwarranted, needs review, and must be checked.

(9) Closer co-operation between different arms of the state and the civil society such as the advocates of child rights, lawyers,

doctors, youth workers, etc. can help in ensuring that the best interests of the child are kept paramount.

(10) It should be made mandatory for the magistrates of the juvenile court/board to record in their judgement the reasons for not considering non-institutional programme while placing a child in an institution. This would check indiscriminate placement of children in institutions.

Strengthening of Non-Institutional Programme

Sabnis (1996) clearly brought out that "in the name of protection and welfare the institutionalised children are tossed from the police to courts/boards and institutions. The saddest part is that these children are seldom motivated or mentally prepared to go back to their real homes Thus the enforcement of legal and administrative provisions prove very expensive without being productive of positive durable results". He opines that protection does not mean merely providing food, clothing, and shelter. These are no doubt important for their physical and mental development but protection must embrace fostering a congenial home environment. It must consist of social infrastructure for building up and strengthening the child's intellectual, moral, and emotional fibre.

There is an urgent need to develop alternatives to institutional care in order to prevent those children who get into institutions due to poverty and destitution. Similarly, children who are in exploitative situations such as street and working children should be encouraged and motivated at an early stage towards non-institutional arrangements.

Early Diversion Programmes

The Minimum Standard Rules for Juvenile Justice lays stress on diversion and discretion at the initial stages so as to avoid bringing juveniles into the criminal justice system. Non-institutional arrangements such as training-cum-production centres, Drop in shelters, Foster care, Sponsorship programmes, Night shelters, Crisis Counselling, Child Help Line, etc. are some such programmes that have been experimented and found effective. In order to make the children into responsible citizens and for avoiding the induction of our children into the criminal justice system at all, such non-institutional programmes need to be expanded and strengthened.

Preventive Programmes

Importance should be stressed on preventive services whereby the basic developmental needs of the individual child could be ensured and the capacity for self-development, such as, sense of discipline, hard work, consistency in personal conduct, etc. be enhanced which no child welfare legislation *per se* can ever achieve. It is well known that prevention is always better than cure. Programmes like youth clubs/groups, mahila mandals, hobby centres, recreation and cultural outlets, balwadis, anganwadis, creches, school counsellors/social workers, child guidance clinics, juvenile service bureau, career and marriage counselling, community outreach programmes, etc. are some of the programmes which have proven to be useful in preventing the individuals from going hey-wire and astray. Such programmes, therefore, need to be strengthened and expanded. There is also the need to develop, innovate and experiment with newer programmes that are preventive in nature. Working partnerships between local people and government as well as non-governmental organisations should be established with a view to identify risk factors and take appropriate protective steps. Understanding and identifying risk factors that place children in difficult and exploitative circumstances would help the neighbourhood to focus on what should be done to prevent the problems and will help in the development and encouragement of positive behaviour and in providing and ensuring timely help for speedy, orderly, and balanced physical, mental and intellectual development of the children. The preventive plan will have to be worked out and implemented in close collaboration with other governmental and local agencies concerned with education, social welfare, housing, urban and rural development, and public health. Each of these agencies shall need to draw their own plans for upgrading the facilities for the welfare of the general population. The perspective plan for child welfare must be dovetailed into and given a proper place and high priority in each of the sectoral plans.

Another important development has been that UNICEF has drafted a Children's Code Bill 1999. The draft Bill recommends basic health facilities, right against exploitation, particularly child abuse, trafficking and child labour, free education for all children below the age of 14 years and these should be made mandatory. The Bill also recommends punishment for those parents who do not allow their children to avail of these facilities. Further, the Bill provides for the constitution of a National Commission and the State Commissions for children; setting up of new courts specially for children, and redesigning of the already existing family courts as children's courts. These recommendations should be implemented at the earliest (Aditya Kant, Delhi Times, *The Times of India*, 23 November 1999, p.1).

The above discussion clearly brings out that the children are being victimized in the institutions also. The objective of institutionalization was to provide protection to those children who were found in abusive situations either in their homes or while on the streets. The institutions in their present form, however, have failed in protecting them from abusive situations. It is, therefore, our prime responsibility to revamp our existing institutional provisions and programmes and strengthen the non-institutional programmes for protecting the interests of the vulnerable children and to protect their rights in particular.

References

Aditya Kant, *Delhi Times, The Times of India, 1999,* November 23, p. 1.

Sabnis, M.S. 1996, *Juvenile Justice and Juvenile Correction—Pride and Prudence,* Somaiya Publications Pvt. Ltd., Bombay.

Sondhi, P. 1989, Psychological Profile of Street Children, Unpublished Masters Dissertation, University of Delhi, Delhi.

The Times of India, 1999, November 19, p. 2.

22

A Study on the Victimisation of Children of Alcoholic Parents

Gia Coombes • Prasanna Poornachandra

Despite newer knowledge about child development we seem to have made little progress in applying our minds to the task of understanding the victimisation of children affected by their parents' behavioural problems due to alcohol abuse.

Since World War II social scientists have been conceptualising child development based on the nature of the parent-child relationship. This relationship often called 'bonding' is a vital aspect in child development, one that develops subsequent relationships with family members and ultimately the world at large. Since the child, after birth, is dependent on the parents for a long period of time there evolves a biological repertoire of behaviours, to 'connect' physically, emotionally and psychologically with parents. The connection is not only oral, it is tactile, olfactory, visual and auditory as well (Bowlby, 1958). A child is stimulated by, shaped by, and focused on the parent from the first moments of life. Most of the parents care for their children adequately enough so that children survive. When either one or both the parents become children an alcoholic stupor, for various reasons, there occurs a failure or aberration in the normal parent-child bond and the consequent development of psychological, emotional and behavioural problems i⁻ the child. Alcoholism is a 'family disease', which affects not only the user but also every member of his or her family. Alcoholics do not drink or recover in isolation. When one person in a family develops alcoholism, the others react to it often with confusion, fear, despair and blame. Alcohol disrupts the consistency and predictability, which should be present in every family. The children, especially, are 'trapped' and left emotionally and situationally helpless. This study attempts to understand and evaluate the intensity and effect of these problems in a growing child.

The Webster's New Dictionary, defines alcoholism as "the habitual excessive drinking of alcoholic liquor, or a resulting diseased condition".

Children of alcoholics face special problems as a result of living in a home disrupted by alcohol problems. No statistical estimations are available on children of alcoholic parents in India. In the U.S. it is estimated that seven million children out of the total 28 million under the age of 18 years, live in households with at least one alcoholic parent (Prevention Resource Guide: Children of Alcoholics, 1991).

A child loses his childhood when he lives with an alcoholic parent. To others, he looks like any other child, dresses like any other child does, walks like any other child, until they get close enough to notice the edge of sadness in his eyes, or the worried look on his brow. He lives life from the standpoint of a victim.

The Study

The study was conducted in the city of Chennai. The sample consisted of 28 children of both sexes chosen using purposive sampling technique. The sample consisted of just 25 per cent males and seventy per cent females in the age group of 11-13 years (25 per cent), and 14-16 years, (68 per cent). Two schools from the North and South of Chennai were chosen for the study. The teachers in these two schools were interviewed initially and asked to identify the children who belong to families with alcoholic parents. An interview schedule formed the tool of the study, which was administered to the children independently. The collected data was analysed using appropriate statistical techniques. The results are presented along with the discussion.

Result and Discussion

The analysis of the data clearly indicates the various aspects of the victimisation of children of alcoholic parents. The effect of these victimisations on the life of the child has been discussed supported by the results.

Effect of Parental Alcoholism on the Parent-Child Relationship

Majority of the children have expressed their love to spend time with their families (80 per cent). Most of them have meals often along with other members of the family (71.4 per cent). The remaining children avoid having meals along with the family. This is probably due to the fact that they do not want to face the alcoholic parent. Nearly half (46.4 per cent) of the children make their own decisions normally and the remaining depend on their parents. Majority of the parents do not go to the movies (64.3 per cent), clubs (100 per cent), or to parties (42.9 per cent).

Research studies show that alcoholic fathers are sometimes very loving and warm. They are caring and interested and promise to get the children all that they want. But, once he is under the influence of alcohol, the same father comes home late, getting the child worried, picks up quarrels and forgets the promises he's made. The parent's behaviour teaches the child that anger means violence, promises can be made but not necessarily kept and creates a dilemma as to what love is all about. They have problems in building positive relationships. In order to cope with these problems the child resorts to a behaviour different from other children.

Majority of the fathers are working in private firms (39.3 per cent) or run their own business (21.4 per cent). More than half of the mothers are housewives (56.7 per cent). A small percentage of mothers work in private firms.

Contrary to other research findings that such children usually deny the fact that their parents abuse alcohol, 92.9 per cent of the children agreed to alcohol abuse by their parents. Majority of the parents have been alcohol users for more than 5 years (75 per cent). The major reason for the abuse is bad company (28.6 per cent) and extra-marital affairs (21.4 per cent) of their parent/s. The children (60.7 per cent) agree that the abuse of alcohol by the parents making their home life unhappy. Compared with non-alcoholic families, research has shown that, alcoholic families demonstrate poorer problem-solving abilities within the family. This increases conflicts in alcoholic families. Further based on clinical observations and preliminary research a relationship between parental alcoholism and child abuse is indicated in a large proportion of child abuse families.

Effect of Parental Alcoholism on the Children's Education

Majority of the children attend school regularly (82.1 per cent) and like going to school (93 per cent). The main reasons for not attending school are ill-health (7 per cent) and not feeling good enough to attend school (7 per cent). Majority of the children are average (53.6 per cent) or below average (36.7 per cent) in their studies. The teachers while identifying the children for the study also stated that these children have a poor academic record. More than half of the sample revealed that even while at school they think and worry about their parents. This affects their concentration in class. Majority of the children (75 per cent) stares blankly at the black-board when the classes are in progress. Surprisingly, 68 per cent of the children get their uniforms ready for school and pack their school bags all by themselves (85.7 per cent). The aspect of learning to be independent is evident here. A small percentage (6.7 per cent) of the children get academic help from their fathers. The rest of them either get help from their mothers (28 per cent) or study by themselves (64.3 per cent). Teachers of these children reported that most of these children are hyperactive and indulge in behaviour that seeks attention and provokes anger. They also have difficulty in remembering and completing their schoolwork.

A child's personality and reaction to parental alcohol dependence is unique. One child may fail in class but another may, to escape stress, study hard for perfect grades. In this sample all the children are probably affected in a negative way, in that they fair not too well in their studies. Informal discussions with the children revealed that they feel they will be failures even if they do well academically. They often do not view themselves successful.

Psychosomatic Effects of Parental Alcoholism on the Child

Children of alcoholic parents are known to experience greater physical and mental health problems than children of non-alcoholic parents. In this study 42 per cent of the children fall sick often. Further, children of alcoholics have physical problems like headaches (33.3 per cent), tiredness (35.7 per cent) and stomach ulcers (16.7 per cent), although no specific illnesses are detected. They do not have nausea or enuresis as some children do. They also do not have any problems to sleep or symptoms of asthma. A quarter of the sample have sensory problems related to noise, bright lights, heat and cold more often than other children.

Effect of Parental Alcoholism on the Child's Behaviour

A good portion (28.6 per cent) of the children have taken up the household chores and duties that the alcoholic parents performed. Some young children from alcoholic families are known to become exceedingly responsible, taking on parental roles towards their siblings and others. Responsible children usually take over the responsibilities of their parents. These children provide stability in the family and makes life easier for the parents by looking after their siblings. They are independent, self-reliant and capable of achievements. They gain an 'early maturity' out of a need for survival.

Nearly fifteen per cent of the children have tried alcohol at some stage in their lives. Nearly ninety per cent of them consume alcohol rarely. There is a strong evidence that alcoholism tends to run in families. Children of alcoholics are more at risk for alcoholism than children of non-alcoholics.

Unlike results obtained from other studies, the children maintain close friends outside the school (64.3 per cent) and also move well with their schoolmates (85.7 per cent). They do not withdraw from their friends because of embarrassment and shame over the parent's drinking habit. Less than-half (42.9 per cent) of the children engaged in frequent fights with the other children. These children probably get irritated easily or show their anger or resentment on the parent by engaging in fights.

The children of alcoholic families generally feel that they are responsible for their parent's alcoholism. They need to recognise that drinking causes their parent's strange and unpredictable behaviour. In this study a majority of them (67.9 per cent) do not feel that they are in any way responsible for their parent's behaviour.

A lot of them (67.9 per cent) have not made any attempt to stop their parent from using alcohol. This is either because they are too young to make this move or that the parent's behaviour frightens them.

In spite of the parent being an alcoholic the children wish to look upon him/her as a role model in their lives (57.1 per cent). Children are not born with standards of evaluating behaviour. They are unable to decide what is right and wrong. When a parent under the influence of alcohol behaves in a certain way, the child 'copies' the behaviour of his/her parent. Even while at play these children act the way the parent behaves. There are also chances that they will grow up to be alcoholics and resort to the behaviour as that of the parent, for example, physical abuse of spouse and children, verbal abuse, lying and cheating, etc.

Psychological Effects of Parental Alcoholism on the Children

Studies reveal that the family members of alcoholics-including children—are high-risk candidates for chronic depression, psychosomatic illness, social aggression, emotional detachment, isolation and suicide.

The children of alcoholics are isolated. They learn at an early age never to talk about what goes on in their homes. They are hence likely to develop emotional and psychological problems. Majority of the children in this study, that is 83.3 per cent, have low self-esteem and 71.4 per cent have high level of aggression. Self-esteemed was measured using the Rosenberg Self-esteem Scale (1965). The scale aims at gathering information on self-opinion, worthiness, successfulness and self-respect. A scale to measure aggression was constructed by the researcher. Items for aggression instincts to kill, cause injury, take revenge, to fight, blame others for things, etc. Children with low self-esteem have a negative self-image and poor self-concept. They do not believe in themselves or others and feels that they have nobody to depend on. No matter what effort they put in they feel it is depreciated.

Conclusion and Recommendations

The disease called 'Alcoholism' can rob a child of his childhood and destroy the opportunities he might have to a bright future. Children can be protected from many problems associated with the growing up in an alcoholic family. If healthy family rituals or traditions such as vacations, meal times, holidays, are highly valued and maintained and the active alcoholic is confronted with his or her problems, the child can be protected from many consequences of parental alcoholism. Efforts should be taken to improve the self-esteemed of identified child. It is sometimes possible to identify child of alcoholic parent and provide intervention services. If the parent is receiving treatment, preventive services such as monitoring can be provided for the child through family counselling. Prevention activities can include information on alcoholism and resources so that assistance can be given to children of alcoholic parents through schools or community agencies. Any programme which aims at prevention of alcoholism should include parents as their target group. Educating and creating awareness about effective parenting would help develop a healthy and positive parent-child relationship. This would pave the way for a child's trouble free, addiction free future.

References

Ministry of Welfare, Government of India, New Delhi, 1989, Alcoholism and Drug Dependency—The Professional's Master Guide.

Nastasi, Bonnie K. and DeZolt, Denise M, 1994, School Interventions of Children of Alcoholics Addictions, ISBN.

Prevention Resource Guide: Children of Alcoholics, 1991.

23

Child Refugees—Socio-Psychological Aspects of Their Victimisation

K. Chockalingam • Prasanna • Poornachandra • R. Hema

Introduction

The previous century has produced the largest number of refugees ever in world history. There are in the world today around 15 million people, two-thirds of whom are children, who have fled their homes and are now living in exile. Behind this abstract figure lies an immeasurable history of indiscriminate sufferings. The past decade has witnesses a series of civil wars and communal conflicts in which masses of people have been forced to flee for their lives—examples are Burundi, Chechnya, Columbia, Liberia, Rwanda and Sri Lanka.

For many people who are confronted with threats to their lives and liberty, fleeing to another country is the only way in which they can find safety. Sadly, it is becoming increasingly difficult for refugees to find a place of safety beyond the borders of their homeland. Confronted with pressing domestic problems and declining international support, a growing number of countries have closed their borders to the impending large-scale refugee influxes. Moreover, in many parts of the world, people who have taken refuge in another country have been harassed, attacked and even forced to go home against their will.

The use of children as tools of war, where they are manipulated and coerced into being unwitting and unwilling perpetrators of the war's inevitable atrocities and inhumanities, is therefore as pernicious as it is cynical. Mass exodus is too often synonymous with a high number of unaccompanied children. Most are not orphans, but have been separated from their parents during conflict or migration. The disintegration of girls particularly, leaves them vulnerable to violence, intimidation and sexual abuse. The children are vulnerable at every stage of their migration—while fleeing a war-zone they risk being raped, physically abused by the soldiers and starved. On arrival at the camps, they risk being sexually exploited by the local security or other refugees. Further, refugees are packed together in refugee camps without hope for their future. Many refugees are worse than the poor of the Third World; aside from lacking proper housing and sufficient food, the refugees, having left their homes, are even more dependent on the outside world. The vast majority of children come from and live in the world's poorest countries and it is their plight that forms the focus of this study.

The United Nations Convention on the Rights of the Child (1989) reaffirms the fundamental place of the family in society, and recognizes that the child should be brought up in the spirit of the ideals in the UN Charter, in particular, peace, dignity, tolerance, freedom and equality. The United Nations High Commissioner for Refugees (UNHCR) was setup to protect refugees. The UNHCR tries to ensure that no refugee is returned involuntarily to a country where he or she has reason to fear persecution.

The victimisation of refugee children is hardly a recent phenomenon. But as we move into the 21st century, knowing the world's desire to protect children, must we accept as inevitable the chronic and escalating pressure of refugee children?

The main aim of this study is mainly to provide a basis for understanding the victimisation faced by the refugee children and not to point to the faults or other aspects of refugee relief efforts by the government, international bodies or NGOs.

The Study

The study examines the various socio-psychological aspects of victimisation of the child refugees. The sample consists of Sri Lankan children of various age groups who live in the refugee camps of Tamil Nadu. The children (N=31), of both sexes, were chosen using purposive sampling technique from three different camps each consisting of refugees from three different districts of Sri Lanka. The sample chosen were individuals ranging from 10-21 years.

An interview schedule formed the tool of the study to gather relevant data. The data obtained was analysed and is being discussed below, along with the results. Unstructured interviews were administered on all the children who have been victimised as young children at the time of migration and who were chosen for the study. Further, for a better understanding of the situation of child victimisation among refugee children, the heads of the camps from among the refugees, social workers and psychologists from NGOs who work with those children on a voluntary basis, were also interviewed.

A tragic fallout of the ethnic conflict has been the cause of the uprooting of its population with external and internal ramifications. The geographical contiguity and ethnic bonds with Tamil Nadu makes it an attractive asylum at the time of crisis.

It appears from this study that the families lived a fairly normal lives, until the situation arrived where they had to leave their homes and flee for two reasons, one is immediate safety to life and the other is to protect their children from joining the militant groups or the armed forces. In the recent years, more children and youth bear arms in internal armed conflict and violent strife than ever before. When the conflict drags on for years or even decades, the root causes, such as poverty or repression, are accelerated, galvanising civilian populations for recruitment into armed groups.

Any conflict has its effect on children. It leaves children and youths orphaned, displaced or responsible as head of households when either one or both the parents are killed or are away at war. Schools, which occupy most of the time in a growing child's life, are either closed for indefinite periods of time, or are destroyed. Their agricultural lands are destroyed. Relatives, neighbours and friends are injured killed or have fled. Such youths are at risk and become receptive to ideological propaganda. Instances of children and youths having been coerced into joining government and armed forces in Burma (now Myanmar), Ethiopia, Angola, Sudan and Sri Lanka have been well documented (Child Soldiers: The Role of Children in Armed Conflicts, A Study on Behalf of the Henry Dunant Institute, Geneva, 1994). In this study, a large majority of the sample (81.3 per cent) have not been forced or coerced to join the forces. This is probably because they have not been direct victims (74.2 per cent) the war and have fled before they were attacked.

Therefore, Post Traumatic Stress Disorders (PTSD) symptoms like cognitive symptoms such as confusion in thinking, difficulty in making decisions and disorientation; physical symptoms such as excessive sweating, dizzy spells, increased heart rate, high blood pressure and rapid breathing that may be found in refugees of other countries are unfound in a majority of the children.

It is interesting to note that emotional (anger, shock, grief, etc.) and behavioural symptoms (changes in food habits, withdrawal from others, prolonged silence, etc.) were also non-existent in these children. The grown up children and youths while relating their experiences revealed that they had to cross dead bodies, some lying just open and mutilated parts of bodies, to get to school. Some of the boys had severe illnesses after seeing mutilated bodies and have not been able to attend school for days. An interesting phenomenon is that, while on their way to school, in groups mostly, when they heard grenades or bombs they laid down flat wherever they were and after the effect just kept moving as if nothing has happened. This shows the effect of their prolonged exposure to war ever since birth.

The families seem to have been financially stable (87.1 per cent) with own house (45.2 per cent), agricultural land (53.1 per cent) and two wheeler or cycle. Majority of them (48.4 per cent) have just left the land and fled, while the remaining have either sold their property (22.6 per cent) or left it in someone else's custody (9.4 per cent).

Impact of Victimisation During Migration

The call for migration comes either when their village or colony is going to be attacked by the armed forces or when they are warned to vacate the village by the forces to form a war-base.

Impact of Victimisation After Migration

On reaching the host country, the families are at first kept in a single camp and thereafter moved to different camps based on the district to which they belong.

The host government provides cash (depending upon the size of the family) and also basic provisions like rice, kerosene, sugar and dal. They are permitted to take up employment, a facility incidentally denied to the Chakma refugees. In some instances the family income is supplemented by funds from relatives abroad. Restrictions on their movements have been considerably relaxed in the recent years. They have been included in the category of 'weaker sections' and stand eligible for a free supply of clothes and cash and a reservation of seats in schools and professional courses.

To be a refugee is to experience an upheaval. They are torn by the roots from their native soil and often denied the possibility of going back home again. They face new conditions in a new country, and a new environment. Among the Sri Lankan refugees there are a configuration of forces contributing in many cases to family tensions and general estrangement in the parent-child relationship in the pre-adolescent and adolescent periods. As with many other refugee groups the Sri Lankan refugees have experienced widespread fatigue and depression resulting from relentless economic pressures and cultural alienation. Thus, their abilities to raise their children in a foreign culture are weakened. Often they lack the energy to discipline their children consistently. Some adults cope with the pressures by abusing alcohol and drugs or by gambling, both of which contribute further to family instability. Half (51.5 per cent) of the children interviewed felt a behavioural change in their parents after migration.

Effects on Children

Many of the families are experiencing crisis in their relationships with their children. These tensions often erupt into child's behaviour, which tends to be destructive to both the children and the families. Such problems include running away, not attending school, engaging in sexual activity, drug and alcohol use, child marriage starting in early adolescence and initiating gangs within the camp. A main factor which alienates the parent from the child while he grows, especially when the child is born and brought up in the host country, is that, the parent tries to bring up the child in their culture while the child adapts to the host culture. The parents refuse to accept the values of the prevailing culture. Moreover, the parents and the older generation in the camp socially isolate themselves and their children from the outside world (outside the camp).

Adolescent marriage is a serious problem in these camps. The reasons are threefold. One is the close proximity of the houses, which are at times, just partitioned by sheets. Each house measures just around 100 square feet. Second is that, as revealed by the children, the one room accommodation forces all of them to sleep together, this brings about a curiosity in the minds of the children as to watch sexual activities between the parents and some of them have revealed that they keep awake till the wee hours of the morning awaiting such activities. This in turn builds in them the urge to indulge in sexual activities. Thirdly, these children are alienated from the outside world. They live inside the camp, which is composed only of Sri Lankans. In many camps where the child marriage problem persists, the schools are inside the camp, run by Sri Lankans. The NGOs, which render help to these camps, are also run by Sri Lankans. The medical officers, social workers and psychologists are all Sri Lankans.

Most of the families have children between two to four (56.3 per cent) and 31.2 per cent have children above five and the remaining to a maximum of nine children. Certainly a catastrophe in the making, with the government providing money and necessities based on the size of the family and increasing the number of camps.

The children, nearly 50 per cent of them, especially the younger children, want to start life afresh. They do feel low at times (48.4 per cent) and generally suicidal tendencies are high. The boys abuse alcohol but not drugs, and do not engage in criminal behaviour. They are treated well in schools of the host country and do not suffer from any problems of discrimination due to their nationality.

A little more than 50 per cent of them like the kind of life they lead in the camps while the other half resent this kind of life and wish to go back to their country some day. Majority of the boys wish to join the armed forces and the girls wish to become doctors. The children who are older and have seen the war and its atrocities are the ones who wish to go back to their country and fight the forces. They miss their friends (92.8 per cent) and school (36.5 per cent). Those who were young when they left their country wish to stay back in this country. A major reason why they do not like life at the camp is not due to restrictions (64.3 per cent) but due to the lack of amenities in the camp (50 per cent) like clean lavatories, clean surroundings, etc. Those who like the camp attribute the feeling mainly to mental (59 per cent) and physical security (65 per cent) that is being away from the war environment.

Nearly all the children attend school and very few of them (22.6 per cent) go to work; all of them are boys. The kind of work in which they engage are stone cutting, tailoring and as wage labourers. They do not face any victimisation at work in terms of wages, working hours, or discrimination.

Common refugee problems like lack of basic necessities

including medical needs is absent in the Sri Lankan refugee camps. The victimisation on the whole is centered on the psychological well-being of the child in various ways. The effect of the migration on the parents and their problems in raising their children is unique to these refugees.

This study has broadened our own understanding of the condition of child refugees in the camps. The psychological victimization they face has confirmed the complexity of issues at the level of policies, programmes and repatriation.

This 'war on children' is a 20th century invention. It is said that only five per cent of the casualties in the World War I were civilians. By the World War II, the proportion has risen to 50 per cent. The civilian share was about 80 per cent most of them women and children (James P. Grant, UNICEF, 1992).

Recommendations

Priority in the list of recommendations would be the need for further research. The psycho-socio impacts of the war and the unique problems faced inside the camp due to camp conditions and the parent society needs to be identified and appropriate steps should be taken to practice innovative and responsive programmes. The children are receptive and look forward to counselling on education, information on education, are interested in computer courses and are also interested in meditation and yoga.

A refugee, therefore, is any person who is unable to return to his or her own country because of persecution on account of race, religion, nationality, membership in a particular social group or political opinion. The line of difference between immigrants and refugees lies in the fact that most immigrants leave their country voluntarily while the refugees have been forced to flee their country of origin and have been accepted to live in another country.

The needs of refugees vary depending on who and where they are. In many cases, refugees need immediate assistance in the form of food, water, shelter or medical care. But the most fundamental need of a refugee is to be granted asylum. Article 14 of the Universal Declaration of Human Rights states, "everyone has the right to seek and enjoy in other countries asylum from persecution".

India is a home to thousands of refugees. Giving asylum has been an age-old tradition for which the Rajput kings sometimes paid with their lives and kingdoms. The independence saw millions of Indians become refugees overnight in what was until then their own homes—over 15 million people crossed the newly formed borders. In the 1960's over 100,000 Tibetans sought asylum in India. They still live here, mostly living in settlements and enjoying almost the same facilities as Indian citizens. In the eighties, thousands of Tamils came from Sri Lanka to Tamil Nadu, fleeing ethnic violence. Many of them are still to be repatriated.

The refugee population of India comprises of people mainly from the countries of Tibet, Sri Lanka, Bangladesh and Afghanistan. As of 1997, there were nearly 2,60,000 refugees living in India and the refugee population has remained more or less stable in the last decade of the previous century. In the recent past 12000 refugees fled to India from Sri Lanka. There are at present 65000 refugees from Sri Lanka in 133 camps in Tamil Nadu, in addition to an unspecified number who live outside the camp.

An information worth mentioning here is that India is not a party to the United Nations Refugee Convention and Protocol, and like the rest of Asia, has no domestic refugee laws. Refugees are treated like other aliens under the Foreigners Act and the Passport Act and are subject to domestic laws governing the entry and stay of foreigners. Refugee problems are handled on the basis of administrative policies which, though ad hoc in nature, are broadly in line with international refugee law principles. Aid to refugees is generally regarded as humanitarian work. As it has been expressed, "Refugee constitutes one of the powerful labels currently in the repertoire of humanitarian concern". Most of the people can look at their own governments to guarantee and protect their basic rights and security. But in the case of refugees, the country of origin has proved itself unable or unwilling to protect those rights. Deprived of the protection by their country, detached from their families and communities of origin, refugees form a group vulnerable to violence, abuse and victimisation of basic human rights.

Infants and children are often the earliest and most frequent victims of violence, disease and malnutrition, which accompany population displacement. A host of studies in war zones around the world, including Jaffna, testify to traumatisation and other extreme adverse effects on children resulting from the ravages of war.

Sample Characteristics

The sample consisted of thirty children with an almost equal number of male (46.9 per cent) and female (53.1 per cent) respondents. All the children were educated or undergoing schooling. Except for one, all are born Sri Lankan citizens. Majority (90.6 per cent) of them have migrated to India before 1994. While in Sri Lanka their parents have either been farmers (31.3 per cent), fishermen (21.9 per cent), tailors (31.3 per cent) or businessmen and their economic conditions while in Sri Lanka was on the whole stable for a large majority (84.4 per cent) of the sample.

Overall Discussion

Victimisation in the life of a refugee starts even before he is labelled a refugee. Children are victimised at all levels of their lives, plunging into a future of total darkness.

The trauma undergone by the Sri Lankan children has been assessed here in different stages namely, before migration (while in their homes in Sri Lanka), during migration (the process of shifting to the host country) and after migration (in the camps at the host country).

Impact of Victimisation Before Migration

Although the problems of refugees have become more distinct in the recent times, it cannot be understood without a historical perspective. A small country with a population of only 18 million, Sri Lanka is one of the largest principal sources of refugees and displaced persons. The origin of flow of refugees can generally be seen in the light of fundamental historical and social processes. The formation of a nation state has been an important process in the case of the Sri Lankan refugees.

Traumatic Experiences and Psychosocial Outcomes

While in Sri Lanka, during the war, the children have been victimised in several ways. They have starved without food (74.2 per cent) and have been shelterless for days (84.4 per cent), unable to go out to the market place (51.6 per cent) or to entertainment or cultural activities (29 per cent) or visit the temple (58.1 per cent) and most of all not being able to attend school (74.2 per cent). Worst, though only a negligible percentage, is that 12.9 per cent of the sample have been sexually abused by the soldiers, that is sexual abuse other than rape, and an equally small percentage (6.5 per cent) have been exposed to sexual abuse. Out of the total 16 girls who formed part of the sample, there was one rape victim.

Two children were exposed to rape of one of their family members by the soldiers and three children have lost a sibling during the war. About 15.6 per cent of the children have been physically injured during the war. There was a case of an adolescent boy who had lost his leg as a result of the war.

As regards PTSD interestingly majority of the children (83.9 per cent) recollect not having experienced any confusion in thinking. This is perhaps true because, firstly they were too young at the time of travel and the second reason is one that can be peculiar to Sri Lankan refugees. War has been an everyday happening for all of them as many have been born and brought up in a war torn situation. Since their birth they have bitter experiences of witnessing the flee of their friends, relatives and other people most frequently and suddenly. Because of such experiences these children do not understand the context in which their friends and relatives were forced to leave their motherland and the consequences which they are going to face. Hence these children had more excitement than apprehension on leaving their own country.

The homes are vacated overnight and the families flee their homes leaving behind most of their movable and all their immovable properties. In a few families (9.4 per cent), the parents are unable to go with the children for various reasons like lack of finance, etc., have sent only the children either with relatives or neighbours.

There was a case of a family who had lost their parents in the war and the neighbours when fleeing had brought these children with them to Tamil Nadu.

Migration is an expensive matter for these families. Especially when they are large families, as most of them are, migration financially drains them—expenses include charges for packing and transporting their luggage and for their own transportation by boat (93.8 per cent) to the host country. It is during these times that almost all of them have starved for three to four days and walked miles to reach the place of embarkation. The children have trekked behind their parents, carrying loads on their backs facing the sun and rain.

Many of the children have expressed that though they were initially excited about going to a foreign country, while crossing the sea they panicked and some of them have also witnessed boats being capsized and many of them being drowned. These scenes come often to their minds leading to depression and isolation. As to PTSD some of them have expressed having felt certain physical symptoms while on migration like excessive sweating, increased heart beat, etc. This could also be due to anxiety of travelling abroad and the mode of travelling, which is by boat in the middle of the night.

Nearly all of those who feel this change agreed that their parents did spend time with them and they care for them. They agree that they provide them with all basic necessities.

The change in their behaviour is attributed to alcohol usage in nearly three-fourths of the parents, 60 per cent of these parents also encourage and force their children to abuse alcohol. However, engaging in criminal behaviour by the parents is negligible. They do not physically abuse the children or force them to overwork or prevent them from attending school. A common problem felt by nearly 50 per cent of the children was that their parents were over-protective about them.

Most commonly the family members fall sick, after the tedious travel and the environmental conditions that are prevalent in the camp. This puts a financial pressure in them forcing them to borrow money from money lenders, who exploit the refugees. The interest mounts and in return the money lender offers a job for the mother, where she entertains and provides sex to her clients. As days go by the mother is replaced with the well-grown daughter and the cycle continues. The mothers are offered work abroad as housekeepers. They send their earnings to their children in the camp.

The children feel that their parents refuse to start life afresh (56.3 per cent). A majority of them (68.8 per cent) feel that their parents are depressed most of the time, are under economic pressure (59.4 per cent) and suffer from cultural alienation (75 per cent).

Contributing to this significant malaise in the Sri Lankan community is the trauma of the early 90's during which period most of the parent generation suffered terribly. Almost all of them have experienced the destruction of family members. They still bear the burden of the previous life of terror, starvation and relentless stress.

Socialisation, as in any other child is therefore lacking. They do not have relatives or friends to visit. Therefore, the kind of affection and love a normal child of that age gets out of socialisation with the family, relatives, the peer group and the school is lacking for the refugee children. Further to this is the fact that they have a lot of spare time. Therefore, boys in their adolescence and girls just around their teens look to each other for love, affection and sex. Another important point that brings them on to the same ground as other children of their age is the mass media. Television is the most common and most accessible form of entertainment to these children. They normally watch two to three movies per day on their own video decks or on common decks. This further instills feelings like love and sex in them. When the parents oppose to a marriage between them, the children usually resort to attempting suicide either by burning themselves or jumping into a well. Getting married when young is a fad among these children. This brings them a lot of attention from other camp members and friends who look upon them as role models, thus increasing the chain. Another interesting factor is that, these children belong to broken home families. They are either single parent families or one where the parents, most often the mother, is working in a foreign land. The children get married with or without their family's consent. The girls stop their schooling from the time of marriage and start having children at a tender age of 13-15 years. A factor worth contemplating about is that, these children who get married do not believe in birth control. Their ultimate motive is to produce as many children as possible and rebuild their lost empire in Sri Lanka.

Surprisingly, a majority of the children (83.9 per cent) do not need any financial help at present. An equal percentage of them feel that educational facilities should be improved. Majority of them (71 per cent) are satisfied with the kind of medical facilities offered but feel the condition of housing and sanitation should be improved (71 per cent).

The statistical records show that a great number of refugees have indeed received help from domestic and international organizations. It is considered that the cooperation on behalf of refugees has saved many millions of human lives, and that it provides a rare example of cooperation among governments for the purpose of giving direct assistance to individuals. Even though organizations on behalf of refugees do not bring peace and security to the world; it is emphasized that they do at least give protection and relief to a number of human beings.

Conclusion

The world 'refugee' tends to evoke images of a sprawling camp, housing large numbers of distressed and impoverished people who had to escape from their own country at short notice and with nothing but the clothes on their back. This perception is very true.

It is here that the refugee families of Sri Lanka wait for the day when it is safe enough for them to go back to their homes and resume a normal way of life.

The Sri Lankan refugee children, in all probabilities, do not seem to suffer the kind of victimization child refugees from Bosnia or the Soviet Union do. They have their own unique stand, based on historical and cultural aspects and the duration of the wars.

Although it is impossible to reach out to the thousands of Sri Lankan children who participate and will be participating in the armed conflicts, we can divert the energies of the young in these camps to go back, not as grown up citizens to die at war but as useful citizens to develop their nation.

What we here can probably do is to understand them not as a threat to us but as threatened victims themselves. Public opinion can go a long way towards encouraging governments to adopt policies that could be helpful to them.

There are particularly vulnerable individuals in each refugee situation and for the Sri Lankans it is no doubt their young citizens. Special attention is being given by local and international bodies in various ways but what they need is not just an asylum or facilities for their physical survival. They need to be understood as a 'unique community with unique needs'—this in turn will safeguard the welfare of the host country too.

Sample Characteristics

Variable	*Categories*	*Freq.*	*percentage*
Sex	Male	15	46.9
	Female	16	53.1
	TOTAL	31	100.0
Educational Qualification	Below 5th Std.	4	12.9
	5th–10th Std.	17	54.8
	Above 10th Std.	10	32.3
	TOTAL	31	100.0
Year of Migration	Before 1994	29	90.6
	1994-1999	2	9.4
	TOTAL	31	100.0
Employment Status of Parents in Sri Lanka	Fishermen	7	22.6
	Agriculturists	10	32.3
	Tailors	1	3.2
	Businessmen	7	22.6
	Others	6	19.1
	TOTAL	31	100.0
Employment Status of Parents in Tamil Nadu	Tailors	3	9.7
	Wage labourers	9	29.0
	Businessmen	2	7.5
	Unemployed	8	25.8
	Others	9	29.0
	TOTAL	31	100.0

VICTIMIZATION OF CHILD REFUGEES

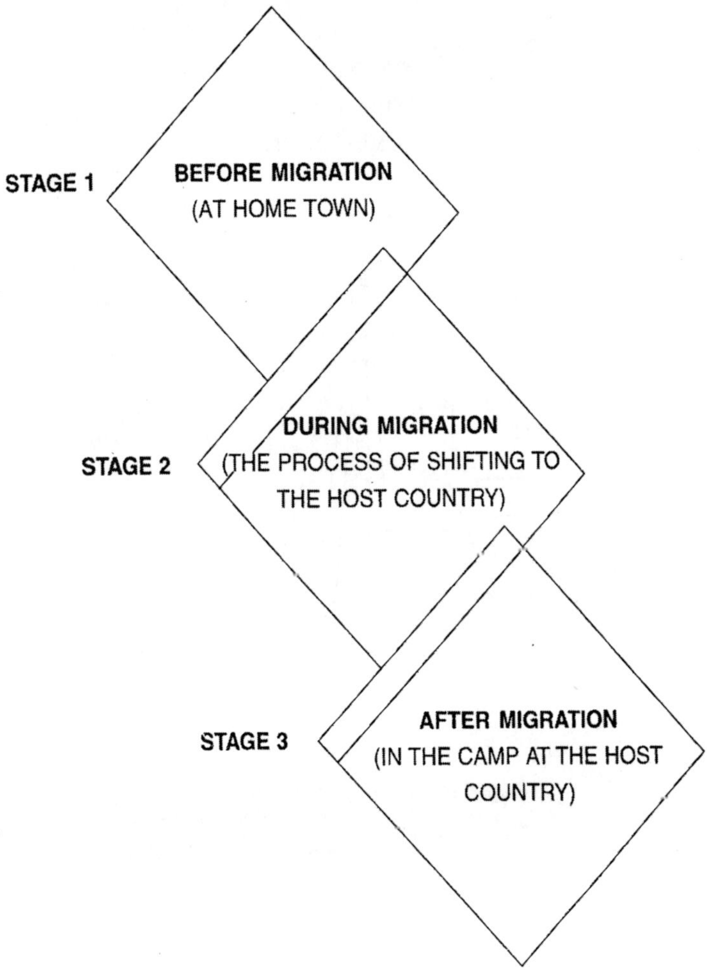

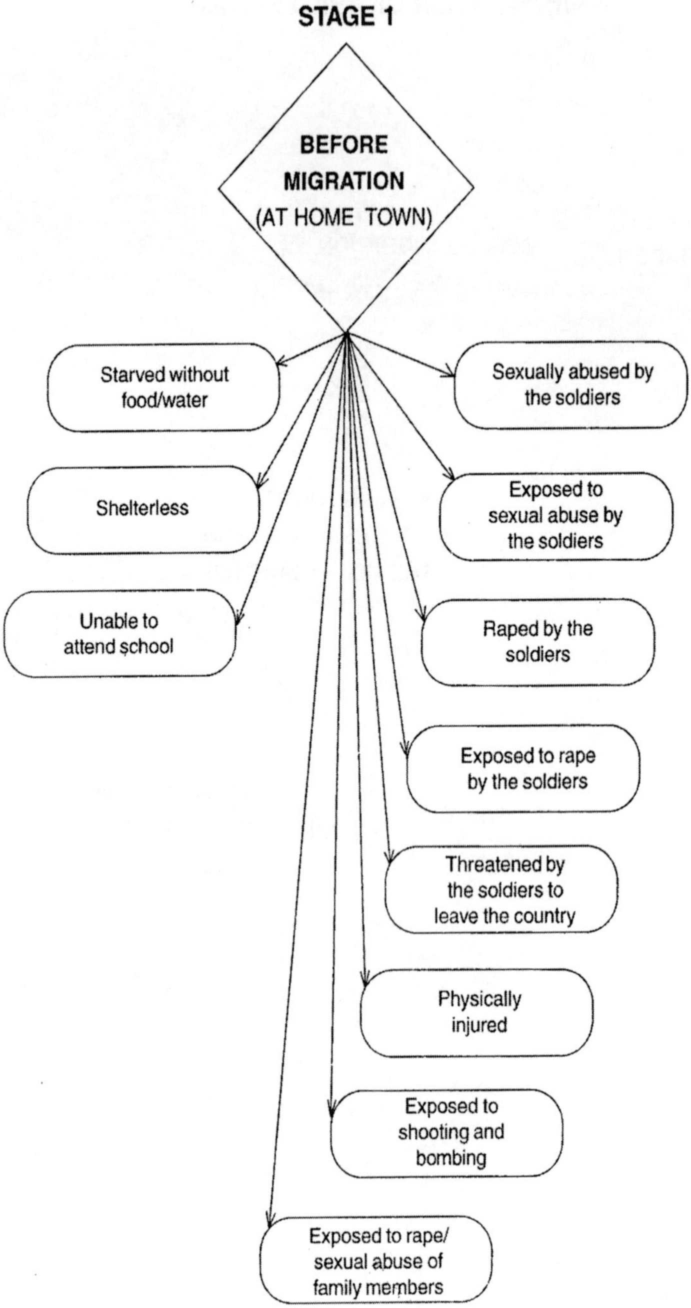
STAGE 1
BEFORE MIGRATION (AT HOME TOWN)
Starved without food/water
Shelterless
Unable to attend school
Sexually abused by the soldiers
Exposed to sexual abuse by the soldiers
Raped by the soldiers
Exposed to rape by the soldiers
Threatened by the soldiers to leave the country
Physically injured
Exposed to shooting and bombing
Exposed to rape/ sexual abuse of family members

STAGE 2

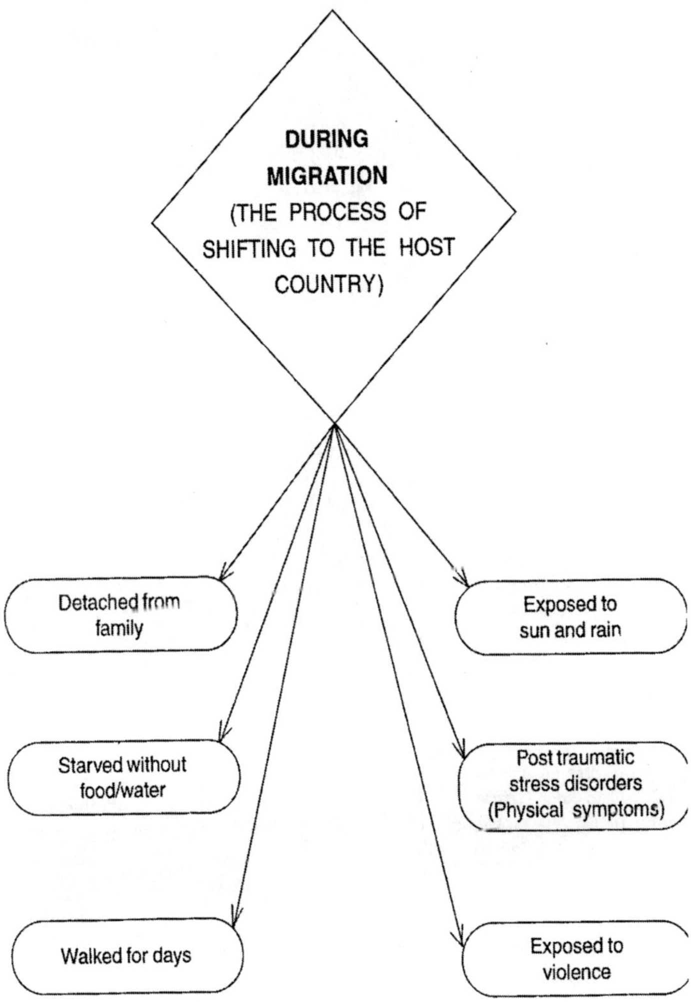
DURING MIGRATION (THE PROCESS OF SHIFTING TO THE HOST COUNTRY)
Detached from family
Starved without food/water
Walked for days
Exposed to sun and rain
Post traumatic stress disorders (Physical symptoms)
Exposed to violence

STAGE 3

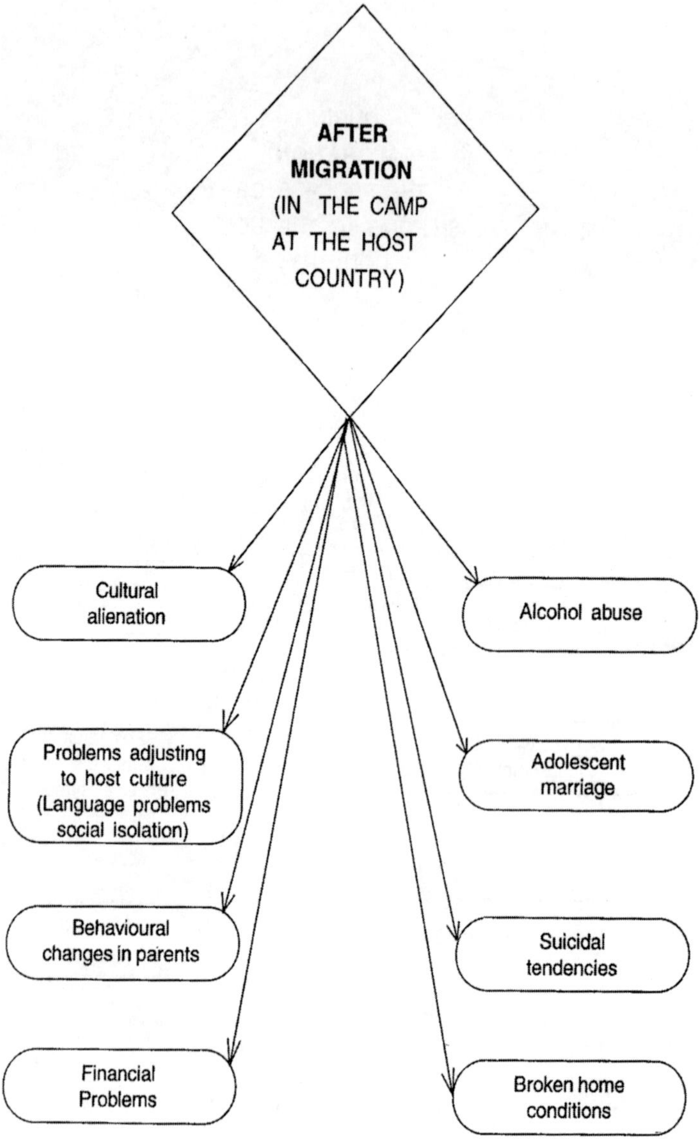
AFTER MIGRATION (IN THE CAMP AT THE HOST COUNTRY)
Cultural alienation
Problems adjusting to host culture (Language problems social isolation)
Behavioural changes in parents
Financial Problems
Alcohol abuse
Adolescent marriage
Suicidal tendencies
Broken home conditions

References

Gill, Guy Goodwin and Cohn Ilene, 1994, Child Soldiers—The Role of Children in Armed Conflicts, A Study on behalf of the Henry Dunant Institute, Geneva, Clarendon Press, Oxford.

Salomon, Kim, 1991, Refugees in the Cold War, Lund University Press, Sweden.

United Nations High Commissioner for Refugees (UNHCR), June 1996, Human Rights and Refugee Protection, Part II, Specific Issues.

United Nations High Commissioner for Refugees (1997-98), The State of the World's Refugees: A Humanitarian Agenda, Oxford University Press.

Appendix

RECOMMENDATIONS OF THE THIRD BIENNIAL CONFERENCE OF THE INDIAN SOCIETY OF VICTIMOLOGY HELD AT THE INDIAN INSTITUTE OF THE PUBLIC ADMINISTRATION, NEW DELHI DURING 26-27, NOVEMBER 1999

1. Resolved to recommend to the Government of India to implement the provisions of the United Nations Declaration on the Basic Principles of Justice for Victims of Crime and Abuse of Power, 1985 by creating a national legislation for Victims of Crime by considering the *Victims (Criminal Injuries) Right to Assistance Bill, 1995 drafted by the Indian Society of Victimology* and already pending with the Government of India.

2. In the Home Ministry of the Government of India and the Home Departments of all the State Governments, a section with suitable nomenclature like *Office of Victims of Crime (OVC)* should be created to deal with all the issues of Victims of Crime and Abuse of Power exclusively.

3. One day in a year should be earmarked as "Crime Victims Day" to remember the countless number of victims of crime who laid down their lives at the hands of criminals and suffered in many other ways. India could earmark *30th January as 'Crime Victims Day'* as this was the day on which our Father of the Nation Mahatma Gandhi became a victim of the bullets of an assassin. On this 'Crime Victims Day', meetings and programmes may be organized at all the villages, towns and cities to propagate the evils of crime and

violence and problems of the victims, besides organizing runs, rallies in remembrance of innumerable crime victims.

4. *Victim Satisfaction Sample Surveys* should be systematically conducted by an agency, independent of the police, in all the States to understand their grievances and improve the performance of the criminal justice agencies keeping the interest of victims in mind.

5. *Crisis Intervention Centres/'Childline'* to render immediate assistance and provide rescue to children in distress should be established in all the metropolitan cities of India to start with, and extended to other towns gradually with the assistance of Ministry of Social Justice, Government of India and the Social Welfare/Child Welfare Departments of the State Governments in cooperation with local NGOs.

Revision in Relevant Laws:

6. The Law Commission may be entrusted with the task of relooking at different laws relating to sexual abuse and exploitation of women and children in regard to evidentiary requirements which often result in their secondary victimization. With regard to crimes against children, the onus of proof should be shifted on the accused.

7. The free and compulsory education for all children under 14 years of age as provided in Part IV of the Constitution of India should be brought under Part III of Fundamental Rights.

The National Commission for Children:

8. The ISV welcomes the proposed constitution of the *National Commission* for Children. While offering its fullest cooperation, the ISV requests the Commission to consult and involve the ISV in matters concerning research, training, awareness building and mobilization of public support and propagation of the Basic Principles of Justice for Victims of Crime and Abuse of Power.

9. The Ministry of Home Affairs, and the other concerned Ministries through their own outfits, may like to conduct macro and micro level studies/researches on the psychological impact of armed

conflicts, communal violence, caste carnages on children, as a measure to devise an effective "Child-Victim-Friendly" strategies of rescue, relief and rehabilitation.

10. The Bureau of Police Research and Development and other relevant agencies funding for research in Criminology/Victimology may be advised by the Ministry of Home Affairs/Ministry of Women and Child Development/Ministry of Social Justice and Empowerment to encourage research in the field of Victimology as a priority area with a view to making available more information on various forms and patterns of victimization o vulnerable groups such as Women. Children/SC/ST etc., and highlighting their problems and plight from the perspectives of police and programme formulation.

11. **Social Mobilization/Awareness Creation:**

Ministry of Home Affairs, Ministry of Women & Child Development and Ministry of Information and Broadcasting may take appropriate measures to create awareness and help mobilise social action in regard to prevention and control of child abuse, exploitation, cruelty and other forms of victimization of women/children. Further, the aforesaid Ministries may like to encourage (through funding and other means) NGOs to undertake social action projects aimed at mobilizing public support for children's cause.

12. **Training of CJS Functionaries:**

The National/Regional and State level training institutions for Criminal Justice functionaries such as Police, Prosecutors, Magistrates/Judges/Correctional Officers need to be advised to devise and develop a training module in Victimology to familiarize all criminal justice functionaries of different cadres with current developments in Victimology and to develop in them the required sensitivity in dealing wth the victims of crime. In particular, the State-level Police Training Institutions may be required to devise, develop and/or adopt similar training module for middle and lower level police functionaries to adopt "human approach" in handling the cases of women/children victims of crime.

13. The Home Ministry, Government of India, should direct all the DGs of police to ensure that the basic rights of the victims of crime are prominently displayed at all police stations in the vernacular language.

14. **Law Enforcement Measures:**

The concerned Ministries/Departments at the Central and State—level need to review the bottlenecks in the enforcement of laws in relation to the prevention of child abuse, exploitation, cruelty, including criminal victimization, and take appropriate measures for the protection of the child victims of crime.

15. The Code of Conduct for Law Enforcement Agencies should be strictly enforced to ensure protection of the rights of women and children involved in the Criminal Justice Process.

Index